IMAGES
of America

BLACK MOUNTAIN
and the SWANNANOA VALLEY

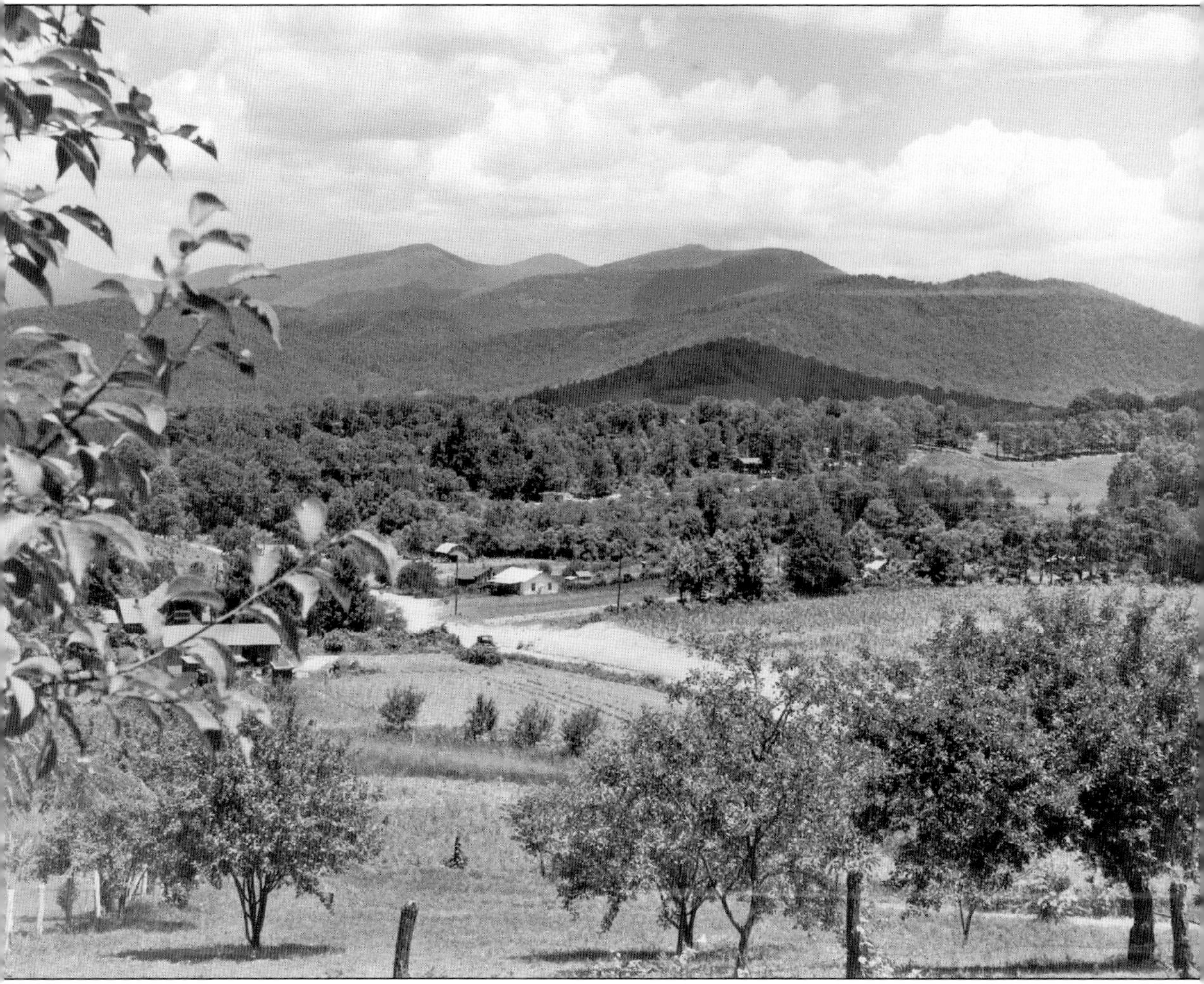

The Essence of the Valley. A view of Buckeye Cove depicts much of the appeal of the Swannanoa Valley—lush, fertile lands, peaceful surroundings, and the scenic beauty of the mountains in the distance. (Noah Collection, courtesy David Rozzell.)

On the Cover: The cool waters of the North Fork and other area streams and rivers refreshed summer visitors to the Swannanoa Valley. Many returned to settle permanently to enjoy the valley's scenic beauty and temperate climate.

IMAGES *of America*

BLACK MOUNTAIN *and the* SWANNANOA VALLEY

Swannanoa Valley Museum

ARCADIA PUBLISHING

ISBN 978-0-7385-1626-4

Published by Arcadia Publishing
Charleston, South Carolina

Printed in the United States of America

Library of Congress Catalog Card Number: 2004100102

For all general information contact Arcadia Publishing at:
Telephone 843-853-2070
Fax 843-853-0044
E-mail sales@arcadiapublishing.com
For customer service and orders:
Toll-Free 1-888-313-2665

Visit us on the Internet at www.arcadiapublishing.com

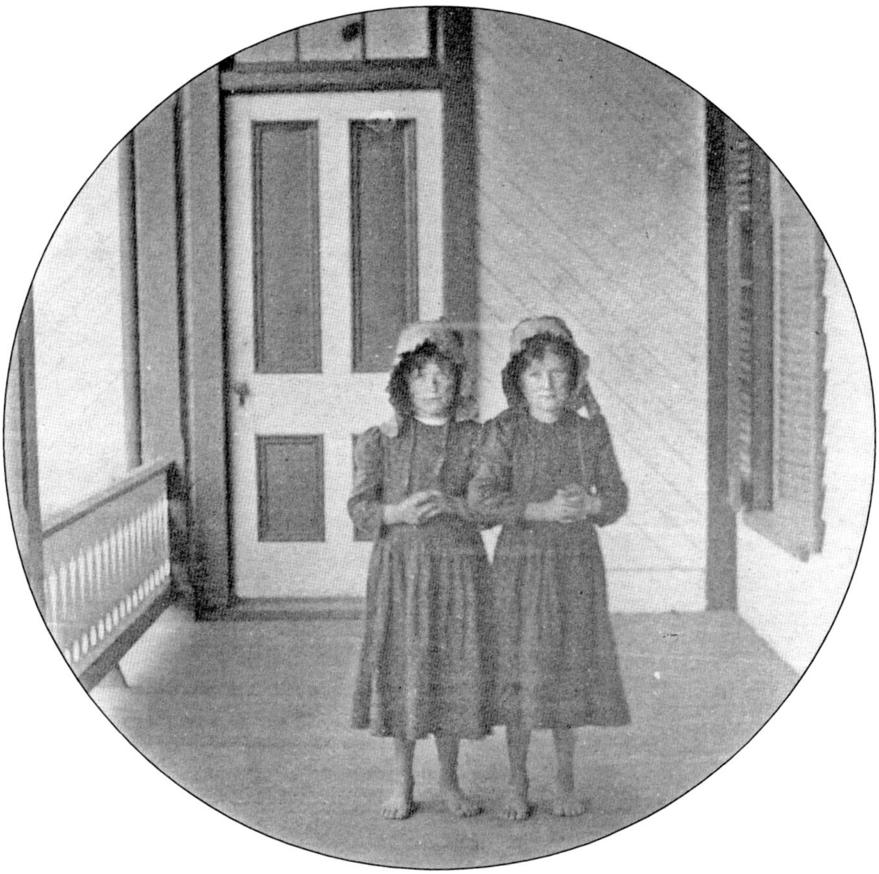

TWINS. These young visitors to Black Mountain were photographed at the turn of the 19th century on the porch of the Black Mountain Hotel by its manager's daughter, Gertrude Sprague. Many of Sprague's images are reproduced in this book. (Swannanoa Valley Museum.)

Contents

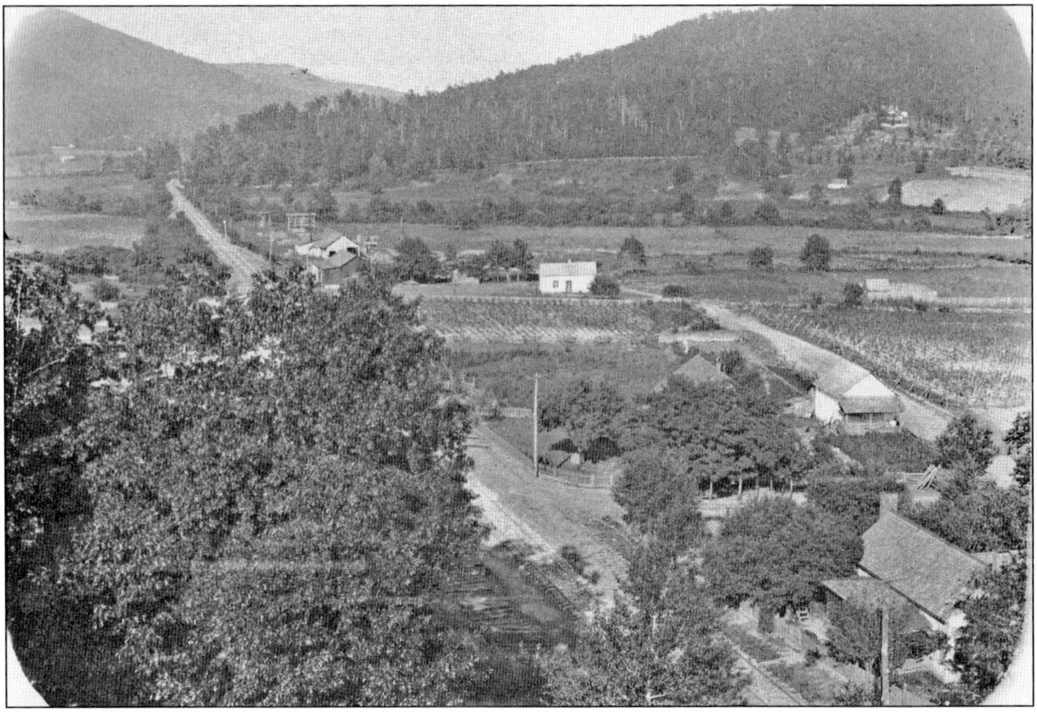

HOTEL VIEW. An unusual view looking east follows the railroad toward Ridgecrest; the image was taken by Gertrude Sprague *c.* 1900 from an upper floor of the Black Mountain Hotel. (Swannanoa Valley Museum.)

ACKNOWLEDGMENTS

The Swannanoa Valley Museum would like to thank its board of directors and the committee who compiled this book: John and Peggy Buckner, Robert Goodson, Arthur Joe and Mary Hemphill, Jill Jones, Sarah Urquhart, and especially Porge Buck and Harriet Styles, who gave many hours of their time throughout the project.

We also would like to thank the many people who generously donated family and other personal photographs, credit for which we have given in each picture. Thanks, too, to Larry Odoski of the Outdoor Paths Map Store and Eric Ringer of Polaris Maps for providing the detailed map on pages 110–111.

INTRODUCTION

The Swannanoa Valley is nestled in the Blue Ridge Mountains in Western North Carolina, reputedly among the oldest mountains in the world. No longer high, jagged, and snow-covered like the Rockies, the still majestic Blue Ridge peaks remain awe-inspiring and yet somehow seem more approachable and hospitable than their Western counterparts.

It is impossible to conceive what these mountains were like in their youth. We can only guess at the species of plant and animal life that inhabited this part of the world millions of years ago. In this book, however, we hope to have captured the story of life in the valley since the American Revolution. What brought the early settlers to the Swannanoa Valley, and what continues to draw people here today?

One obvious answer is the spectacular scenery, but the rugged pioneers who came to the valley after the Revolutionary War weren't looking for great views. They wanted land they could till and forests in which to hunt. For years, the valley and surrounding mountains had been Cherokee hunting grounds, but the Cherokee allied themselves with the British during the Revolutionary War, and when the British were defeated, the new American government opened the land west of the Swannanoa Gap to white settlement.

The Native Americans did not give up their territory easily. One legend is the story of Samuel Davidson, one of the first white settlers to come to the valley. Davidson staked a claim and built a cabin at the foot of Jones Mountain. He then returned to Old Fort for his wife, child, and a servant woman. Davidson kept a bell tied to his horse so he could easily locate it. A renegade Cherokee hunting party approached the cabin, grabbed the horse, and jangled the bell, luring Davidson outside. They shot him and left his body on the mountainside. The women and child escaped back to Old Fort and later Sam Davidson's twin brother, William, and a party of men returned to the cabin, buried Sam's body, and took revenge by killing many of the Indians.

Treaties forced the Cherokee to move on, leaving the valley to the newcomers, who built homes and rustic churches/schools in the early communities of Bee Tree and North Fork. At one time, North Fork boasted more of a population than Asheville. The town of Grey Eagle gradually formed along the old wagon road that became the Western Turnpike, and when the railroad came through the Swannanoa Gap in 1879, the town changed its name to match the one given to the station: Black Mountain.

Rail travel changed the economy of the valley from an agricultural base to one that encompassed logging, mining, tourism, and land development. Boarding houses, hotels, and inns sprang up in the late 19th century to accommodate the many tourists who came by train from lower, hotter climates. Some of these "summer people" returned to stay for good, starting businesses, building homes, and raising their families in the valley. The climate and peaceful ambience of the area appealed to those who were seeking sites to build religious retreats. Montreat Assembly, Blue Ridge Assembly, and Ridgecrest Assembly were all established before 1910.

Visitors to the valley in the early 1920s resulted in new industry coming to the area. Charles D. Owen decided to relocate his blanket manufacturing facility, Beacon Manufacturing, from New Bedford, Massachusetts, to Swannanoa. During the rest of the 20th century, the Owen family's industry employed hundreds of valley residents. Raphael Guastavino II, a famed Spanish architect who came to Western North Carolina to work on the Biltmore House, decided to stay and built his own estate, Rhododendron, just outside of Black Mountain. Franklin Terry built InTheOaks as a vacation home.

The valley continued to prosper during the first quarter of the 20th century but, like the rest of the country, was affected by the Great Depression. During the 1930s, many people came to the area to be treated for tuberculosis, and health care became an important enterprise in the valley, with many small sanatoriums being built. The Western North Carolina Sanatorium was completed in 1937, consolidating much of the care of TB patients until the invention of penicillin obliterated the disease. Black Mountain College was also formed during this era, bringing to the valley one of the most avant garde methods of education in America.

World War II took people from the valley and brought others here. Moore General Hospital, a 1,520-bed facility, was built in just four months in Swannanoa by the Army Corps of Engineers. After the war, the hospital grounds were used as part of the North Carolina prison system, and later the sanatorium became a treatment center for drug and alcohol abuse and Alzheimer's disease.

Today, tourism and the thriving religious assemblies comprise the main industries in the Swannanoa Valley. Visitors continue to find the valley so appealing that many move here permanently. Development and air and water quality are issues of concern as the population grows.

The mountains remain as beautiful as ever. The use of the valley's fertile soil has changed, but bucolic scenes still abound. It is part of the mission of the Swannanoa Valley Museum to educate people, especially the youth of the valley, about the importance of preserving the environment and protecting its ecology for future generations.

Mission Statement: "To preserve and interpret the social, cultural and natural history of the Swannanoa Valley for the education of the community, its children and future generations."

One

Fertile Valleys, Scenic Mountains, Crystal Waters

With a temperate climate and many natural resources, the Swannanoa Valley has been home to farmers, hunters, and fishermen since the first humans crossed the mountains and discovered the richness of the land.

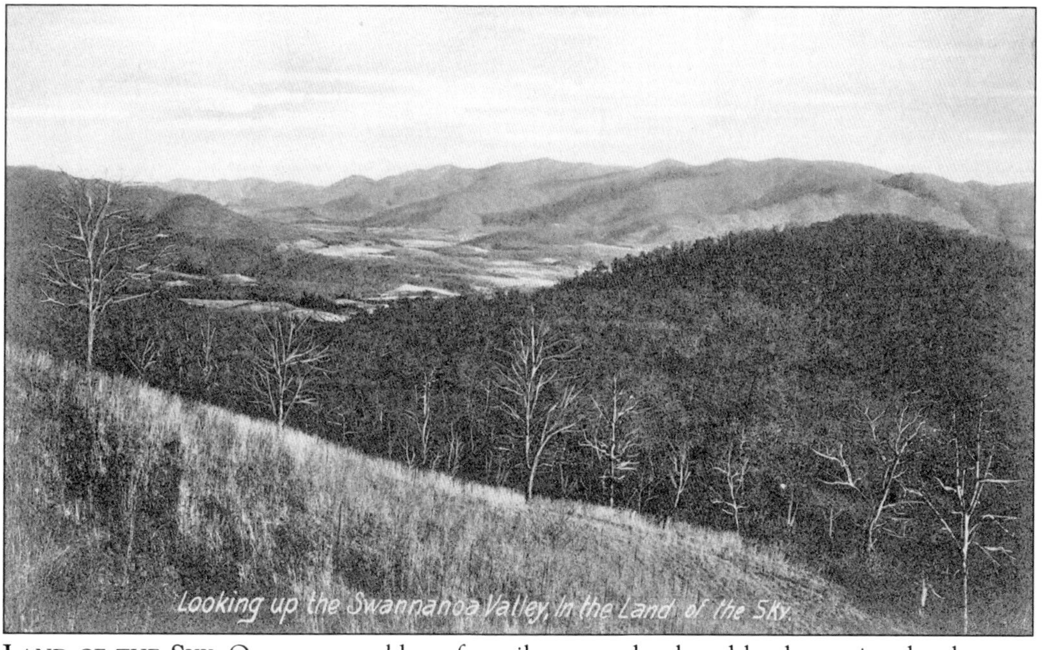

Land of the Sky. Once one could see for miles an undeveloped landscape in what became known as "The Land of the Sky," a name derived from the title of a popular 1870s novel by Christian Reid. (Postcard, Swannanoa Valley Museum.)

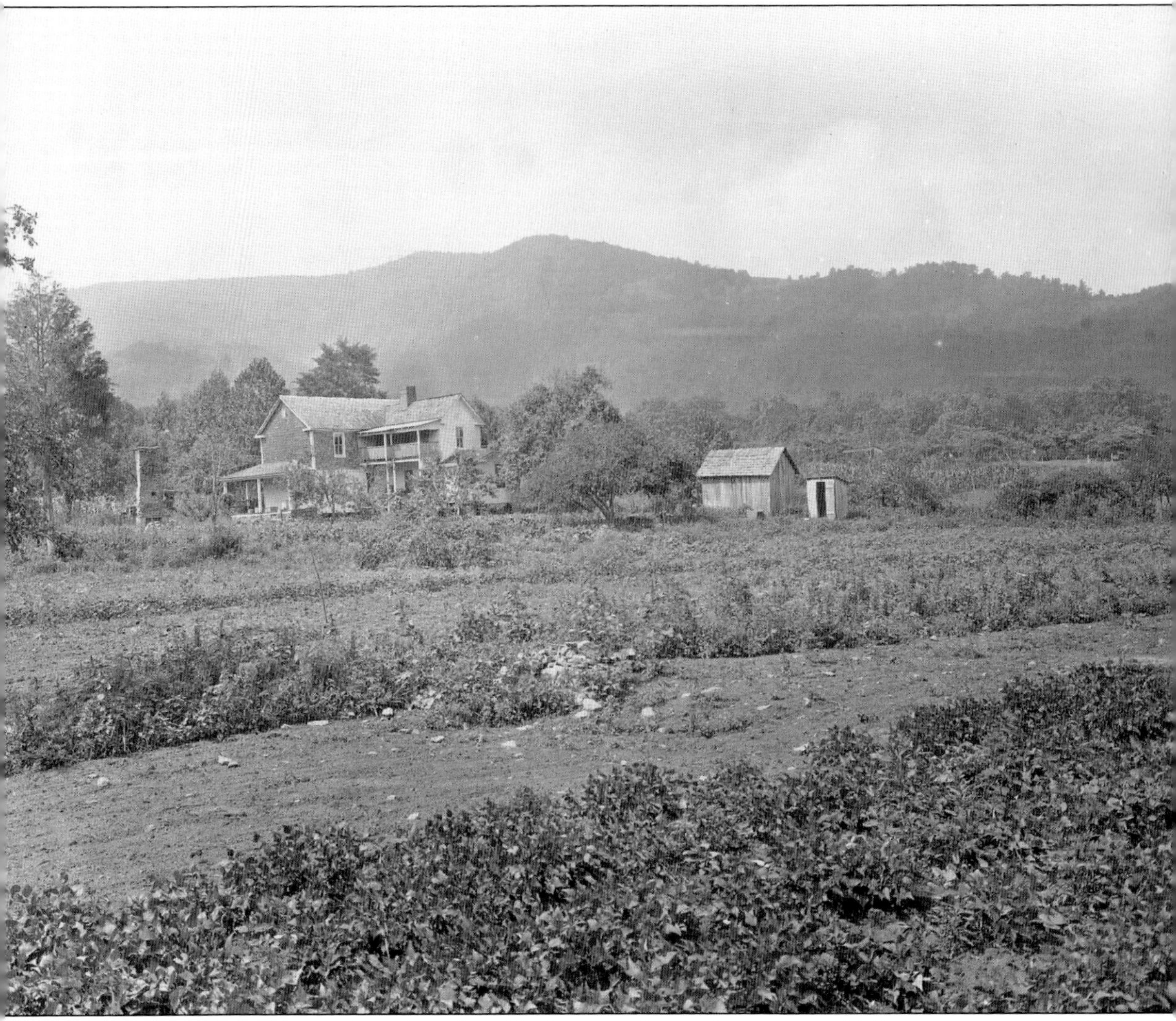

Early Farm. The rich soil and mild climate of the Swannanoa Valley encouraged early farmers who settled homesteads in the lower elevations. This farmstead overlooked part of the garden at Blue Ridge Assembly, *c.* 1920. (Herbert. W. Pelton photo, courtesy YMCA Blue Ridge Assembly.)

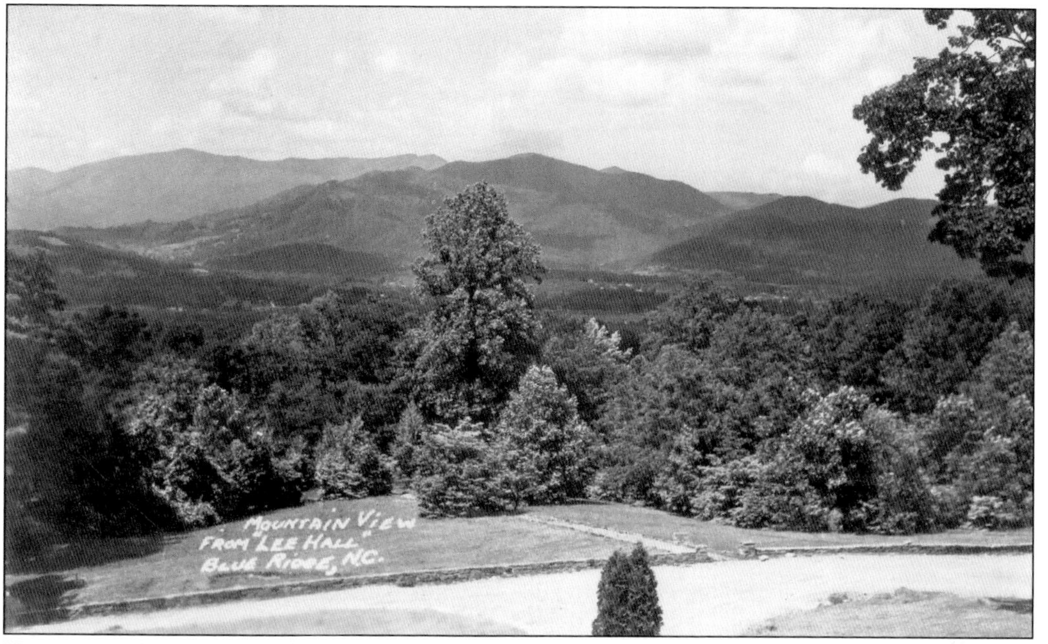

VIEW FROM LEE HALL. Taken from the front porch of the Robert E. Lee Hall, *c.* 1920, this view looks north to the Craggies. (J.C. Wolcott photo, courtesy YMCA Blue Ridge Assembly.)

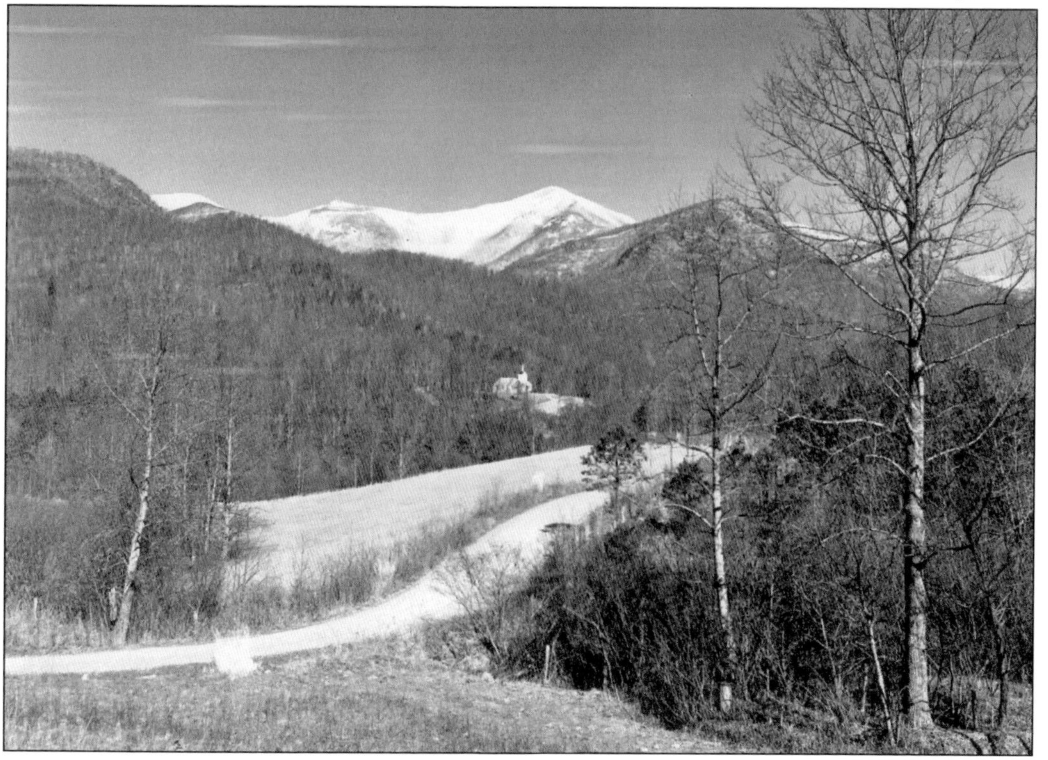

YEAR-ROUND CHARM. The valley's beauty is showcased year round, when winter's bare trees reveal snow-covered mountains rising above the rolling lowlands. (Ed Dupuy photo, courtesy Hemphill Collection, Swannanoa Valley Museum.)

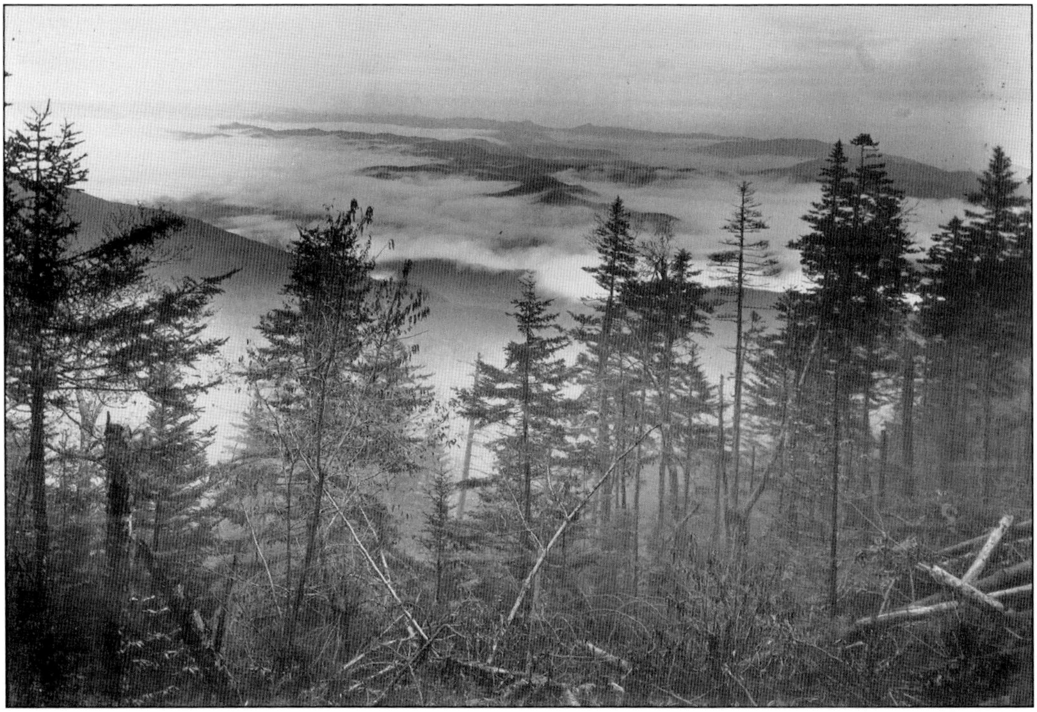

ABOVE THE CLOUDS. Another version of the origin of the name Grey Eagle derives from the clouds that often hang low in the valleys, reminding some of large gray eagles hovering over the landscape. (Courtesy Larry Glenn, Swannanoa Valley Museum.)

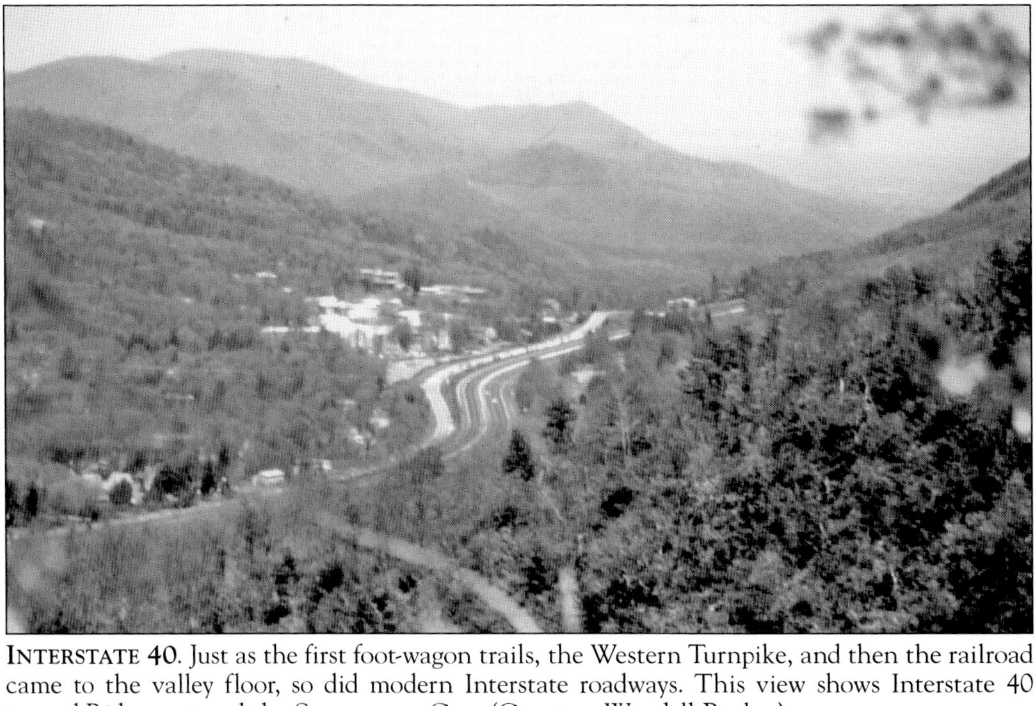

INTERSTATE 40. Just as the first foot-wagon trails, the Western Turnpike, and then the railroad came to the valley floor, so did modern Interstate roadways. This view shows Interstate 40 toward Ridgecrest and the Swannanoa Gap. (Courtesy Wendell Begley.)

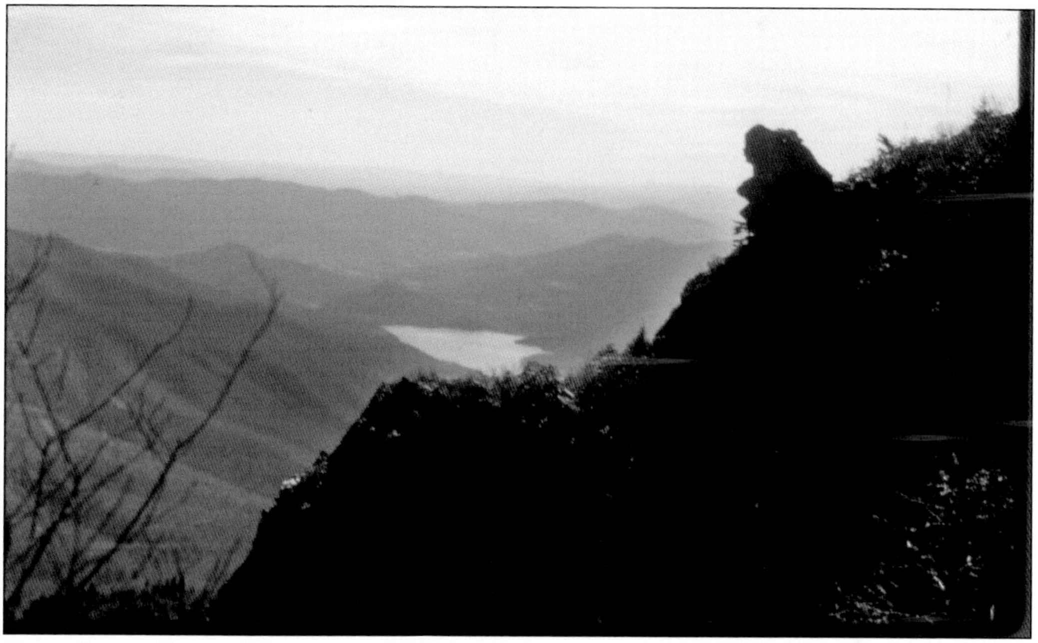

GREY EAGLE ROCK. The town of Black Mountain was originally known as "Grey Eagle." Legends abound concerning the origin of the name; some say this rock formation, high above the North Fork valley, is the image of an Indian named Grey Eagle, who watched over the valley and kept it from harm. Visible in the valley below is the Burnett Reservoir, part of 20,000 acres of protected watershed that provides water to the city of Asheville and surrounding communities. (Courtesy Wendell Begley.)

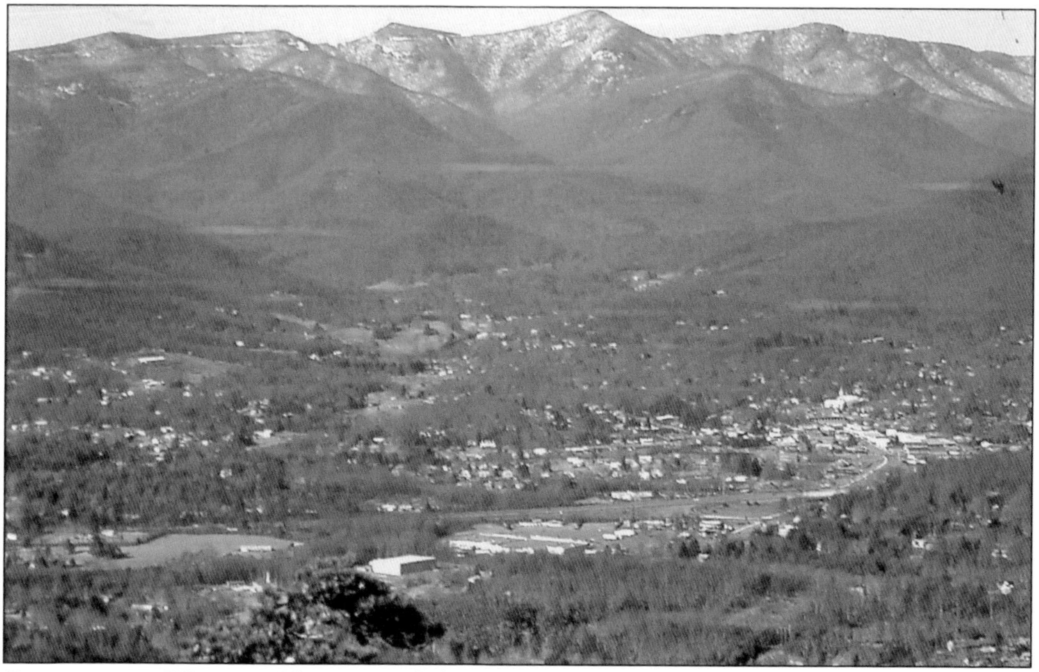

CRAGGIES IN WINTER. This view of the town of Black Mountain shows the snow-covered Craggy range in the distance. (Courtesy Wendell Begley.)

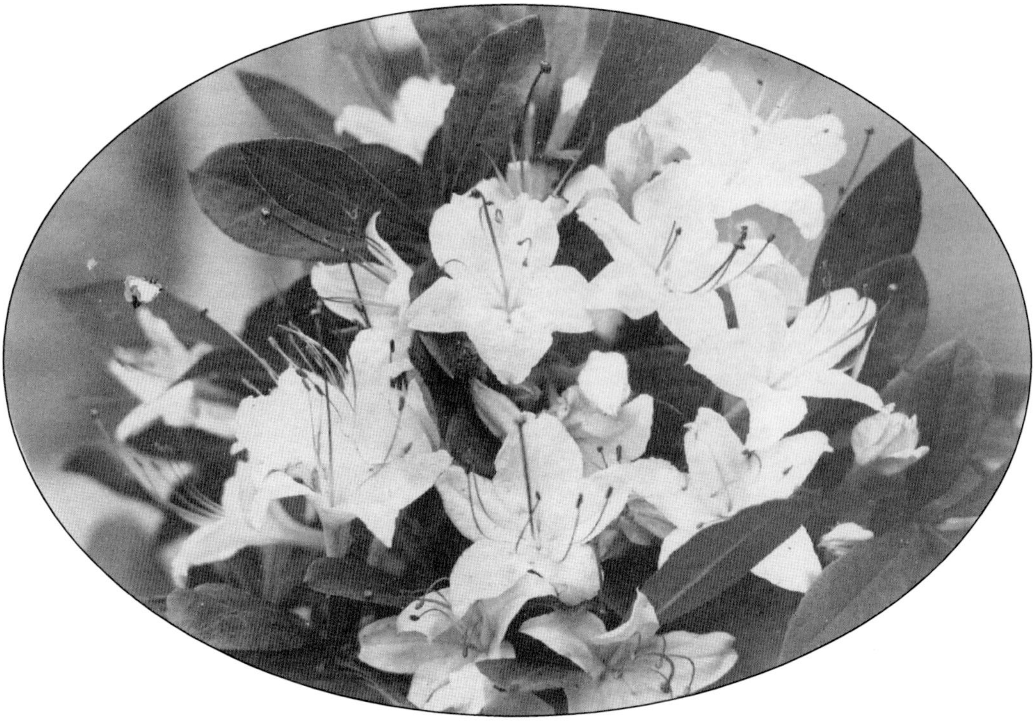

AZALEAS. Early settlers called this honeysuckle.

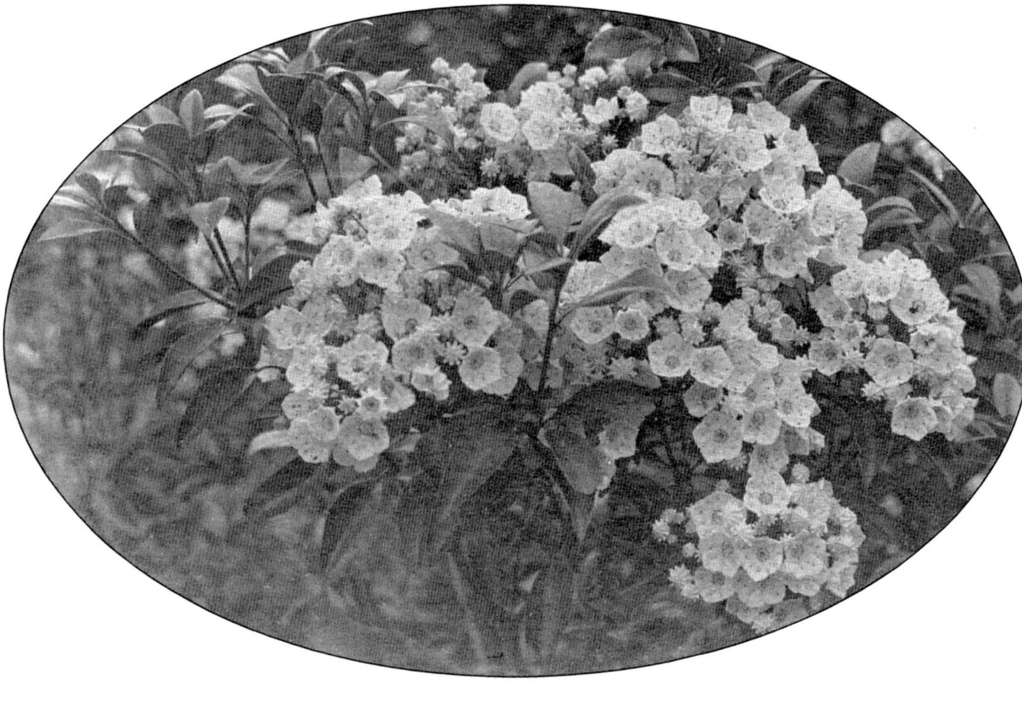

MOUNTAIN LAUREL. This was known as "calico bush."

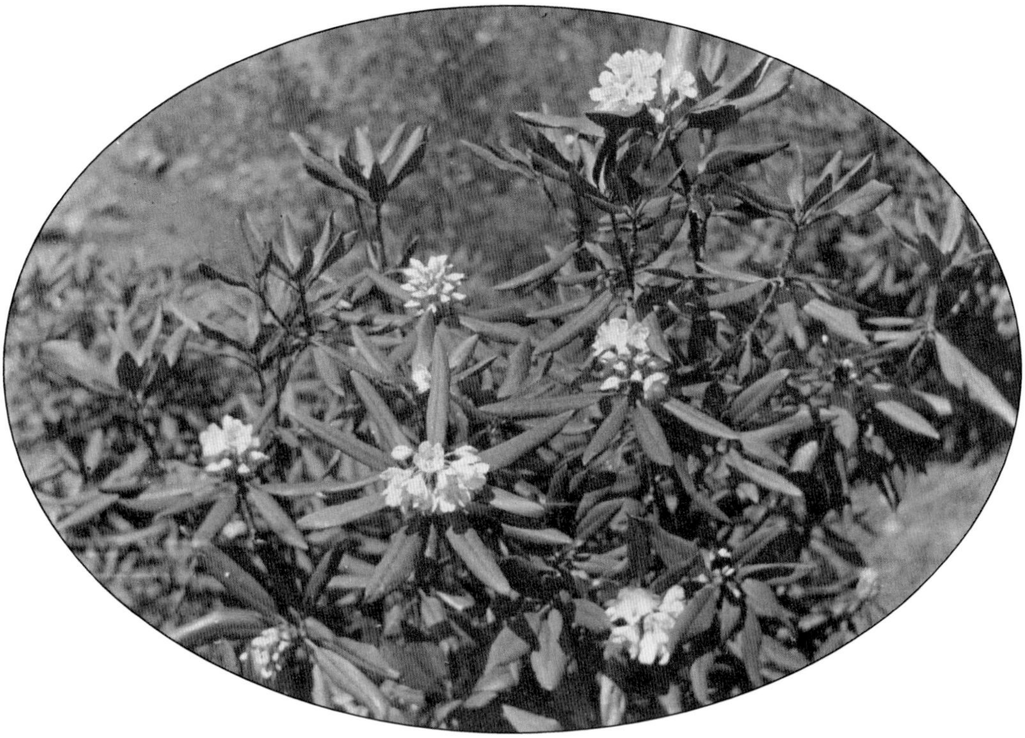

RHODODENDRONS. These were called mountain laurel at that time. Cyanotypes created by Gertrude Sprague, *c.* 1900, show some of the valley's showiest spring and summer vegetation. (Swannanoa Valley Museum.)

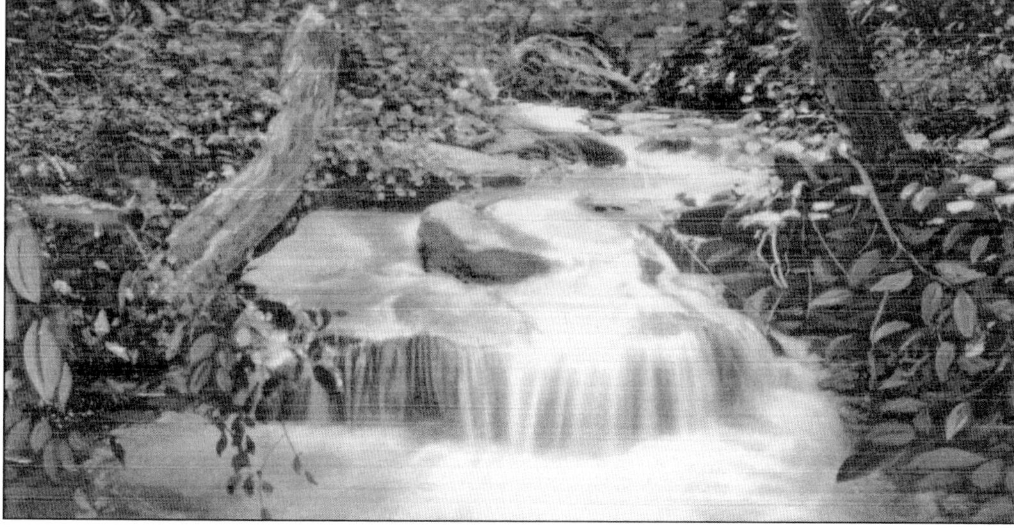

FALLS ON MOUNTAIN STREAM. This postcard image was taken in the rhododendron thickets at Blue Ridge Assembly. (Courtesy Don Talley.)

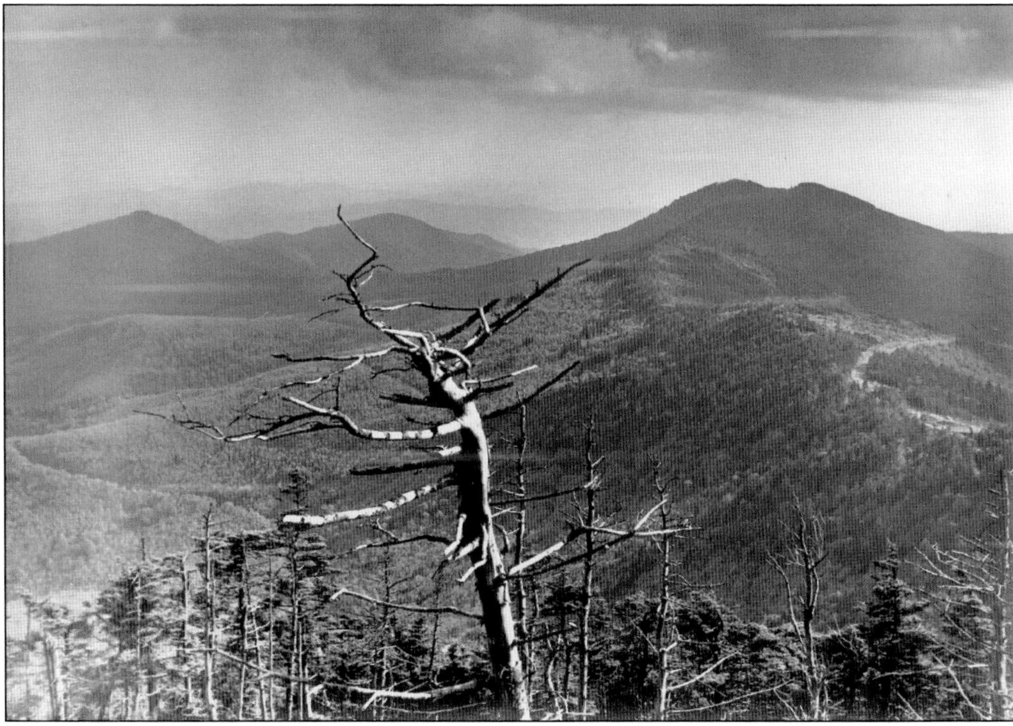

VIEW FROM MT. MITCHELL TOWARD CLINGMAN'S PEAK. Mt. Mitchell, the highest peak in the eastern United States (6,684 feet) is north of the town of Black Mountain in the Black Mountain Range. (Swannanoa Valley Museum.)

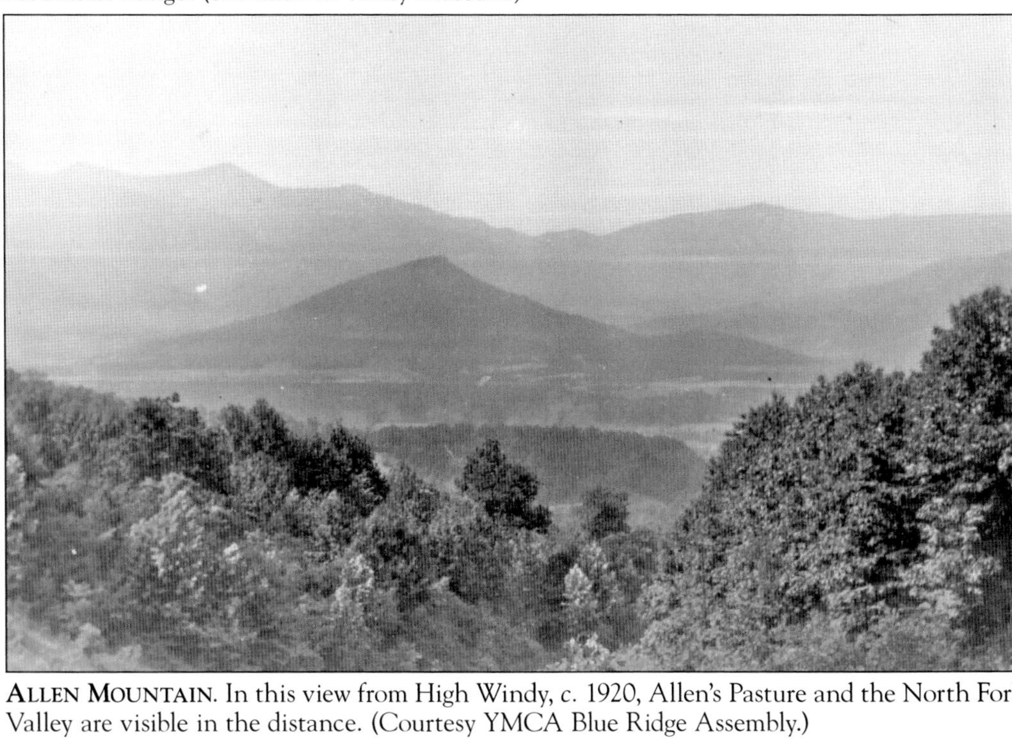

ALLEN MOUNTAIN. In this view from High Windy, *c.* 1920, Allen's Pasture and the North Fork Valley are visible in the distance. (Courtesy YMCA Blue Ridge Assembly.)

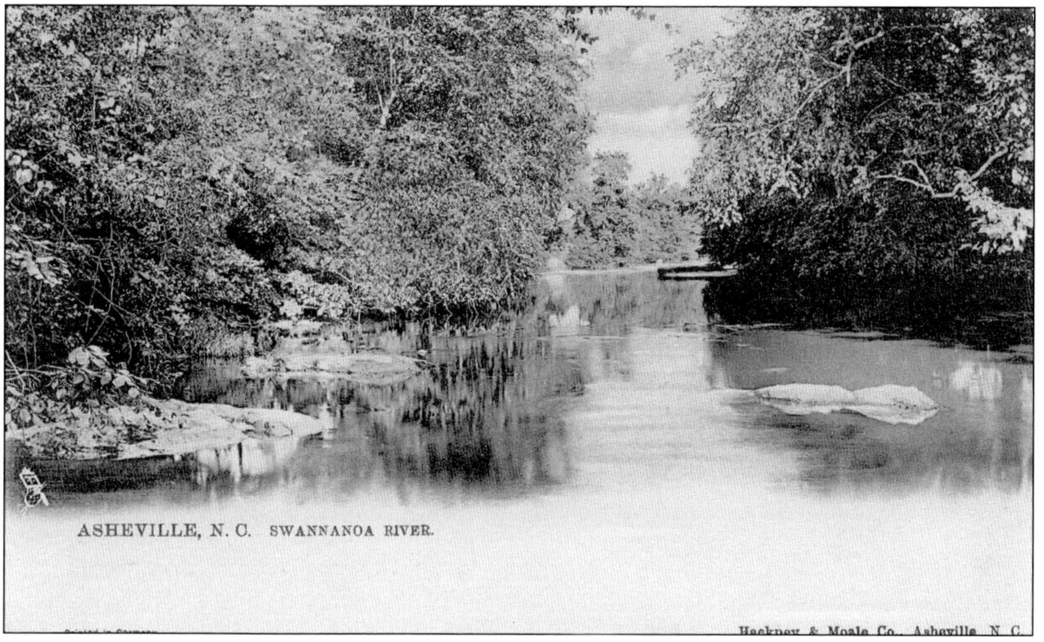

SWANNANOA RIVER SCENE. This postcard view of the Swannanoa River shows a full, slow-moving stream as it was before land use patterns changed to serve a growing Buncombe County community. (Courtesy Don Talley.)

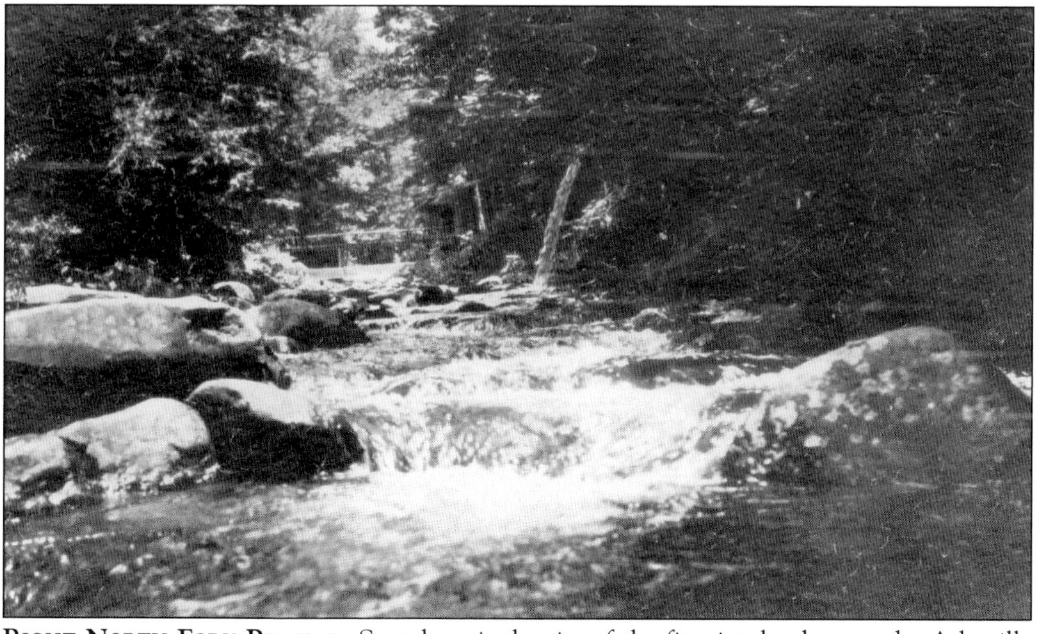

RIGHT NORTH FORK BRANCH. Seen here is the site of the first intake dam on the Asheville watershed. The crystal rush of creeks and streams have lured fishers, waders, and rock-sitters to the Swannanoa Valley for generations. These waters eventually empty into the Swannanoa River to later join the waters of the French Broad River in Asheville. (Robert Goodson Collection, Swannanoa Valley Museum.)

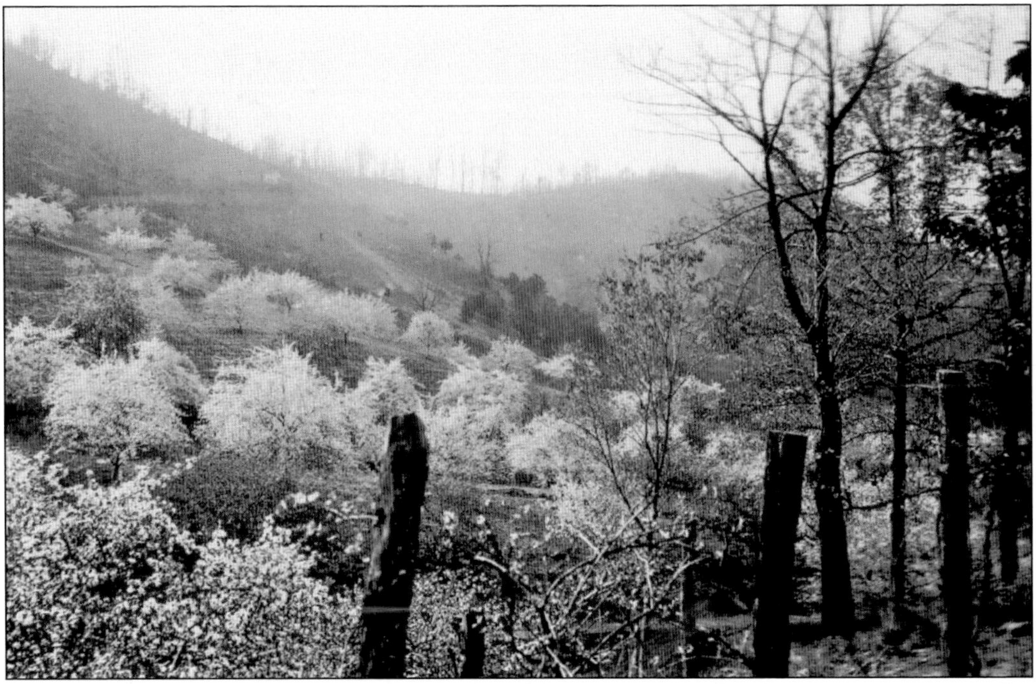

ORCHARD VIEW. High Top orchard at the top of Lynch Cove in Black Mountain is pictured c. 1920. (Courtesy Andy Cook collection.)

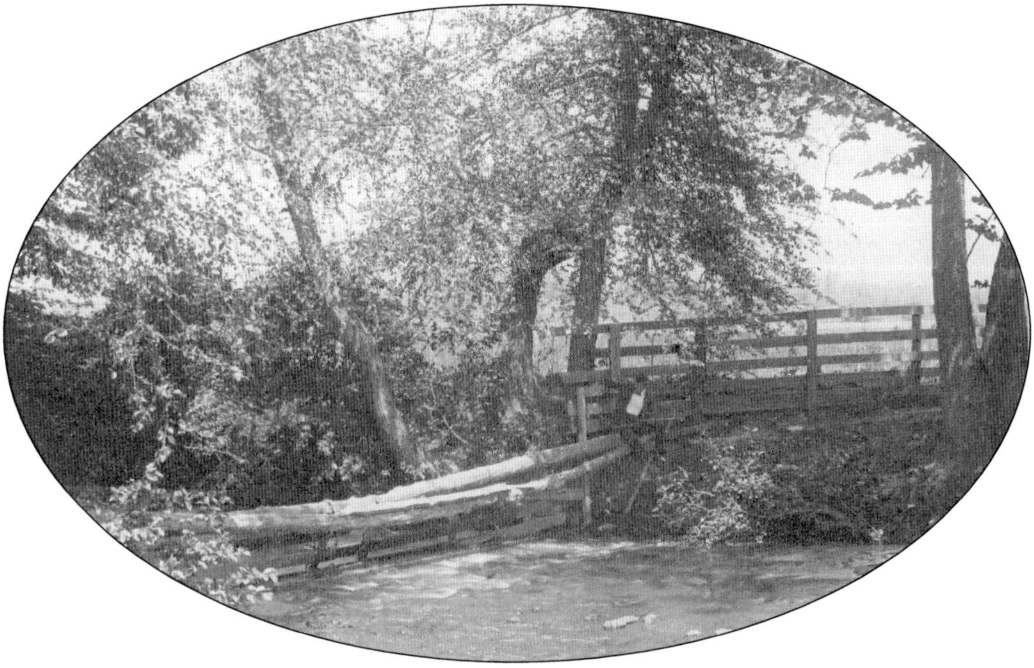

OLD LOG FOOTBRIDGE. This Cyanotype image, taken by Gertrude Sprague, shows an idyllic country scene with a rustic log footbridge crossing a valley creek. (Swannanoa Valley Museum.)

Two

FARMING, LOGGING, AND MINING

In 1776, Col. Griffith Rutherford led more than 2,000 troops through the Swannanoa Valley headed west, going as far as the Little Tennessee River, where they destroyed many Cherokee villages in retribution for Native-American raids to the east. The soldiers saw the rich lands of the valley and were among many others who returned after the Revolutionary War to stake a claim. Some turned to farming, others to logging, and some mined the mica and vermiculite from the mountains.

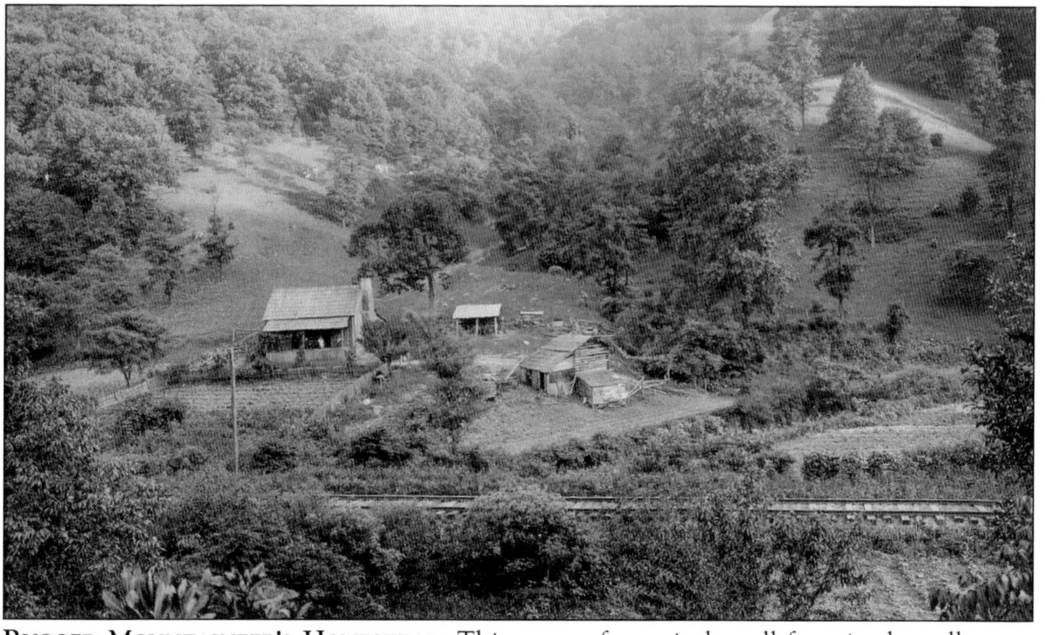

RUGGED MOUNTAINEER'S HOMESTEAD. This scene of a typical small farm in the valley was taken near the present-day Blue Ridge Assembly. (Herbert W. Pelton photo, courtesy YMCA Blue Ridge Assembly.)

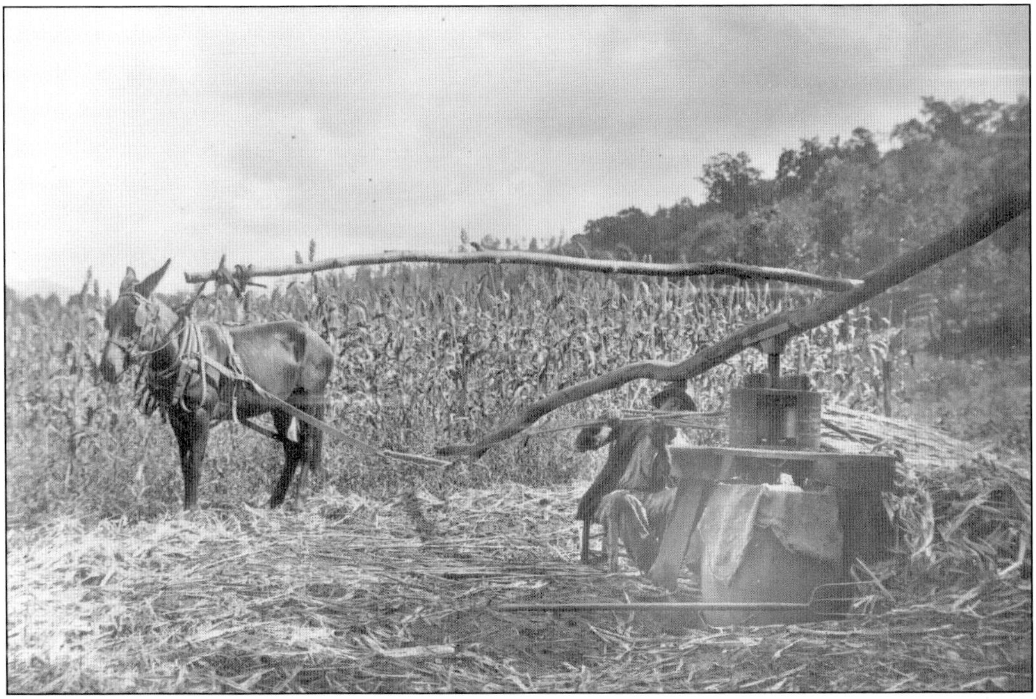

SORGHUM HARVEST. This farmer and his mule grind the cane of recently harvested sorghum to produce molasses. (Barnhill photo, courtesy Pack Memorial Library.)

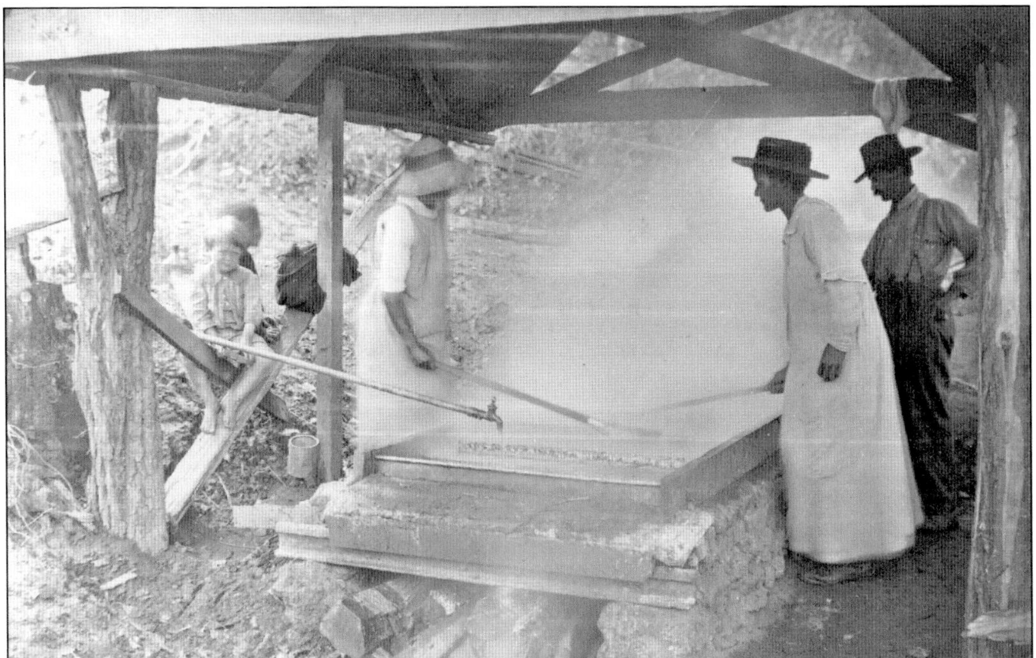

BOILING SORGHAM. Workers—attended by a barefoot boy—boil the sorghum cane juice, skimming off impurities as it reduces to a thick syrup. (Barnhill photo, courtesy Pack Memorial Library.)

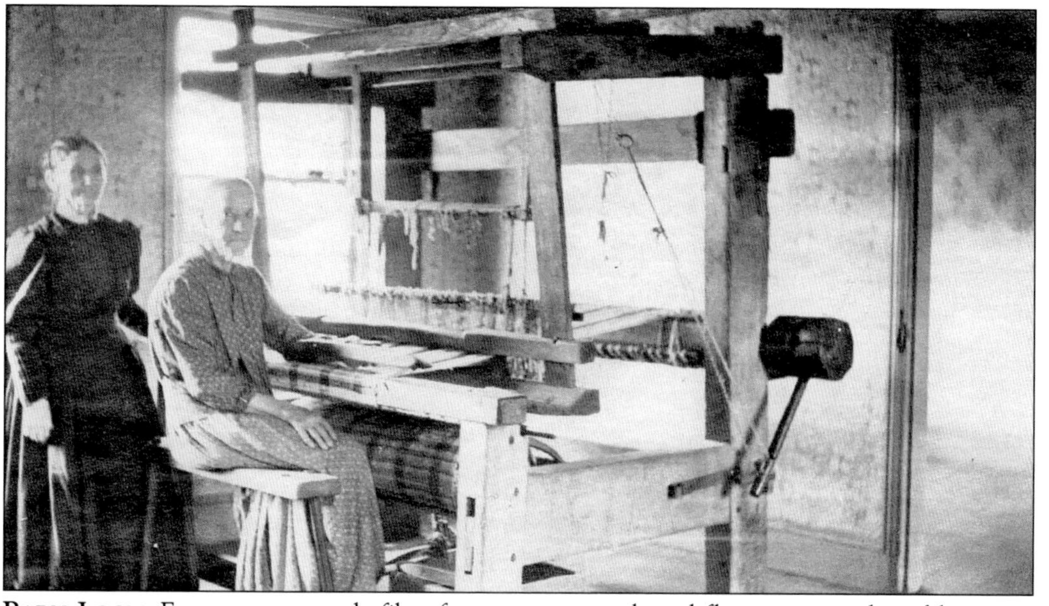

BARN LOOM. Farm women made fiber from cotton, wool, and flax, weaving their fabric into clothing for their families. This typical loom of the day was known as a "barn loom" or "porch loom," because it was usually too large to bring into a house. A barn loom donated by Nancy Wrenn is on display at the Swannanoa Valley Museum. (Swannanoa Valley Museum.)

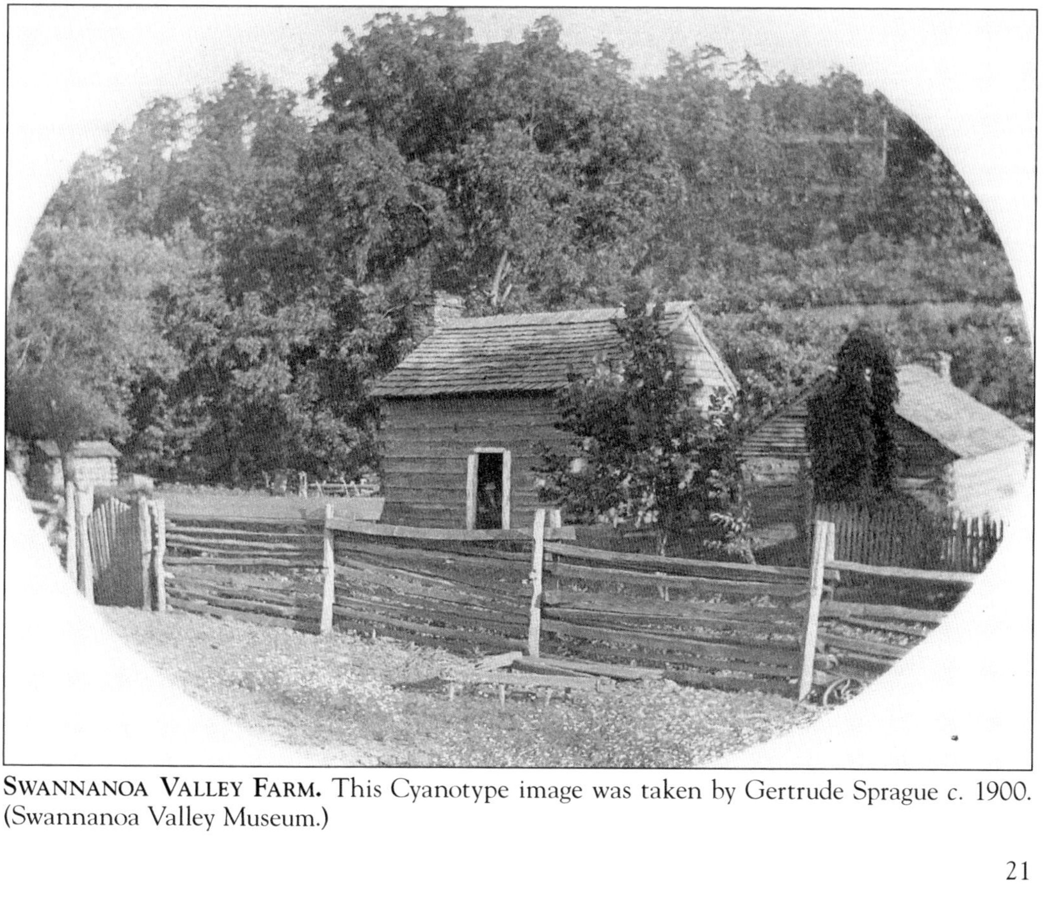

SWANNANOA VALLEY FARM. This Cyanotype image was taken by Gertrude Sprague *c.* 1900. (Swannanoa Valley Museum.)

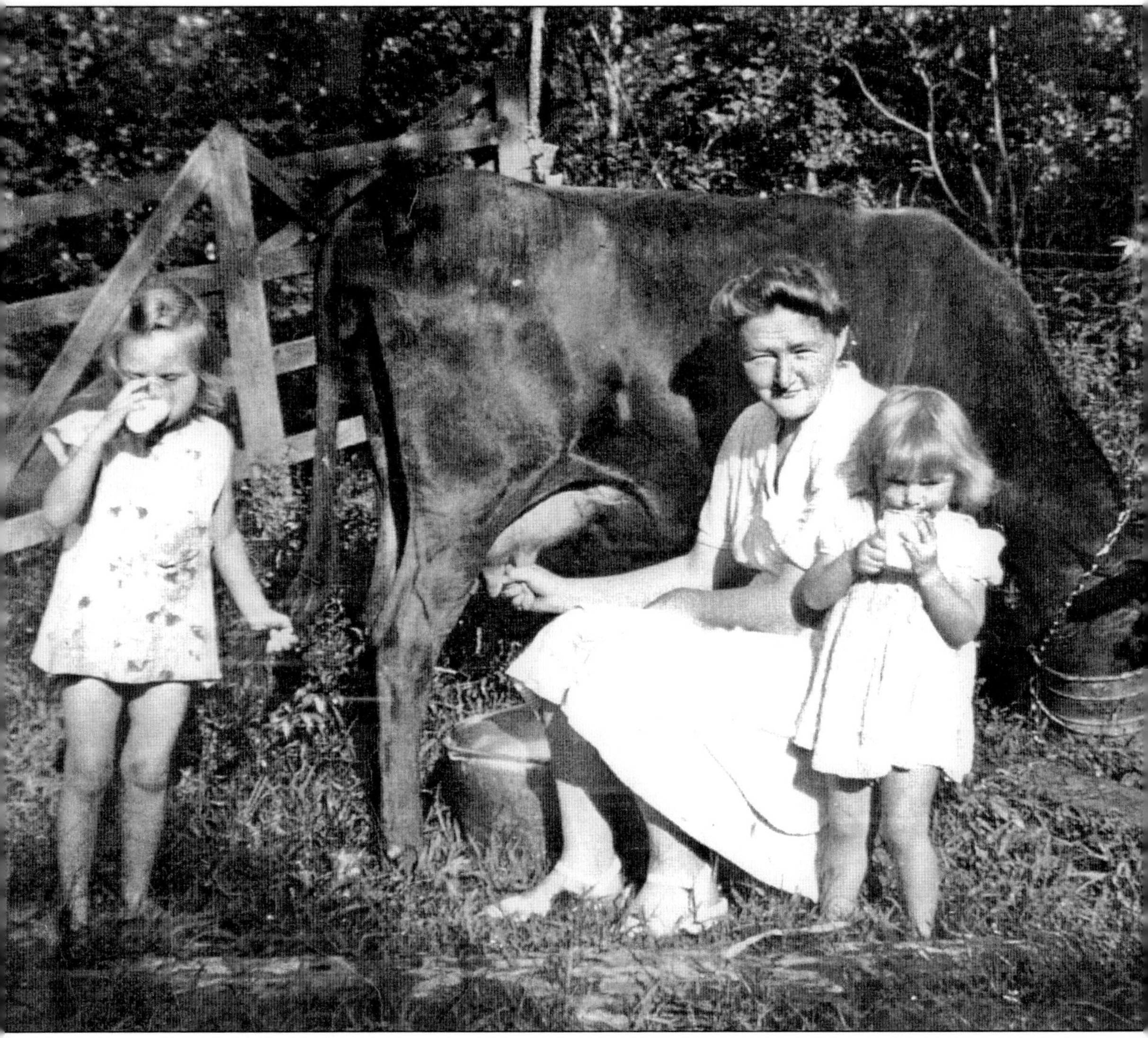

IT DOESN'T GET FRESHER THAN THIS. Reta Allison (left) and Mary Jo Allison (right) enjoy milk straight from the cow, milked by their mother, Lucille Gilliam Allison, *c.* 1946. (Courtesy Jean Allison Hyatt.)

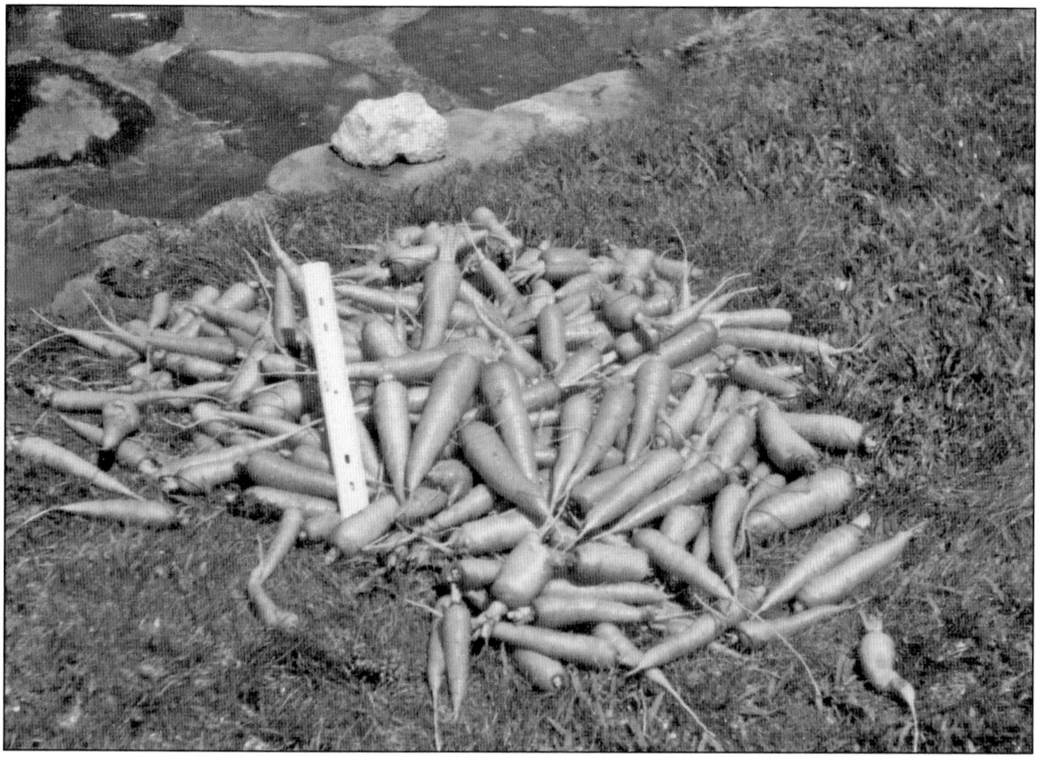

MEASURABLE HARVEST. A ruler shows the size of this hearty carrot crop produced in a garden in Lytle Cove, Swannanoa. (Courtesy Harriet Styles.)

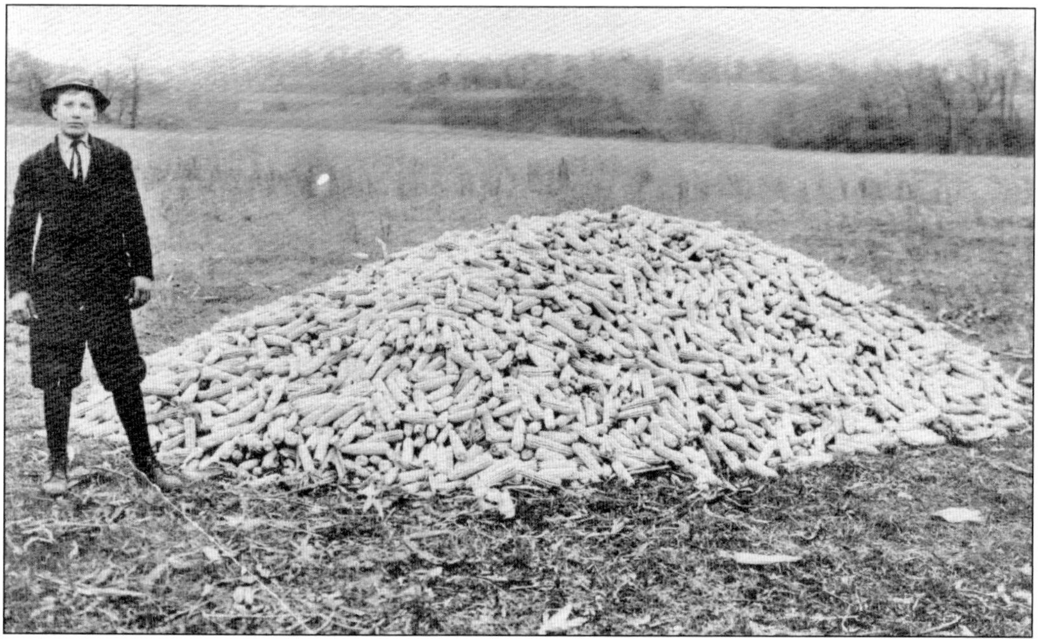

CHAMPION CORN GROWER. Corbett Alexander was named the champion corn grower in an 11-county area in Western North Carolina in 1910–1912, beating out the famous Biltmore Estate. (Swannanoa Valley Museum.)

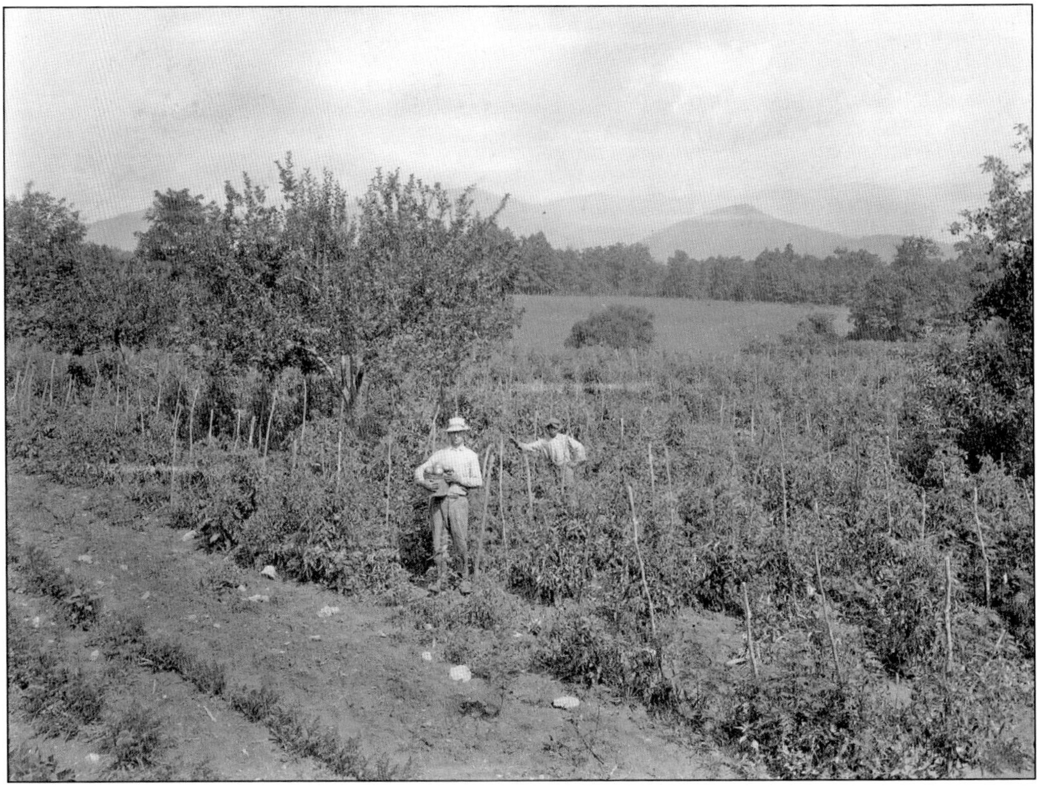

TOMATO BONANZA. Bascombe Burnett and a helper harvest tomatoes on Blue Ridge Farm in 1920. (Courtesy YMCA Blue Ridge Assembly.)

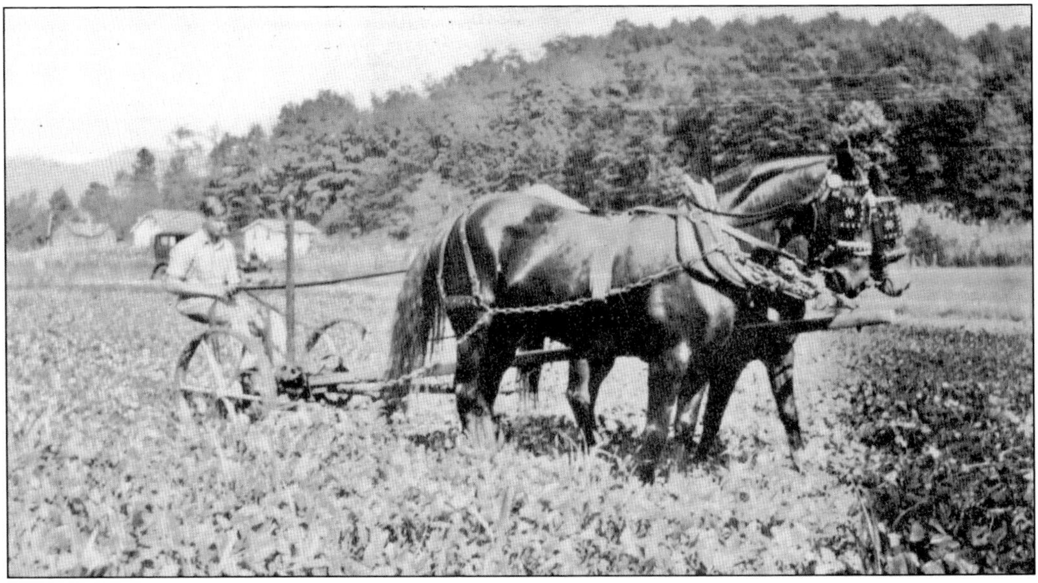

WORKING IN THE FIELDS. Bill Phillips guides his horse-drawn cultivator through a field. (Swannanoa Valley Museum.)

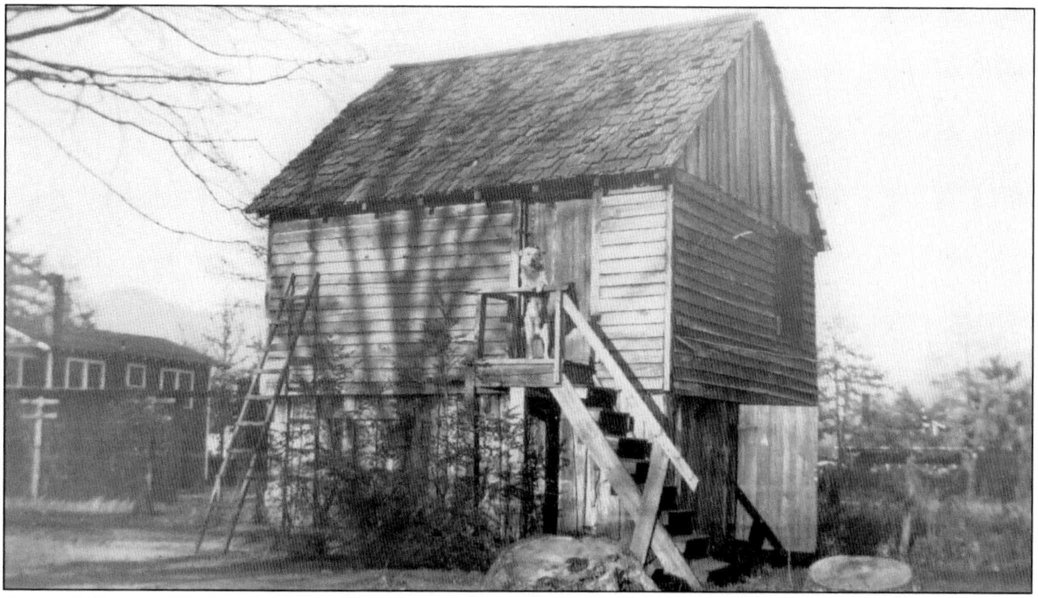

APPLE HOUSE. Built to store apples grown on Tyson's land in Black Mountain, this apple house appears to be happily guarded by a pet dog. (Courtesy Mary Elizabeth Tyson.)

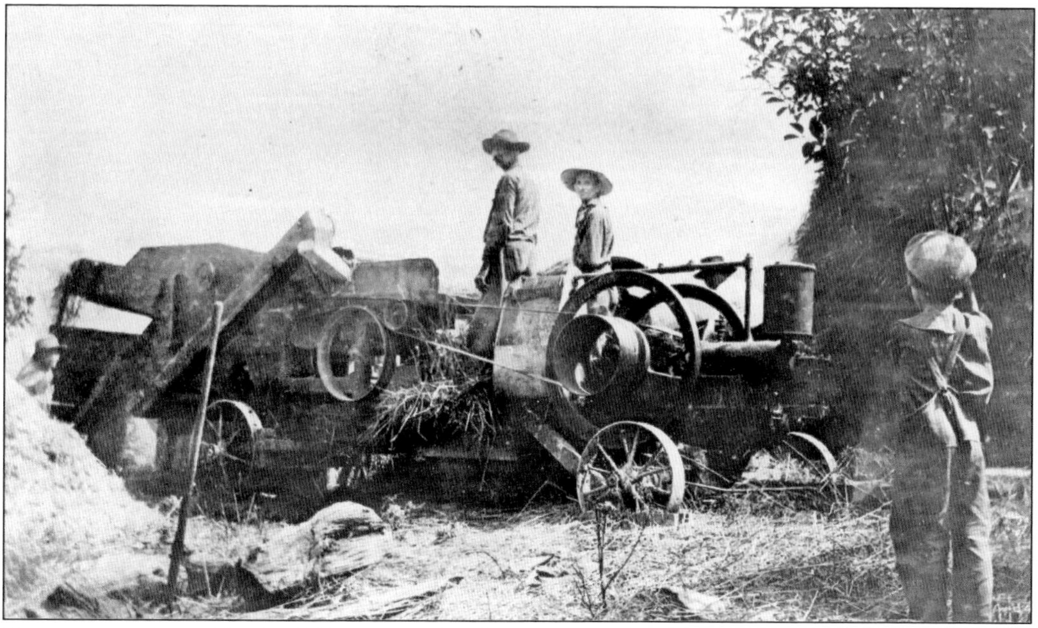

THRESHING DAY. Charles Whitson and helper operate the threshing machine while a young child looks on. In the early 1900s, threshing machines were often owned in partnership in the valley. (Swannanoa Valley Museum.)

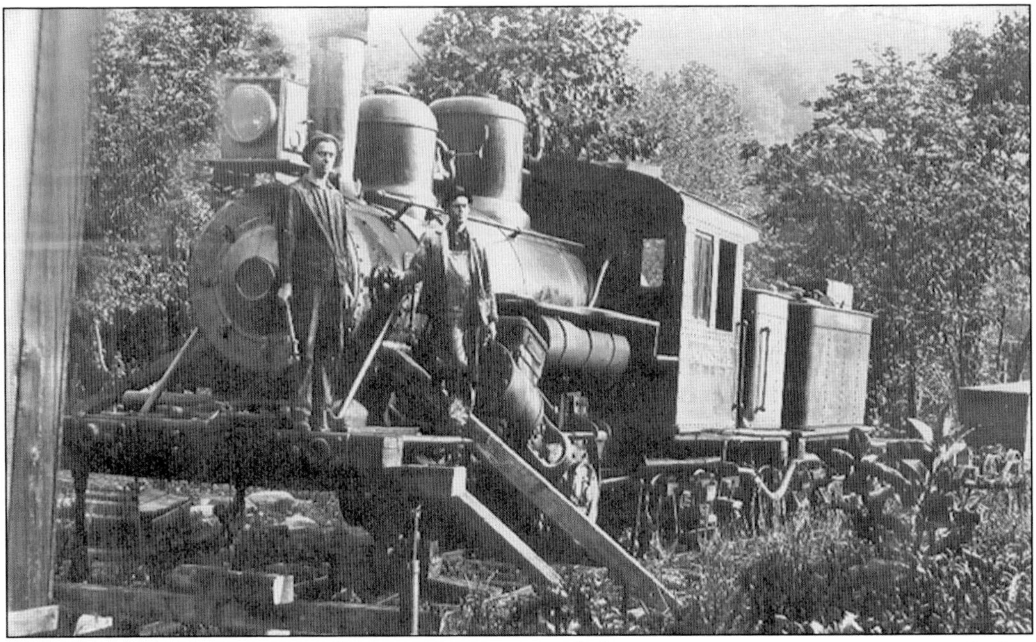

LOGGING TRAIN. Loggers in the Bee Tree area used this narrow gauge train to move timber to the main line of the Southern Railway in Swannanoa. Engine: A.M. Kistler; Engineer: Voll Pruett, Foreman: Cam Penland. (Swannanoa Valley Museum.)

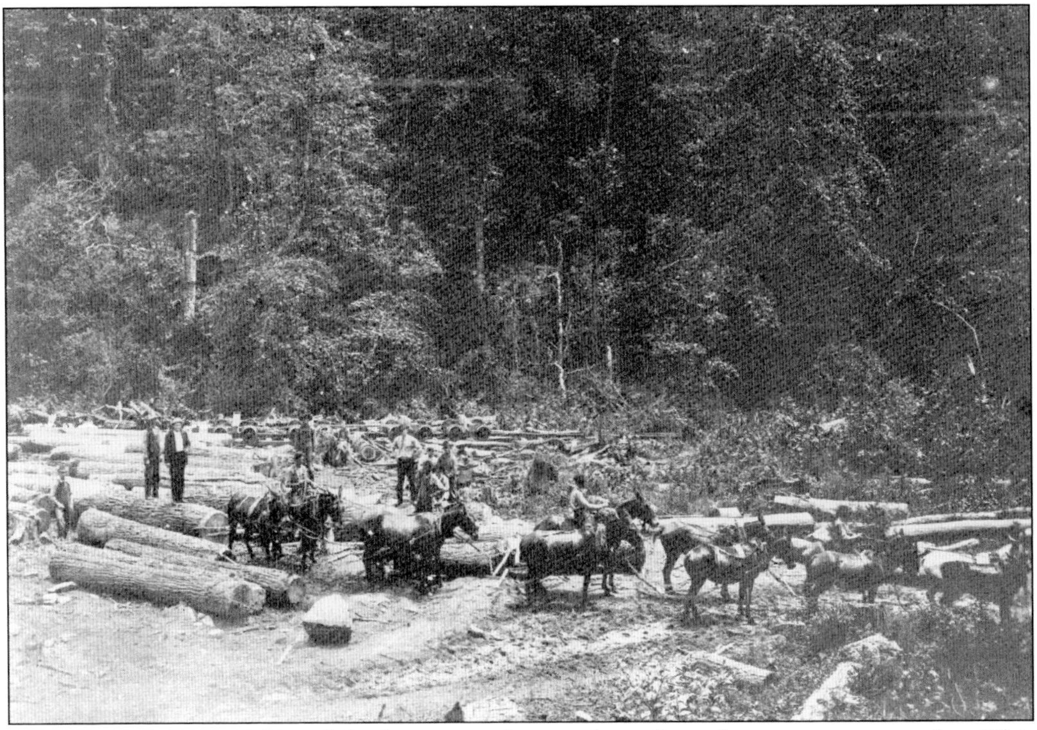

MULES AND MUSCLES. It took both to move logs to the railway for transport to market. This photo was taken in Bee Tree, *c.* 1915. (Swannanoa Valley Museum.)

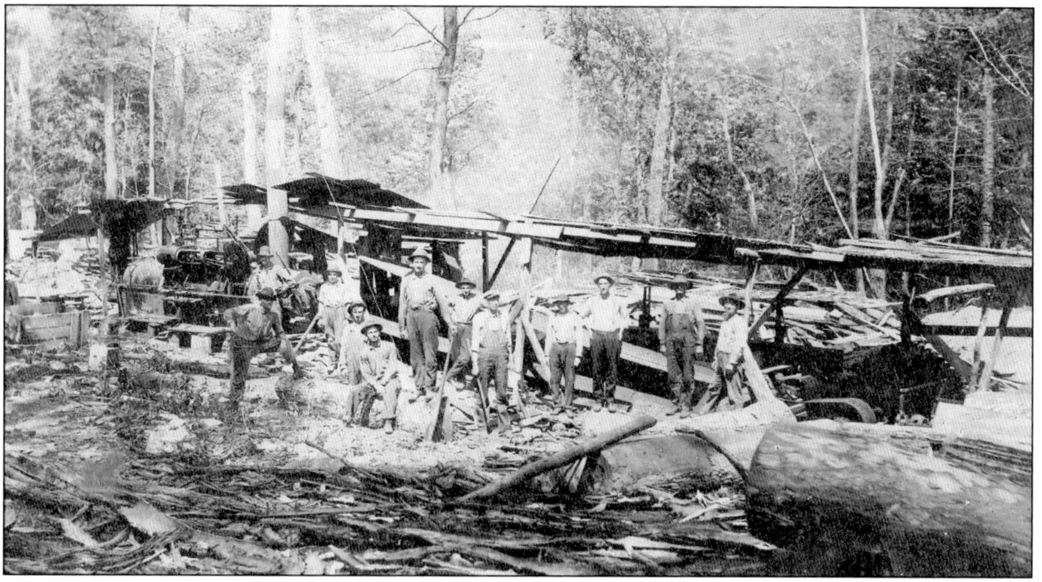

WOODLAND SAWMILL. Sometimes trees were sawn into lumber not far from where they were harvested. Others were moved by mule to larger mills closer to the railroad. (Swannanoa Valley Museum.)

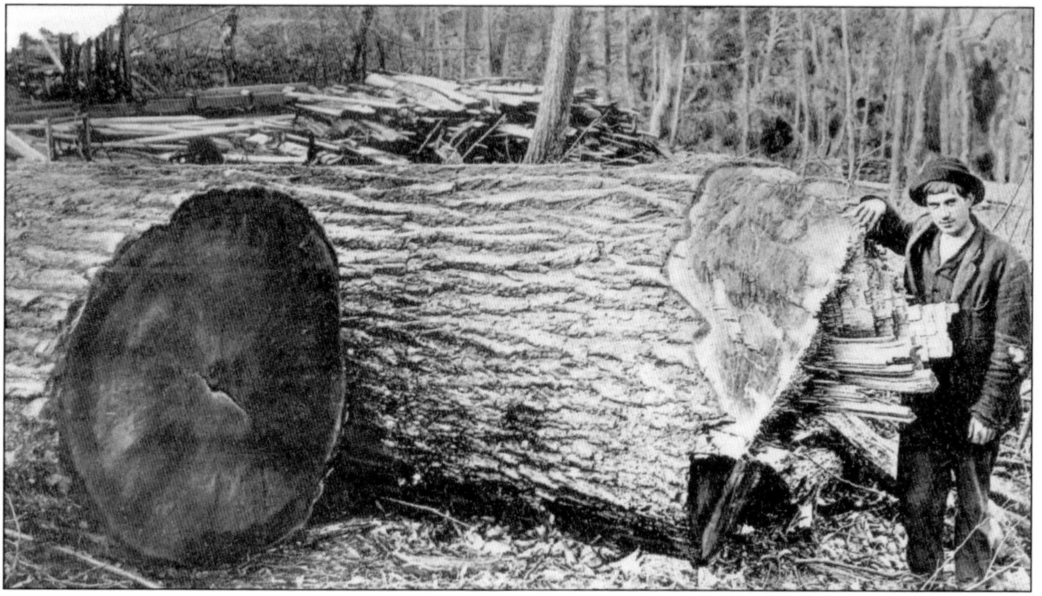

BIG TIMBER. This huge tree was felled on the grounds of Blue Ridge Assembly during the heyday of lumbering in the valley, c. 1915. (Herbert W. Pelton photo. Postcard, Swannanoa Valley Museum.)

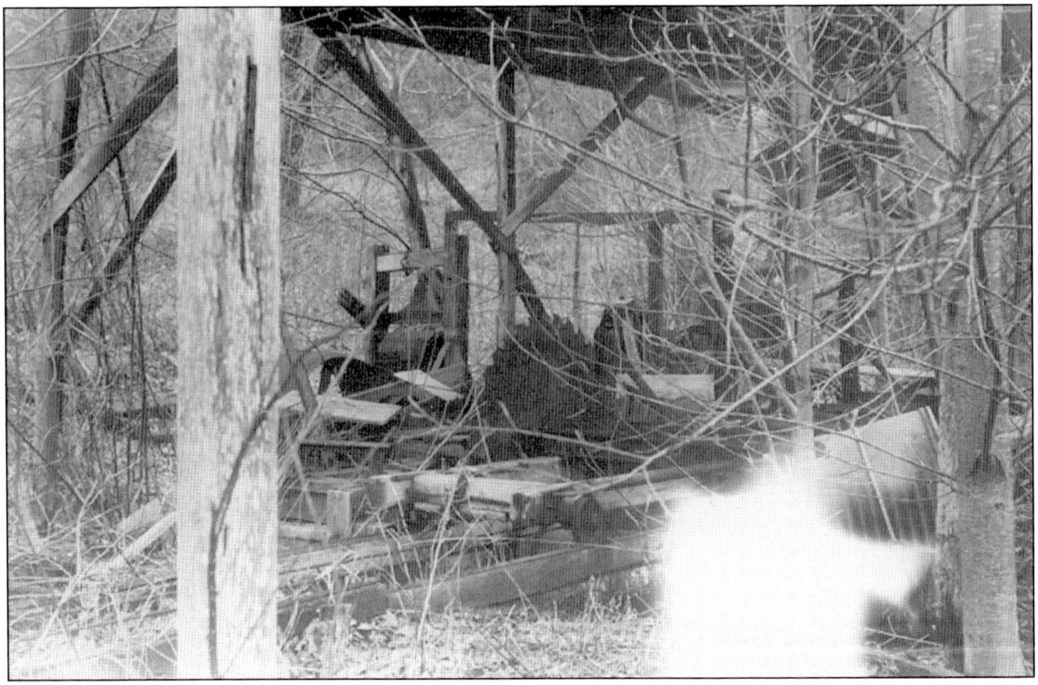

SMALL SAWMILL. Individuals as well as larger companies operated sawmills throughout the valley between 1910–1920. Elmore Burnette ran this sawmill in Bee Tree. The blade shown in this photo is now in the collection of the Swannanoa Valley Museum. (Courtesy Gary Bartlett.)

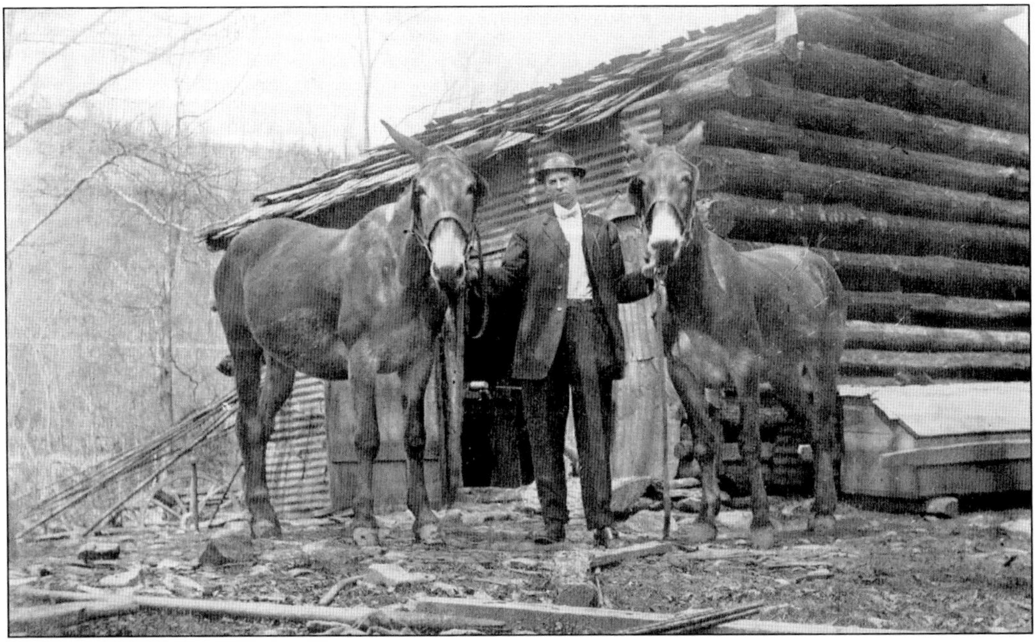

BEE TREE LOGGER. Raymond Shope was one of many settlers in the Bee Tree area who logged the land for a living; he is shown here with his mules in 1913. (Courtesy Catherine Pruett.)

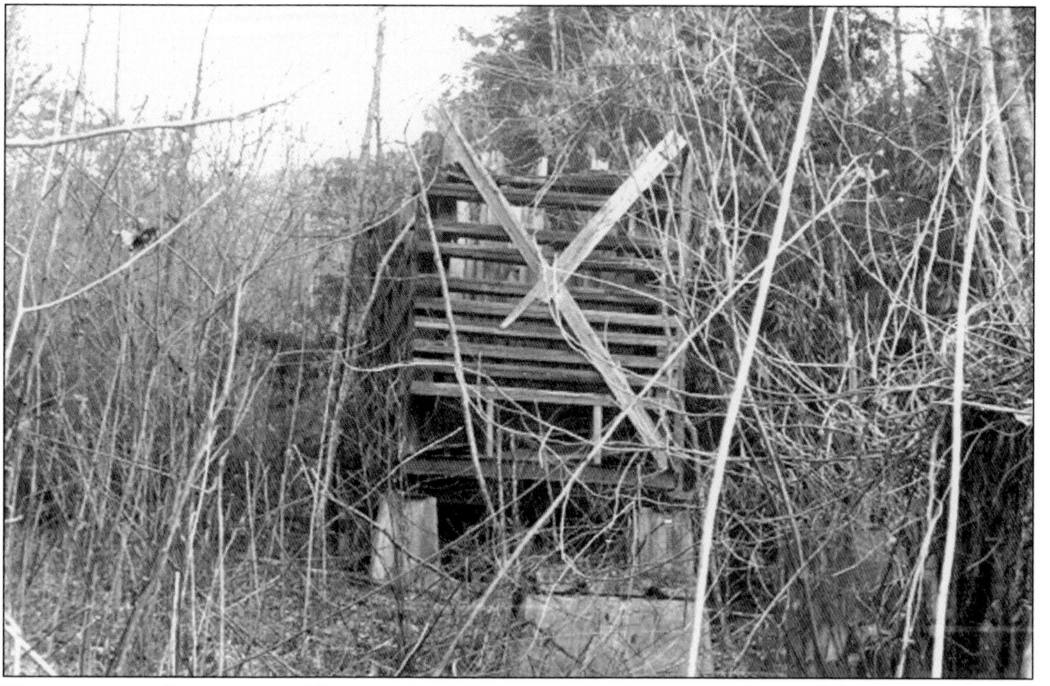

VERMICULITE PROCESSOR. The remains of a vermiculite processing bin and furnace in the Bee Tree community are pictured *c.* 1969. (Courtesy Gary Bartlett.)

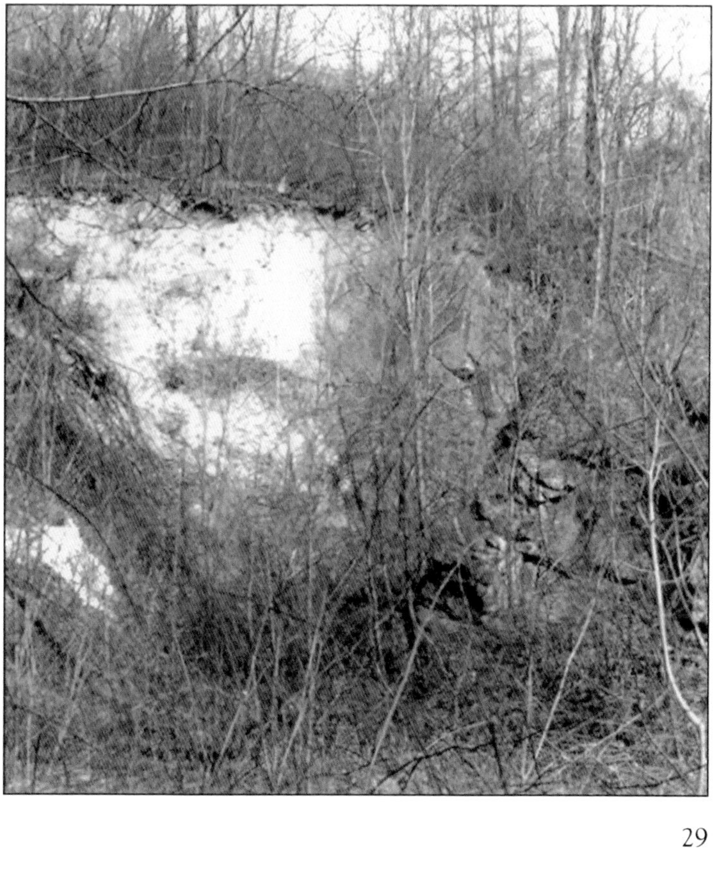

MICA MINE. Henry Allen Coggins mined and marketed mica, which was used in making stoves. This mine ruin was in Chestnut Cove in the Bee Tree community. The photo was taken c. 1969. (Courtesy Gary Bartlett.)

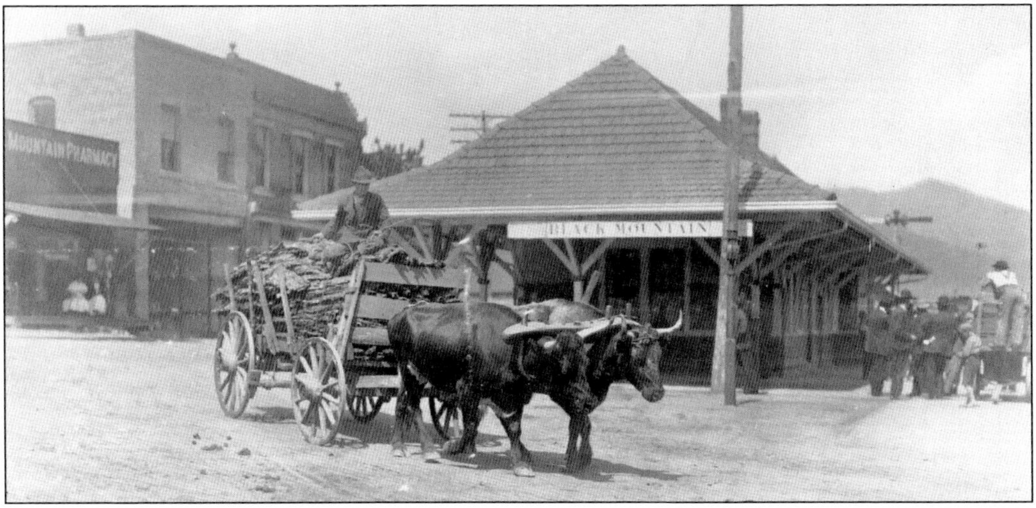

TANBARK TO MARKET. A valley farmer hauls a wagonload of tanbark to the Black Mountain station for transport to the tannery in 1907. (Swannanoa Valley Museum.)

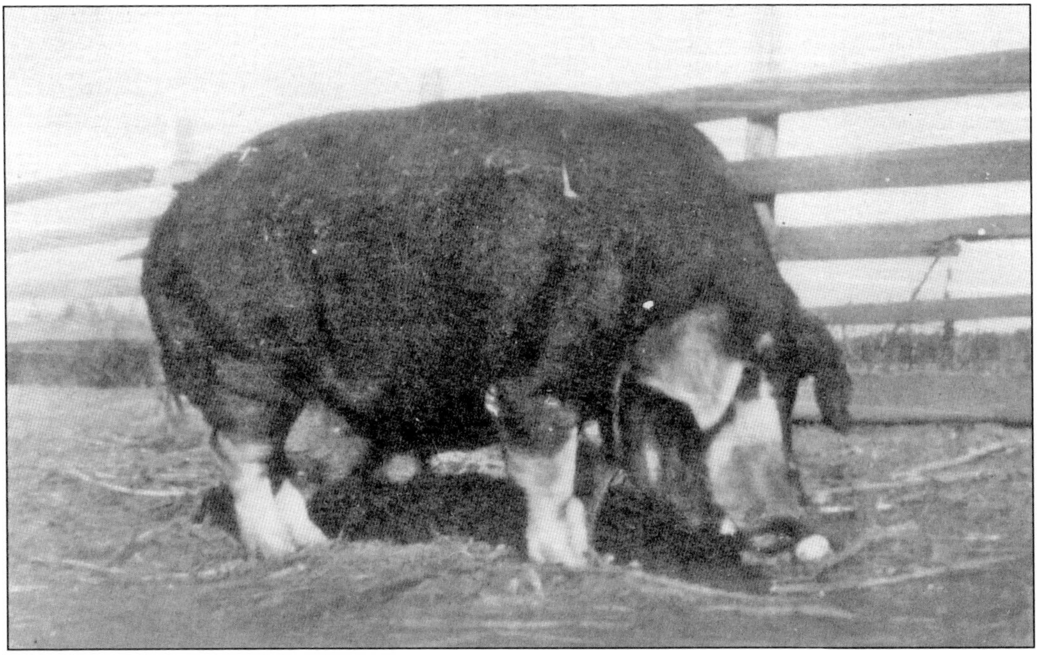

"BIG BOY." Claimed by owner Lyle Sanders of Black Mountain to be the world's largest hog, "Big Boy" weighed in at 1,904 pounds on January 5, 1939. (Swannanoa Valley Museum.)

Three

TRAINS AND TOURISM

On March 11, 1879, James J. Wilson, president, superintendent, and chief engineer of the Western North Carolina Railroad, telegraphed Gov. Zebulon Vance, "Daylight entered Buncombe County today through the Swannanoa Tunnel. Grade and centers met exactly." The coming of the railroad changed life in the Swannanoa Valley dramatically, allowing for greater ease of commerce and the influx of tourists.

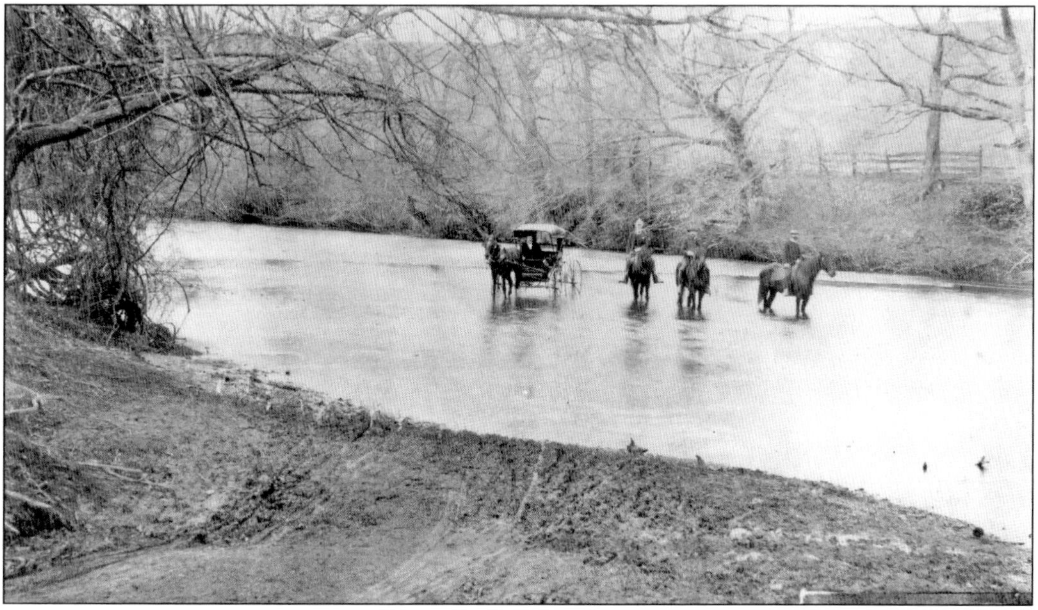

HORSE AND BUGGY DAYS. These gentlemen are crossing Connally's Ford on the Swannanoa River before the automobile brought bridges and highways to the valley. (Courtesy Pack Memorial Library.)

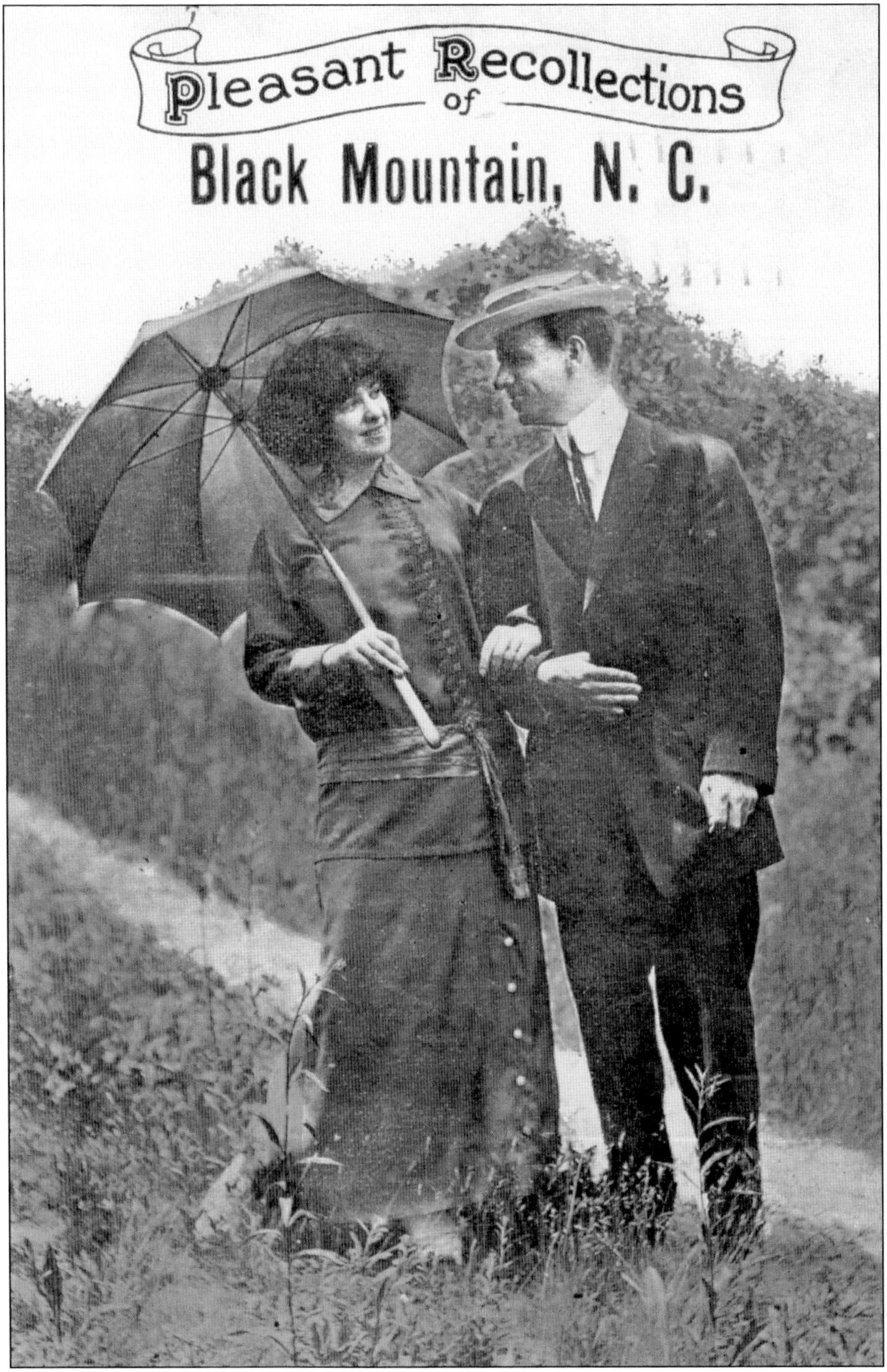

PICTURE PERFECT. "Pleasant Recollections of Black Mountain," states a card postmarked in 1914, depicting a tourist couple who would have been typical of the many visitors to Black Mountain and the Swannanoa Valley in that era. (Swannanoa Valley Museum.)

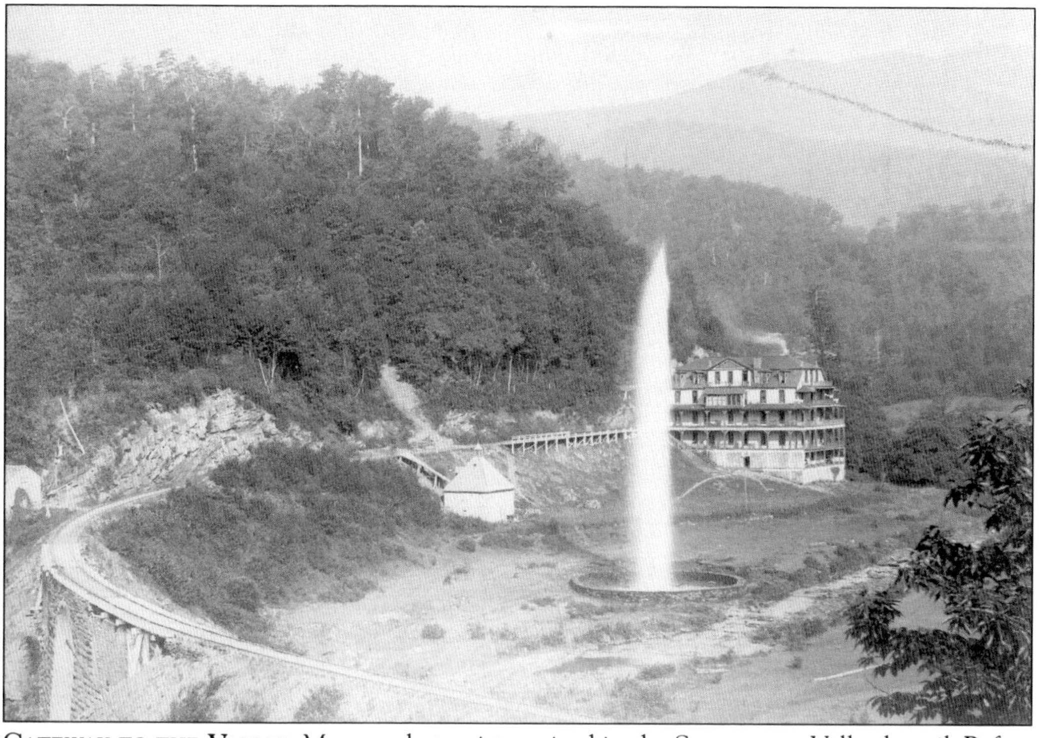

GATEWAY TO THE VALLEY. Many early tourists arrived in the Swannanoa Valley by rail. Before the Western North Carolina Railroad crossed the Blue Ridge, it passed the Andrews Geyser and the Hotel at Round Knob, shown here. (Courtesy Pack Memorial Library.)

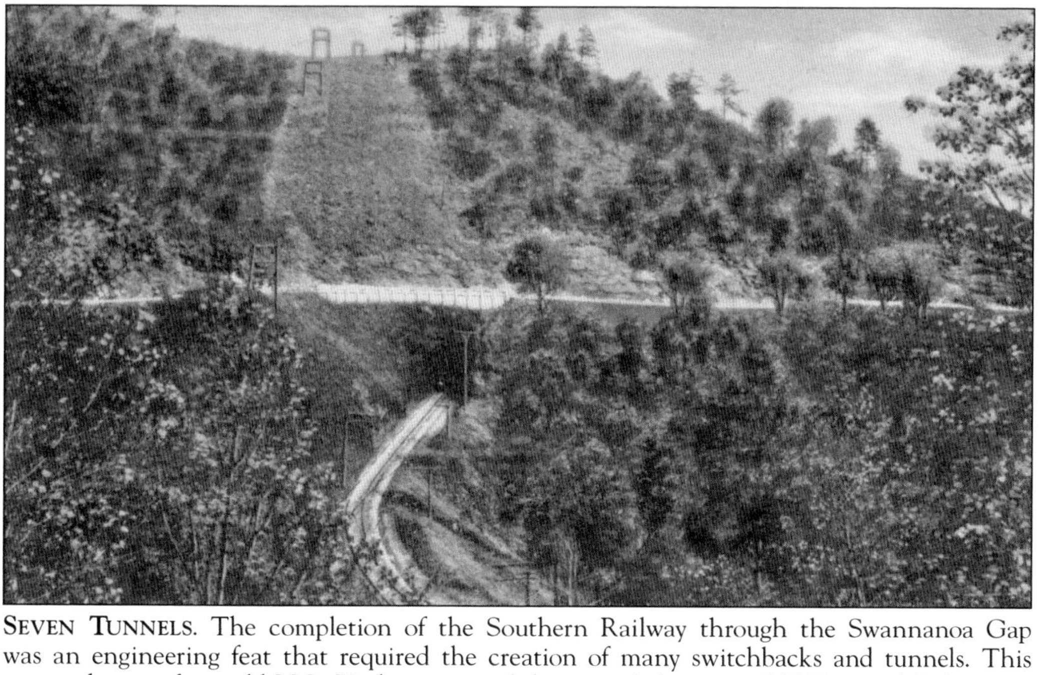

SEVEN TUNNELS. The completion of the Southern Railway through the Swannanoa Gap was an engineering feat that required the creation of many switchbacks and tunnels. This postcard scene from old U.S. 70 shows one of the tunnels between Old Fort and Ridgecrest. (Courtesy Don Talley.)

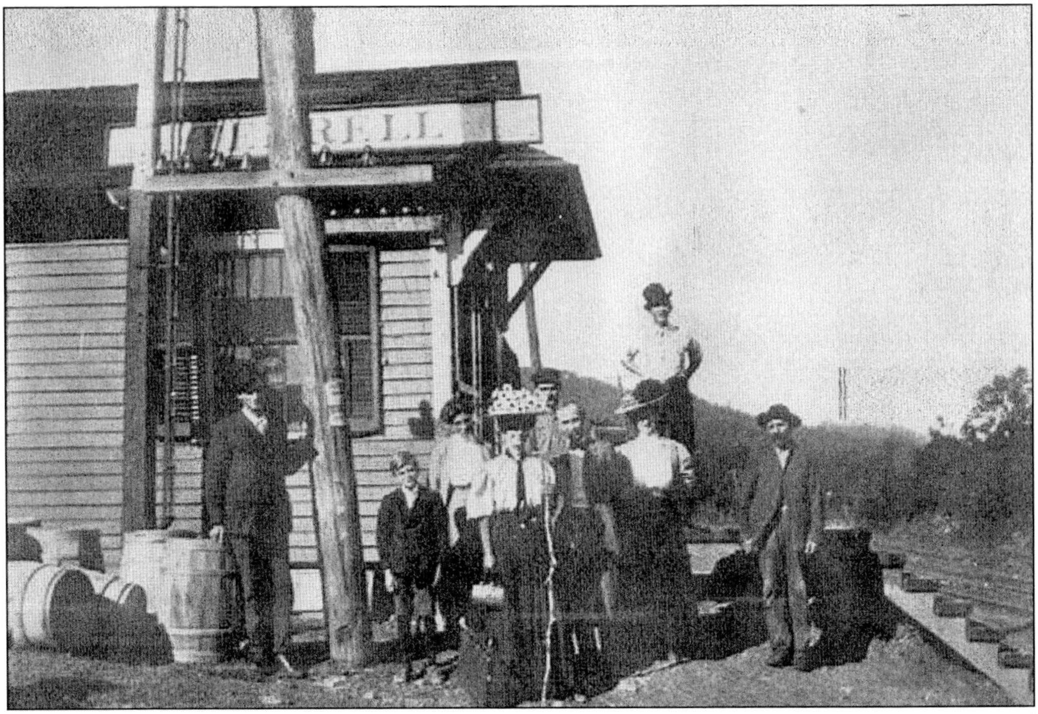

TERRELL STATION. The original Southern Railway station at Ridgecrest, at the eastern end of the Swannanoa Valley, was named for William Pitt Terrell, the first engineer to bring a train through the newly-constructed tunnels into the valley. The photo was taken in 1905. (Swannanoa Valley Museum.)

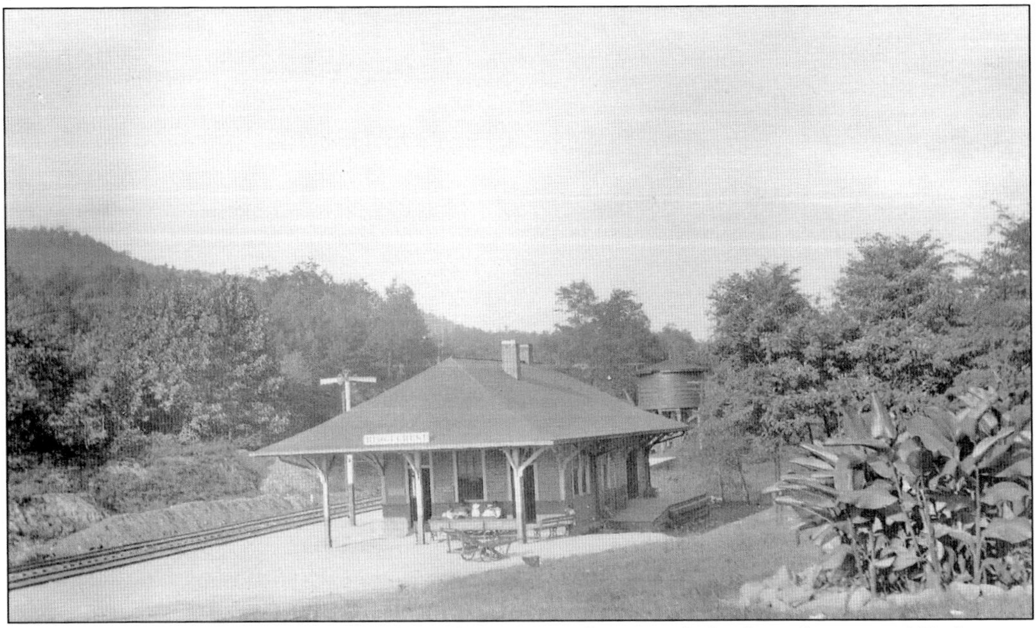

RIDGECREST STATION. A more modern depot was subsequently built and renamed Ridgecrest Station. Visitors to the famous Baptist conference center, Ridgecrest, arrived and departed from this station. (Swannanoa Valley Museum.)

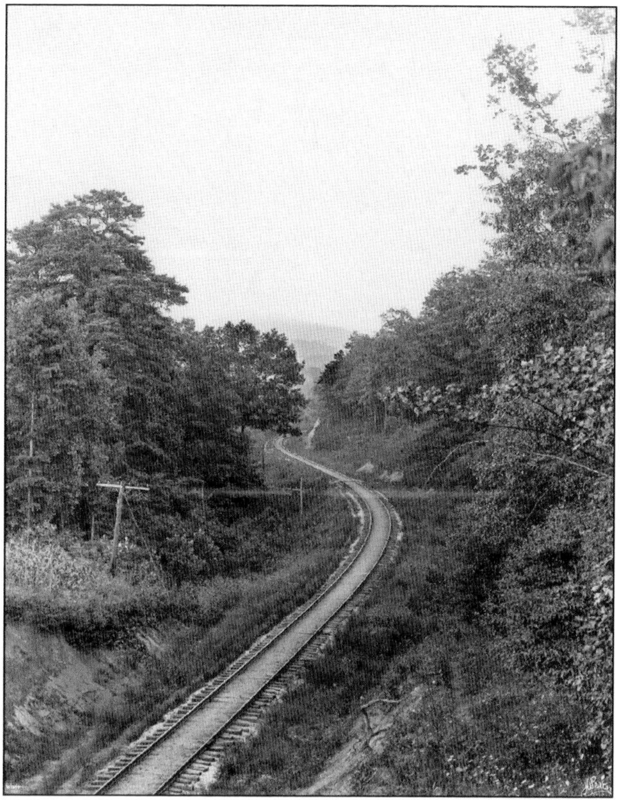

Winding Through the Valley. After leaving Black Mountain station, traveling west, the Southern Railway meandered along the valley bed toward Swannanoa. (Courtesy Blue Ridge Assembly.)

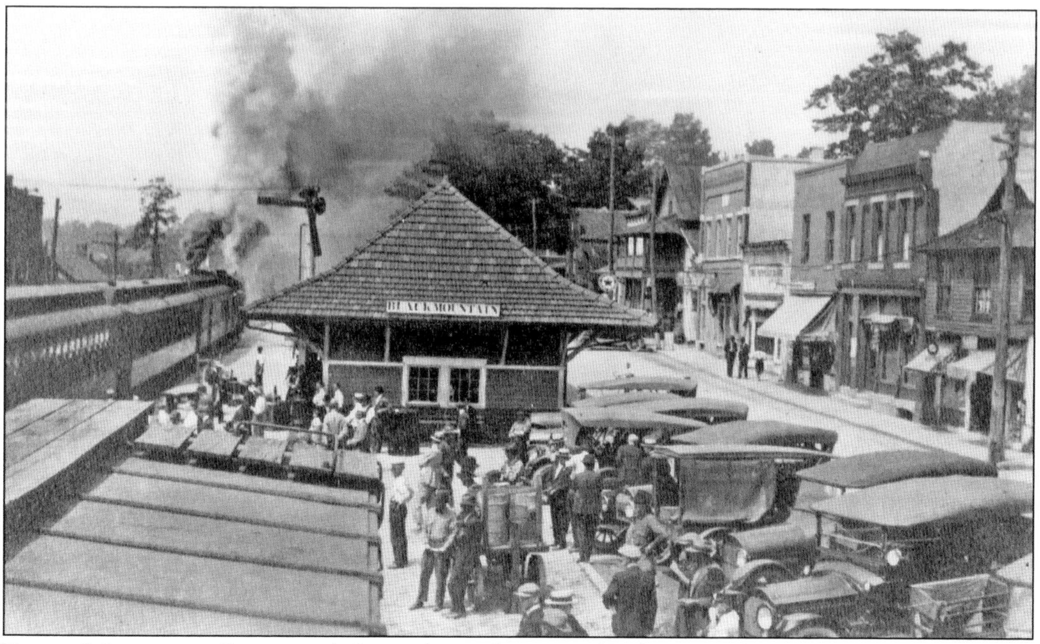

Black Mountain Station. A few miles to the west of Ridgecrest, the town of Black Mountain was a major tourist destination by the early 1920s. This photo shows the town's busy station and thriving commercial center. (Swannanoa Valley Museum.)

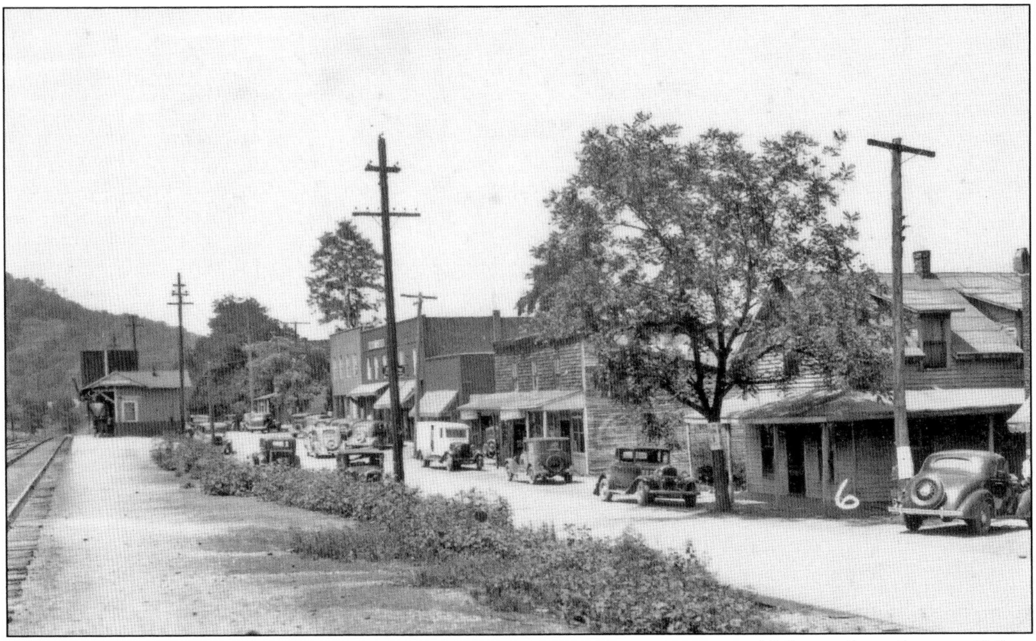

SWANNANOA STATION. Arriving in Swannanoa in 1933, visitors would have found a small but thriving village built near the newly constructed Beacon Manufacturing plant. (Herbert W. Pelton photo, Swannanoa Valley Museum.)

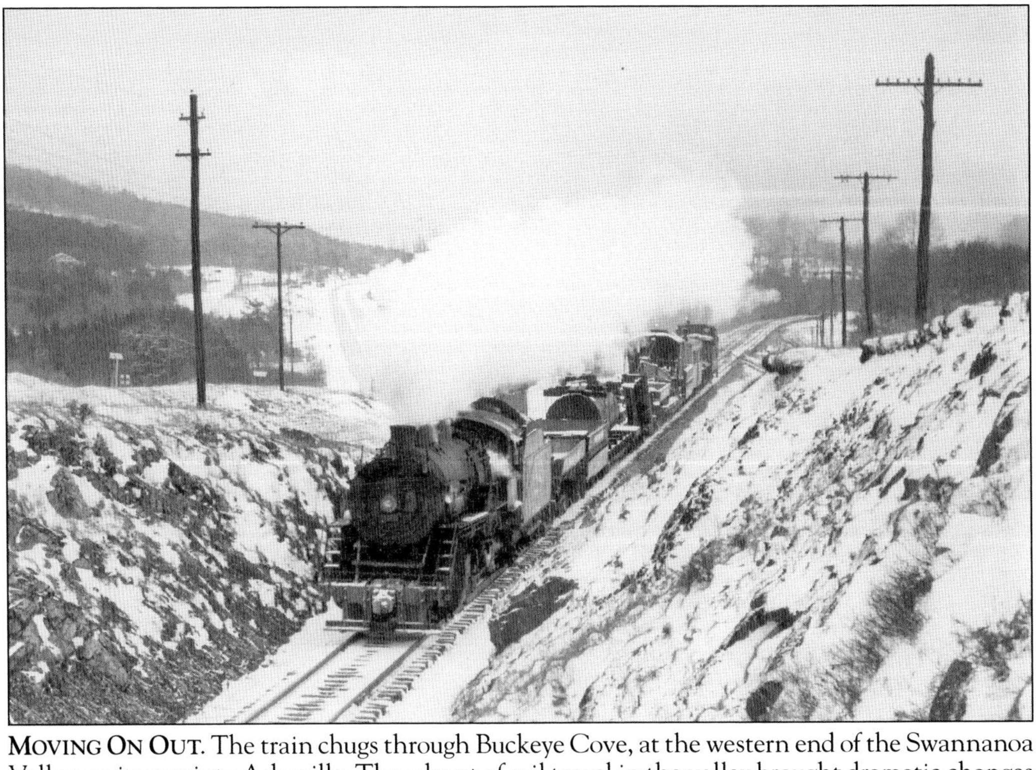

MOVING ON OUT. The train chugs through Buckeye Cove, at the western end of the Swannanoa Valley, on its way into Asheville. The advent of rail travel in the valley brought dramatic changes all along the way. (Noah Collection, courtesy David Rozzell.)

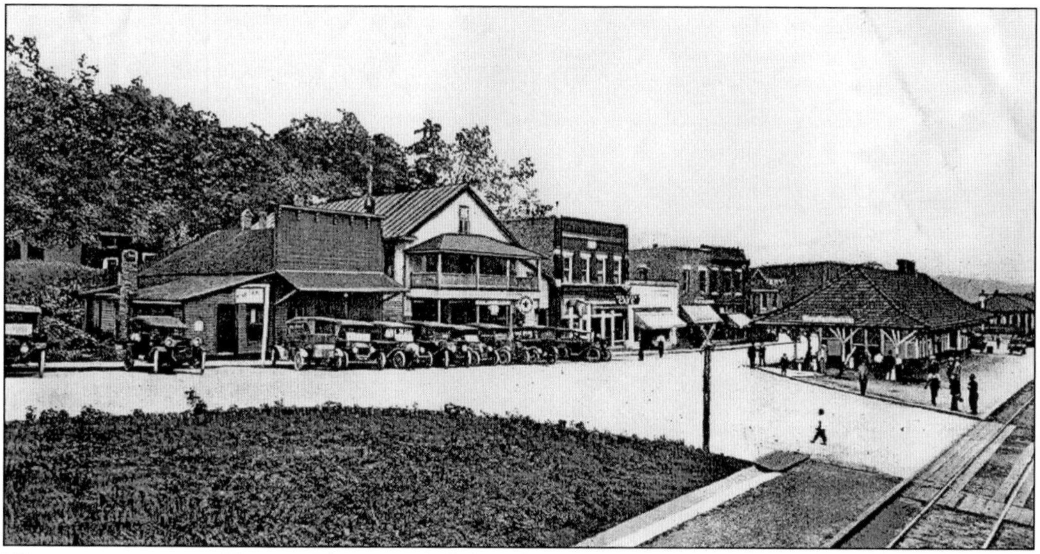

WAITING FOR THE TRAIN. This view of the Black Mountain train station is looking east up Sutton Avenue in 1920. (Swannanoa Valley Museum.)

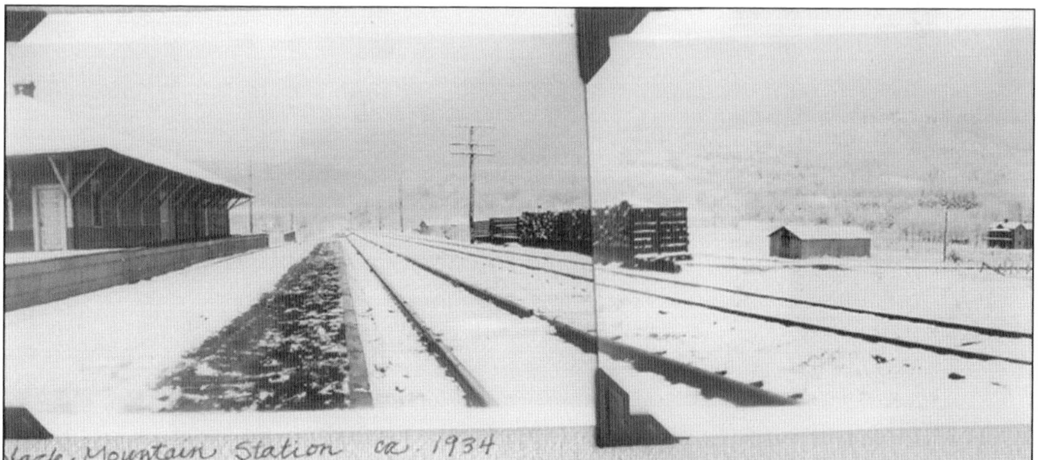

WINTER SCENE. Perhaps a wintertime visitor to Black Mountain captured the railroad station and surrounding fields in these snapshots of the town in snow, c. 1934. (Swannanoa Valley Museum.)

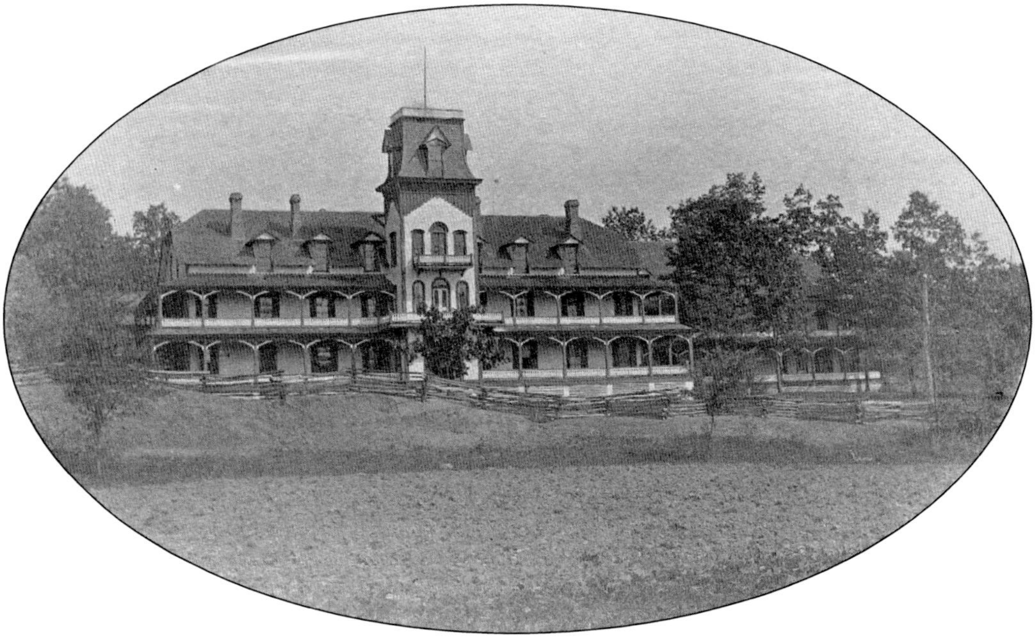

BLACK MOUNTAIN HOTEL. Built in 1882 at the very edge of the railroad tracks in the center of Black Mountain and owned by Mr. and Mrs. Mont Stepp, the Black Mountain Hotel was often the first stop for incoming tourists. This cyanotype image was made by Gertrude Sprague, daughter of the hotel's manager, c. 1900. (Swannanoa Valley Museum.)

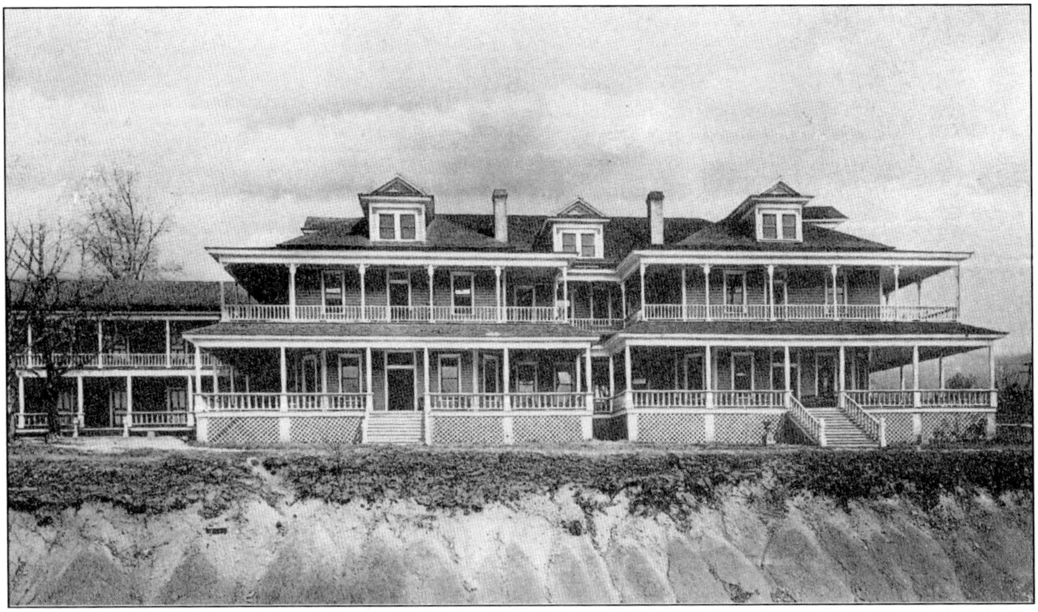

GLADSTONE HOTEL. Constructed on the site of the former Black Mountain Hotel, which was destroyed in 1906 when embers from a passing train caught the building on fire, the Gladstone was built by Mr. Bell and Mr. Manley of Mt. Olive, North Carolina. It was sold in 1917 to Emory L. Wilson, who renamed it the Gresham Hotel. The photo was taken in 1910 by Herbert W. Pelton. (Swannanoa Valley Museum.)

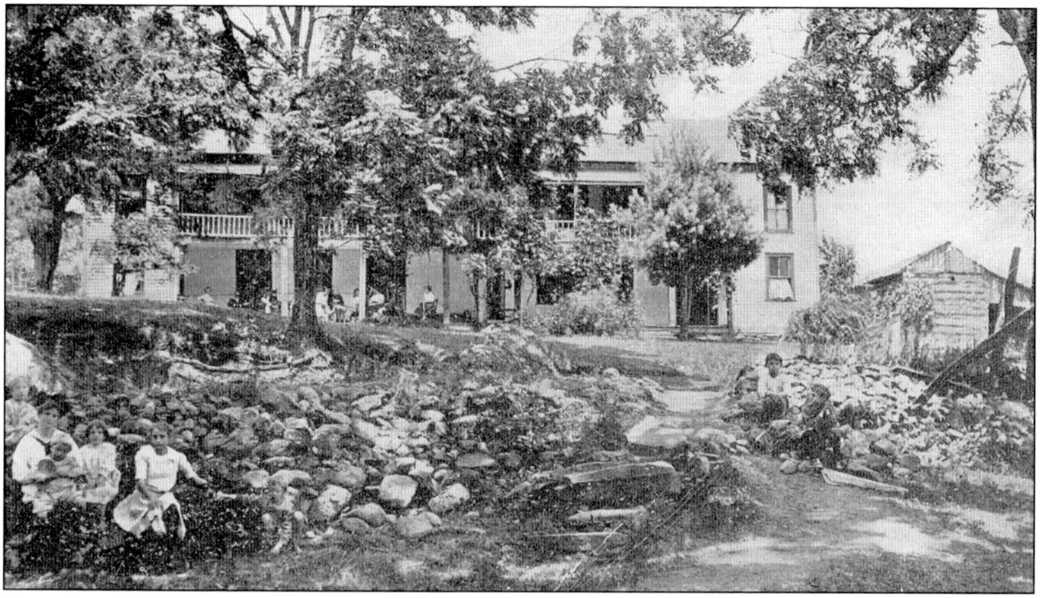

ALEXANDER INN. One of the early inns to provide lodging for tourists in Swannanoa belonged to George C. Alexander. The inn operated continually from 1818 until it closed in the 1930s. This photo was taken *c.* 1914. (Swannanoa Valley Museum.)

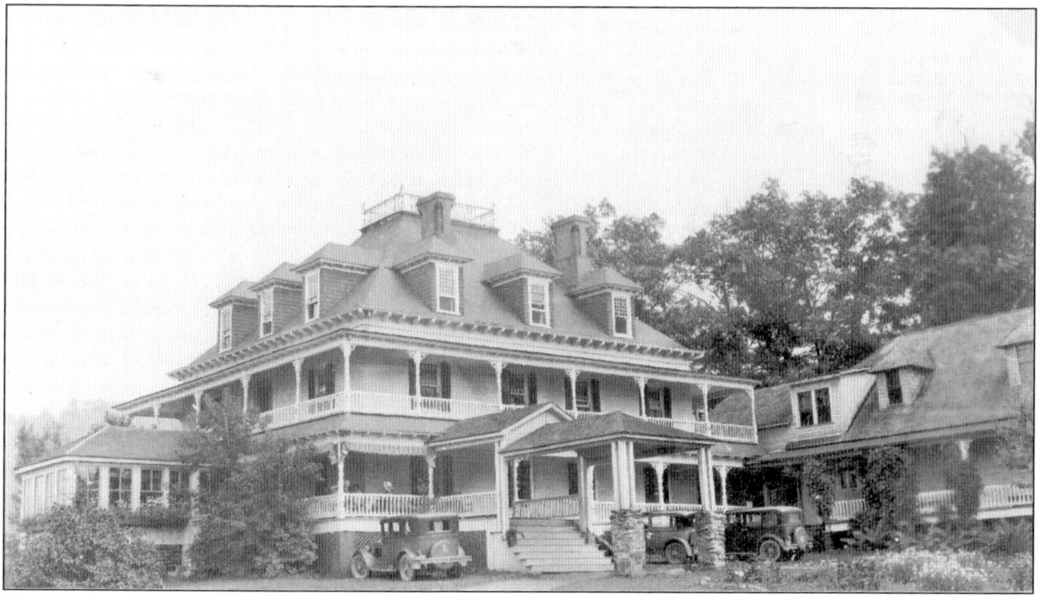

BLACK MOUNTAIN INN. Three stories high with a gabled roof and a sunroom, the house was built by T.K. Brown as his residence. It became a hotel in 1898, owned by A.E. Stevens. The Black Mountain Inn offered guests the latest luxuries and rural views of the valley and surrounding mountains. (Swannanoa Valley Museum.)

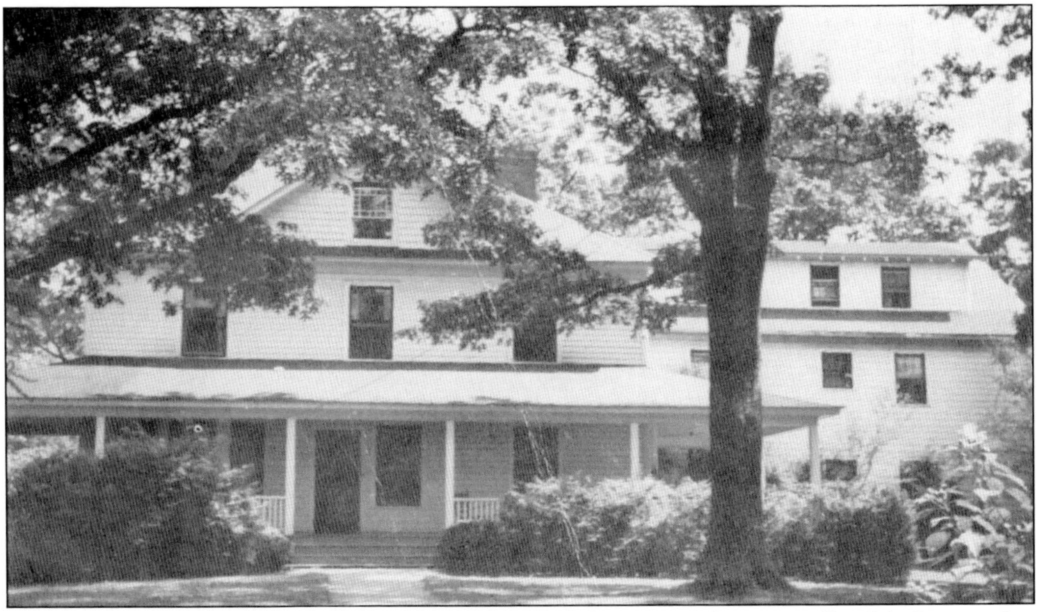

Dougherty Heights Inn. Built in 1898, the Dougherty Heights Inn offered lodging a few blocks away from the depot in Black Mountain. One of the few early inns to remain in the valley, it operates today as the Red Rocker Inn. (Swannanoa Valley Museum.)

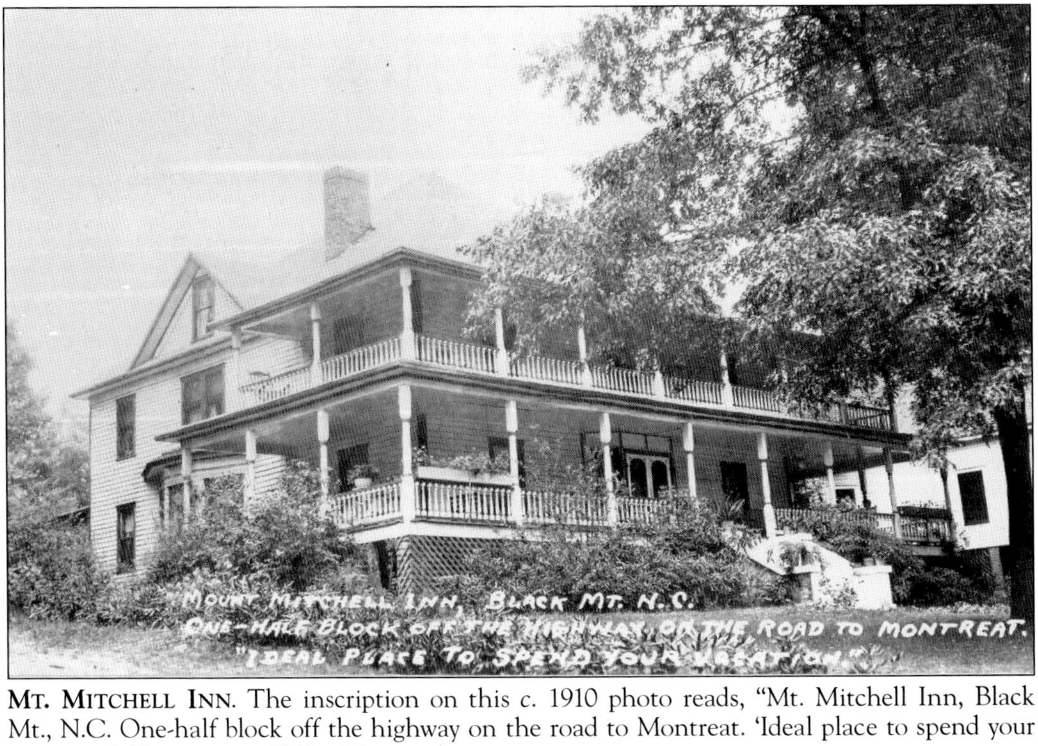

Mt. Mitchell Inn. The inscription on this c. 1910 photo reads, "Mt. Mitchell Inn, Black Mt., N.C. One-half block off the highway on the road to Montreat. 'Ideal place to spend your vacation.'" (Swannanoa Valley Museum.)

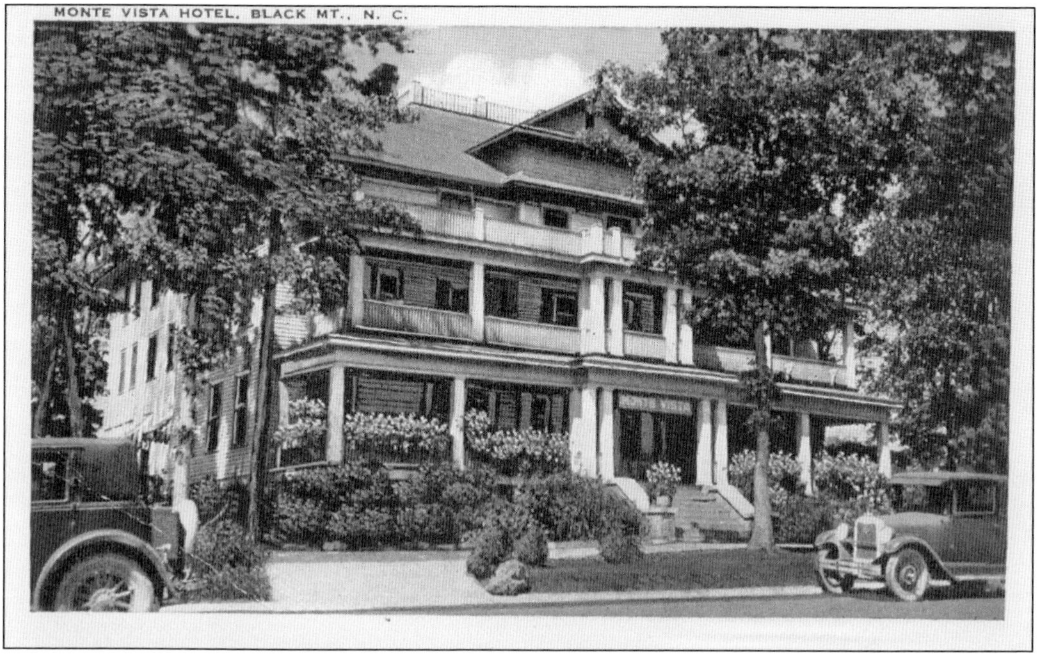

FIRST MONTE VISTA HOTEL. Mrs. L.E. Phillips bought this building, which was the Old Black Mountain School, in 1919. In addition, an annex was built in 1926. (Swannanoa Valley Museum.)

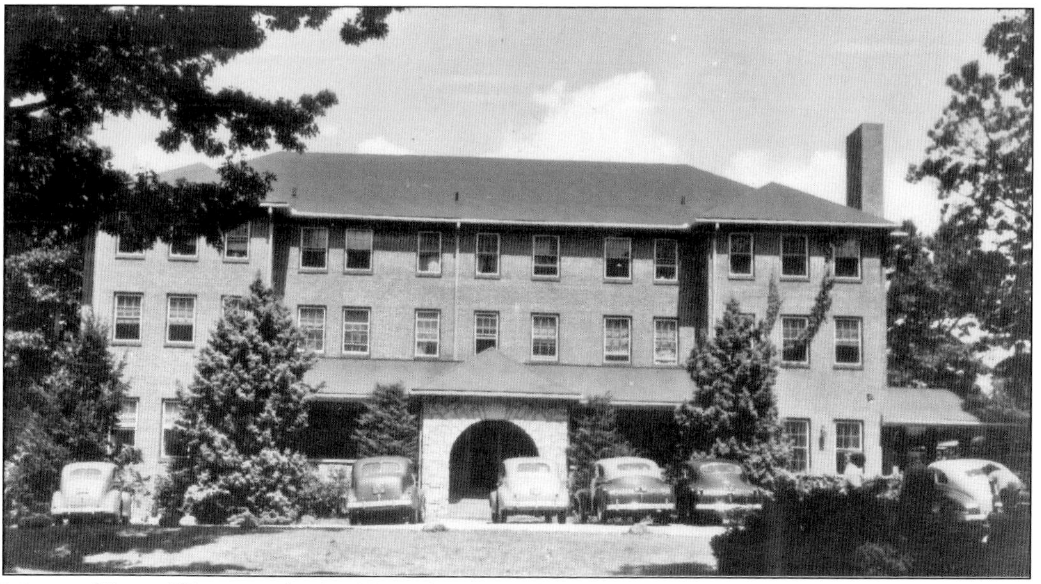

MONTE VISTA HOTEL. The building shown in this postcard is the "new" Monte Vista Hotel, which was built in 1935. All three buildings were operated as the Monte Vista Hotel until 1964, when the original wooden structure was torn down. The wood was used to build a radio station on the site of the former Black Mountain Airport. (Swannanoa Valley Museum.)

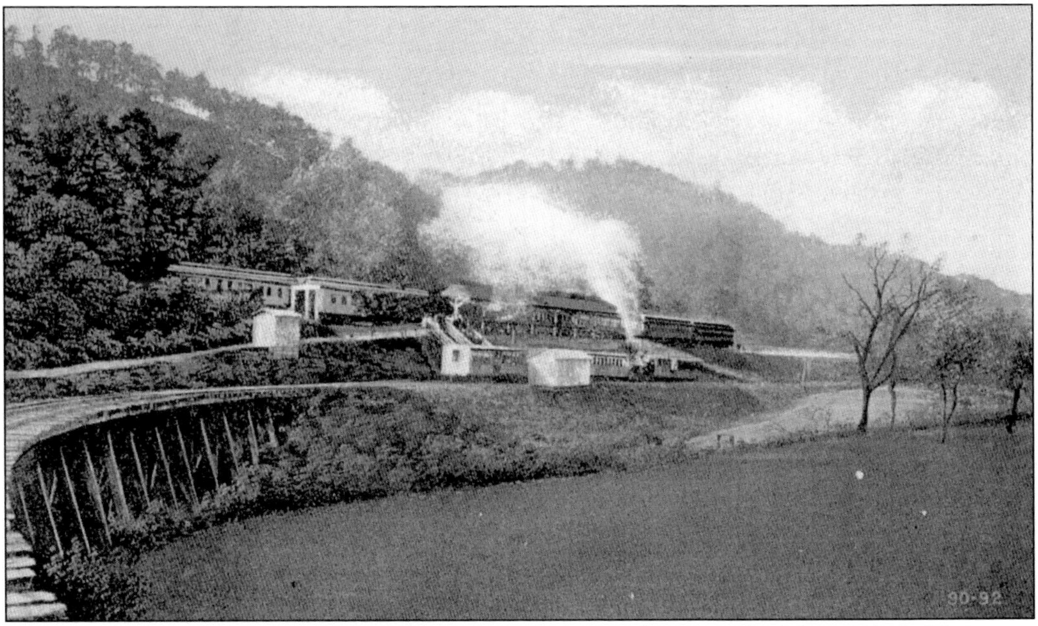

TOURIST TRAINS. Although originally a narrow gauge railway was laid from Black Mountain to Mt. Mitchell for the logging industry, in the early 1920s it was used more and more for tourist excursions. This postcard image shows the station in Black Mountain from which the Mt. Mitchell train departed. (Swannanoa Valley Museum.)

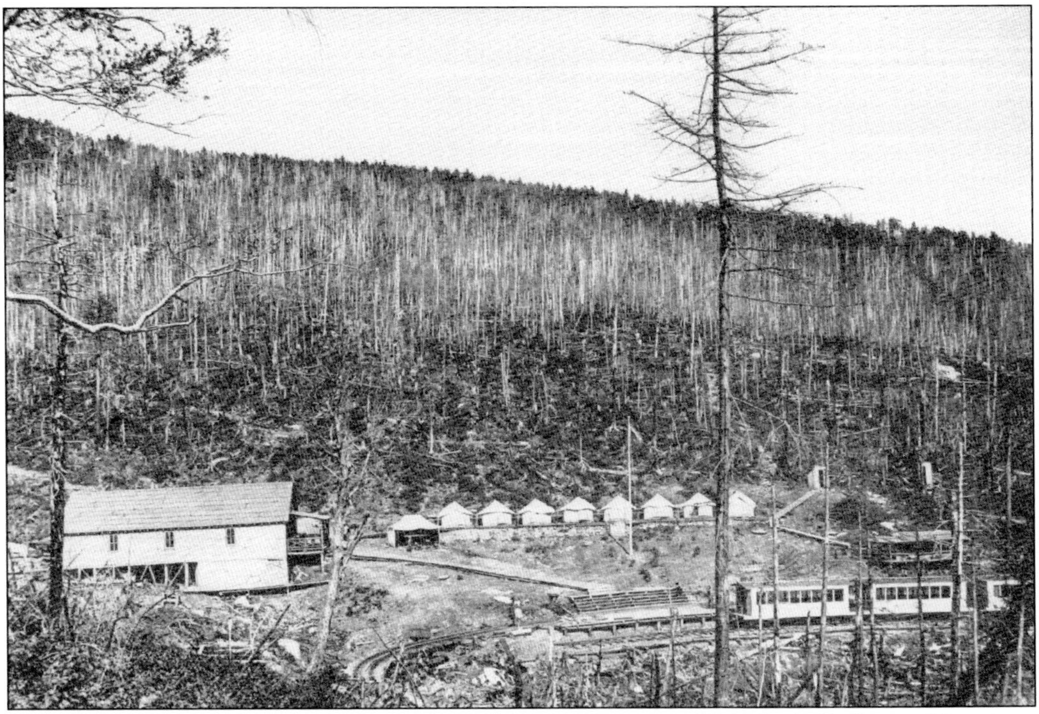

CAMP ALICE. First established to provide shelter to loggers near Mt. Mitchell, Camp Alice later served tourists who rode the train into the high mountains and afforded overnight lodging for Mt. Mitchell hikers. (Swannanoa Valley Museum.)

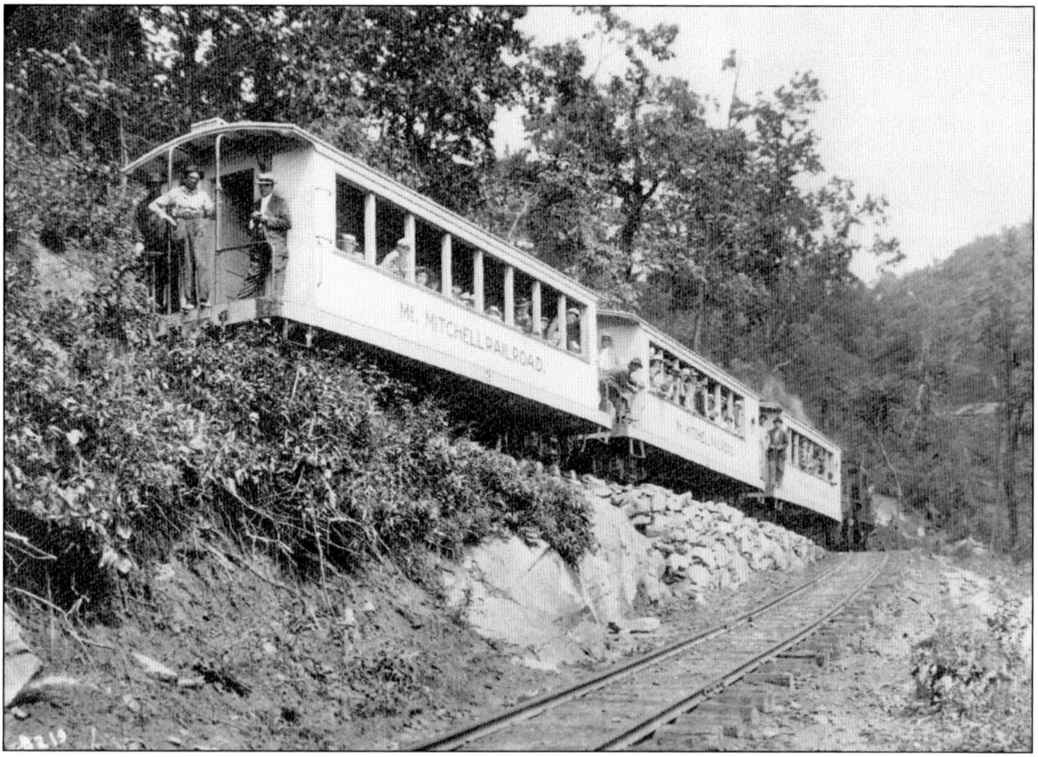

A DAY'S OUTING. Mt. Mitchell Railroad cars on a switchback are filled with tourists traveling to Mt. Mitchell. (Swannanoa Valley Museum.)

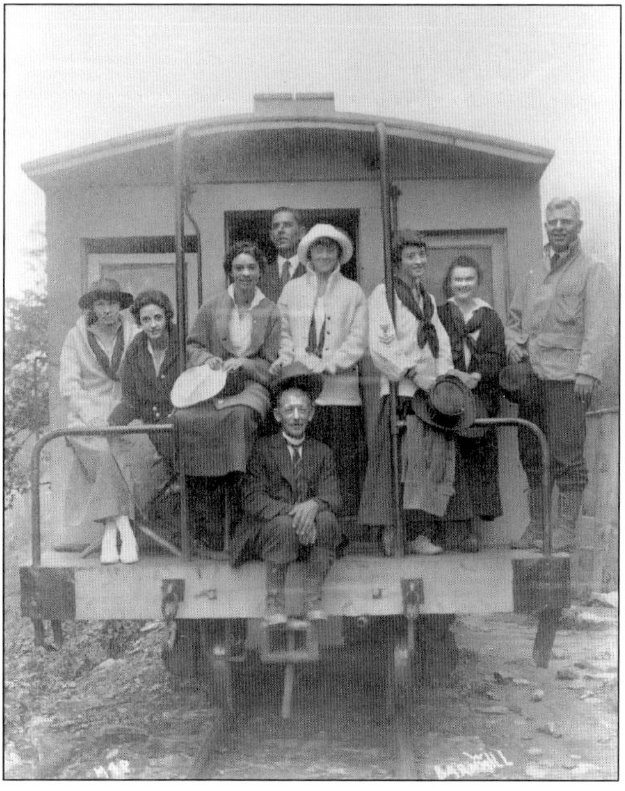

TRAINFUL OF TOURISTS. A group of travelers poses at the rear of a train car on an outing to Mt. Mitchell, the highest mountain east of the Mississippi. (Barnhill photo, Swannanoa Valley Museum.)

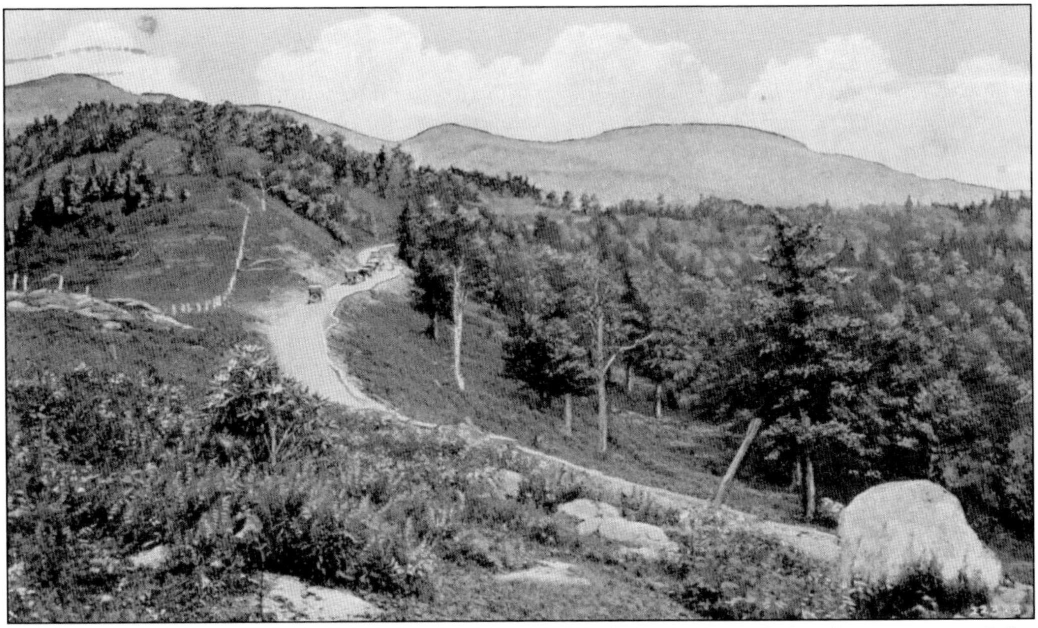

MT. MITCHELL MOTOR ROAD. In the early 1920s, when logging ceased, developers removed the train track and turned the roadbed into a toll road. Traffic was one way only on the narrow road; tourists would depart Black Mountain in the morning no later than 11 a.m., and begin their return no later than 3 p.m. (Courtesy Don Talley.)

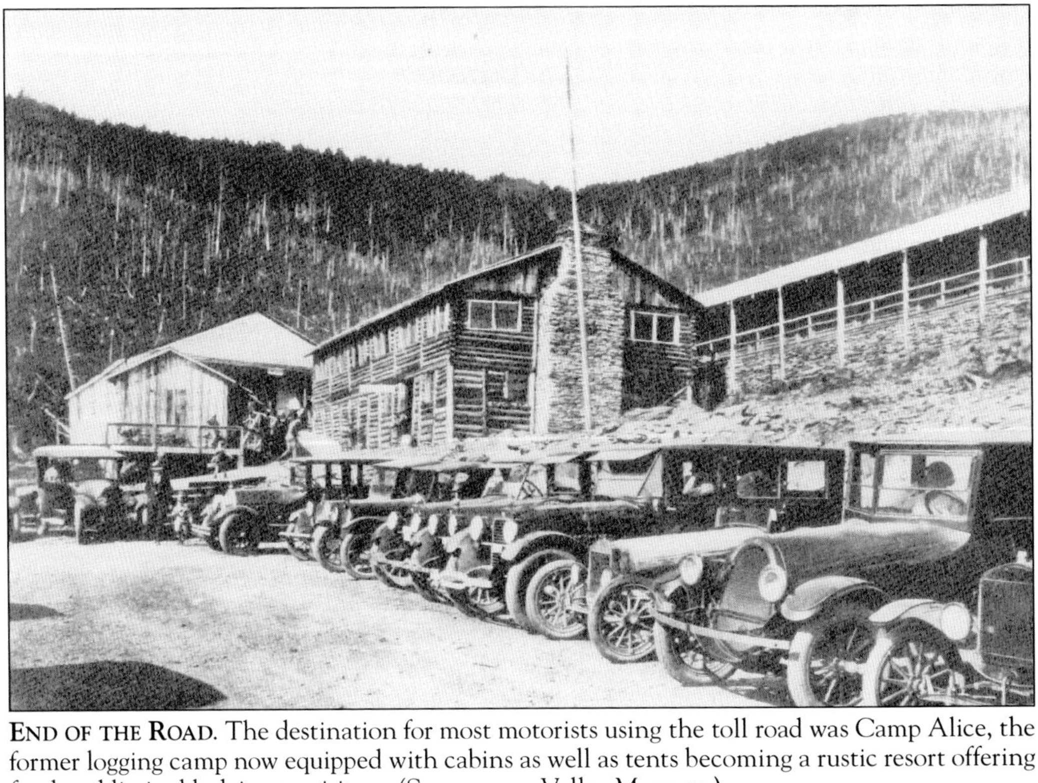

END OF THE ROAD. The destination for most motorists using the toll road was Camp Alice, the former logging camp now equipped with cabins as well as tents becoming a rustic resort offering food and limited lodging to visitors. (Swannanoa Valley Museum.)

Four

ASSEMBLIES AND CONFERENCE CENTERS

Many tourists who visited the valley experienced its restful and restorative qualities and found it the ideal site upon which to establish religious retreats and conference centers. Montreat Assembly was created first, followed by Blue Ridge Assembly and Ridgecrest Assembly. Over the decades of the 20th century, other denominations followed, including the Disciples of Christ's, Christmount, Cragmont, Dorothy Walls and Billy's Graham's Training Center, The Cove.

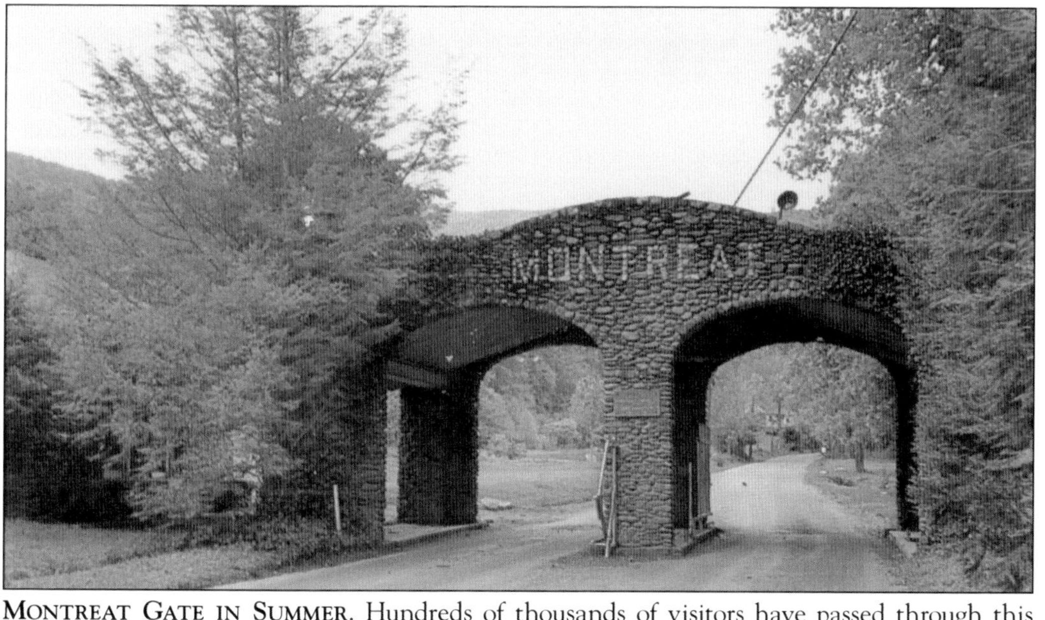

MONTREAT GATE IN SUMMER. Hundreds of thousands of visitors have passed through this gate. The Montreat community was first organized when a group of businessmen purchased 4,000 acres of land north of Black Mountain at the foot of the Black Mountain range. It began as an ecumenical retreat, but later was purchased by the Southern Presbyterian Church. (Swannanoa Valley Museum.)

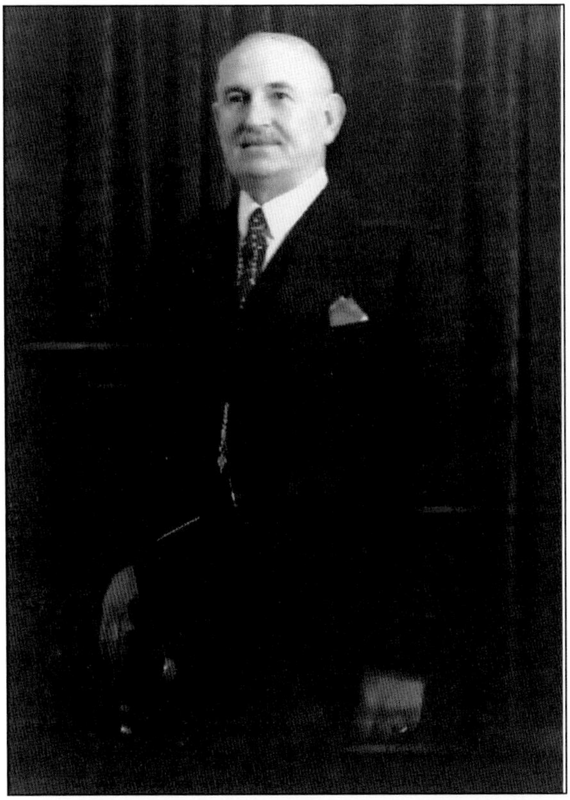

MONTREAT COLLEGE FOUNDER. Dr. Robert C. Anderson founded Montreat College in 1916. Its name was later changed to Montreat-Anderson College in his honor. Dr. Anderson served the college and the Mountain Retreat Association for 35 years. He designed Montreat's early buildings: Gaither Hall, Howerton Hall, and the Assembly Inn. (Swannanoa Valley Museum.)

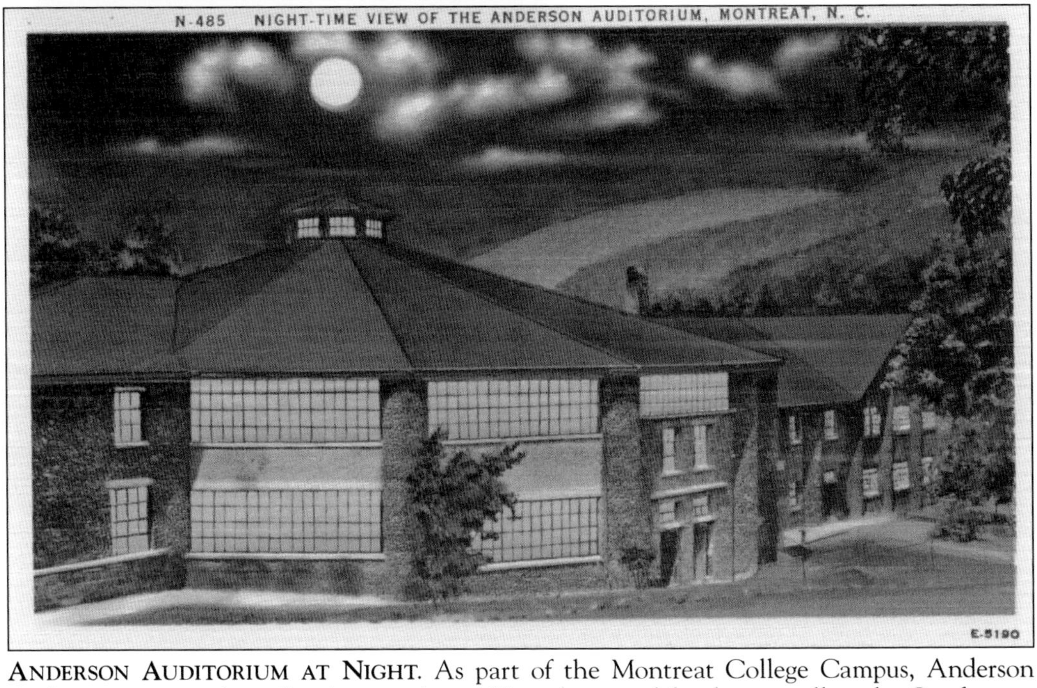

ANDERSON AUDITORIUM AT NIGHT. As part of the Montreat College Campus, Anderson Auditorium serves the college's more than 400 students and faculty, as well as the Conference Center. (Courtesy Don Talley.)

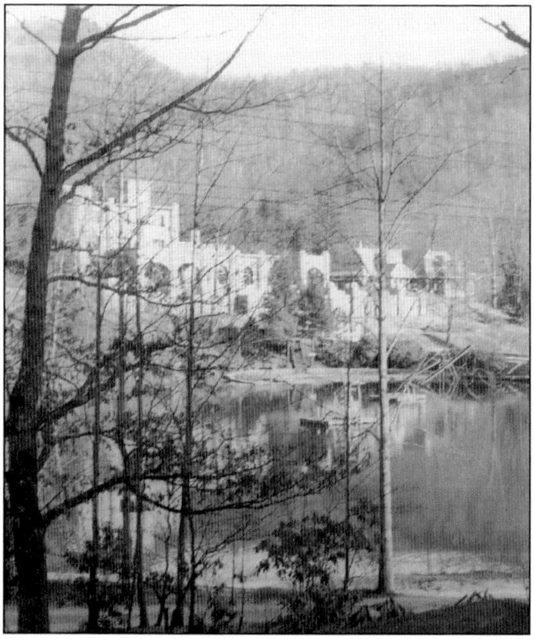

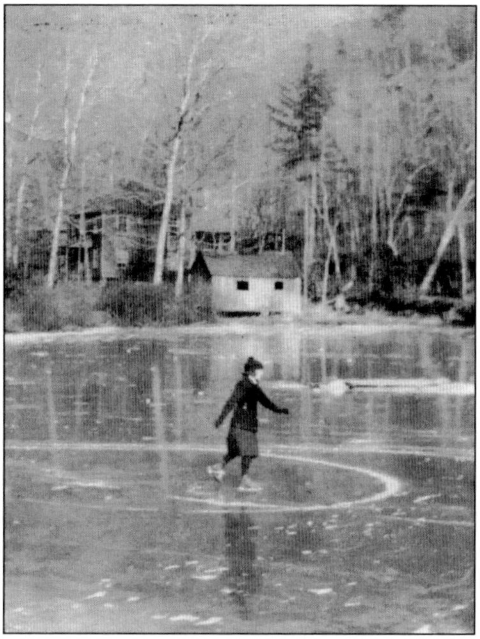

(*above, left*) **ASSEMBLY INN.** Montreat comprises a conference center, Montreat College, and private residences. The Assembly Inn overlooks picturesque Lake Susan and provides lodging for the many camps and conferences hosted in Montreat. (Noah Collection, courtesy David Rozzell.)

(*above, right*) **SKATING ON LAKE SUSAN.** Not just for summer visitors, Lake Susan holds an attraction for winter sports as well. (Swannanoa Valley Museum.)

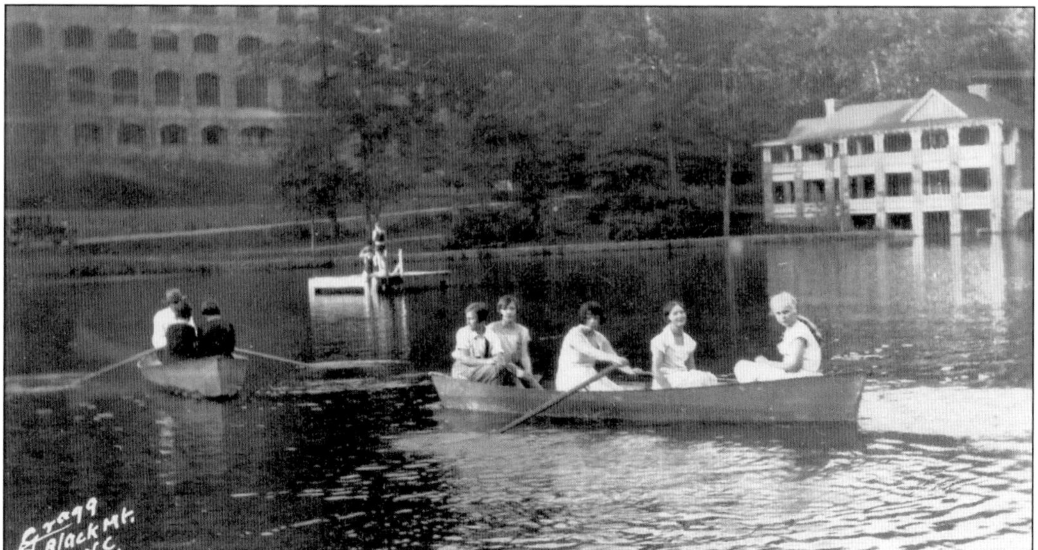

CANOEING ON LAKE SUSAN. This small lake, impounded in 1900 with an earth dam, was made permanent by a stone and concrete dam in 1924, a gift of Allen Graham and his mother Mrs. C.E. Graham. Five generations of the family were named Susan, and so, therefore, was the lake. For decades it has been a place of both recreation and quiet reflection for visitors. (Courtesy Pack Memorial Library.)

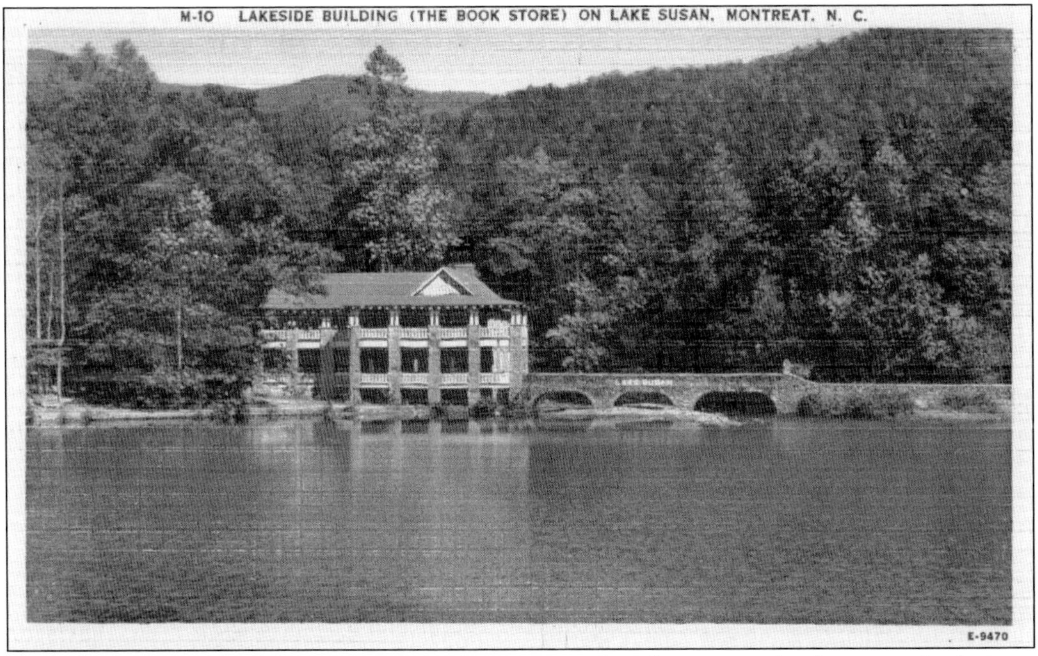

LAKESIDE BUILDING. This native stone structure served as the campus bookstore and gift shop. It is presently a recreation center. (Courtesy Don Talley.)

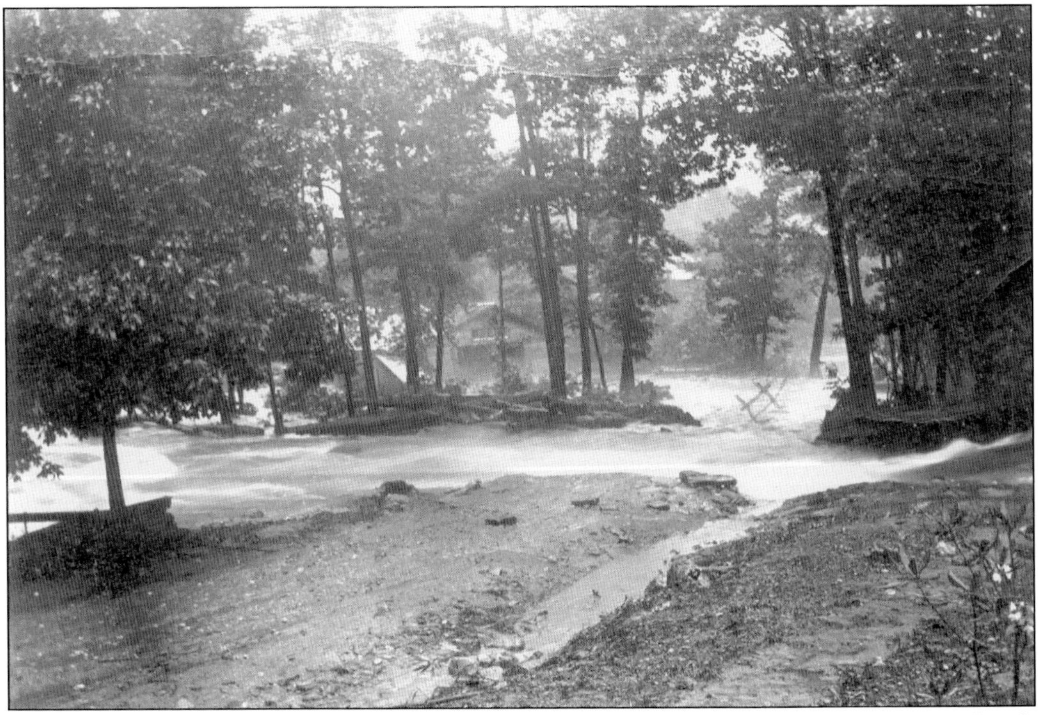

FLOOD ON LAKE SUSAN. In 1916, the Swannanoa Valley was ravaged by one of the worst floods in valley history, and tranquil Lake Susan was not spared. Raging waters pouring down from the mountains burst the dam as they gushed onto the valley floor and into the Swannanoa River. (Swannanoa Valley Museum.)

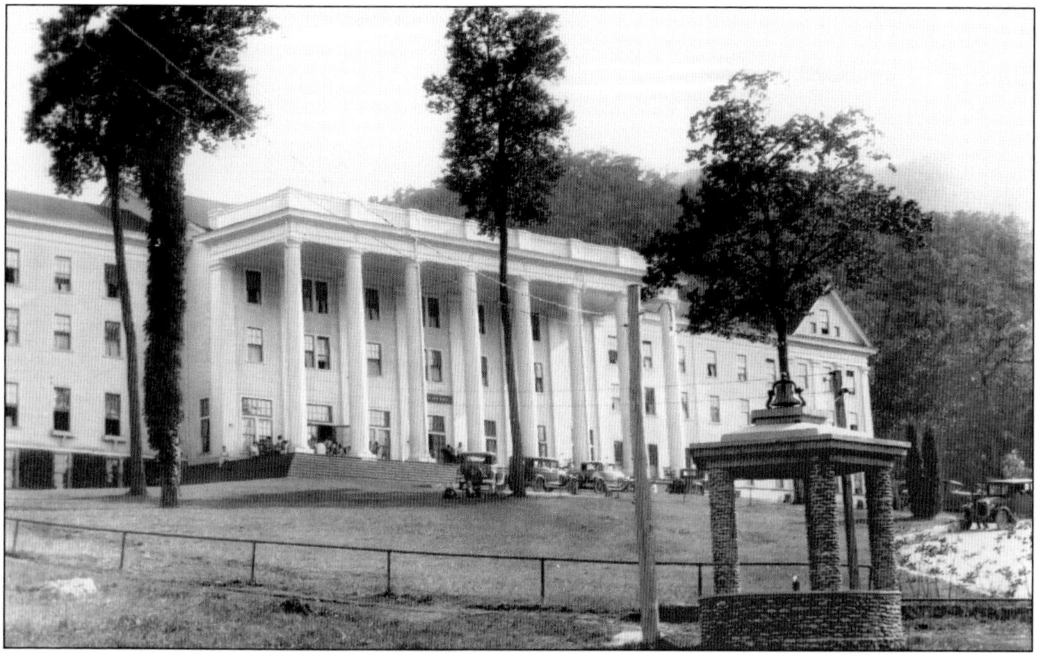

ROBERT E. LEE HALL. YMCA Blue Ridge Assembly was founded in 1906, and Lee Hall was the first structure built to provide lodging for the YMCA's new conference center. The Robert E. Lee Military School for Boys used the facility for four years, beginning in 1917, and it housed Black Mountain College from 1933 to 1940. Lee Hall had its own hydroelectric plant. (Courtesy Pack Memorial Library.)

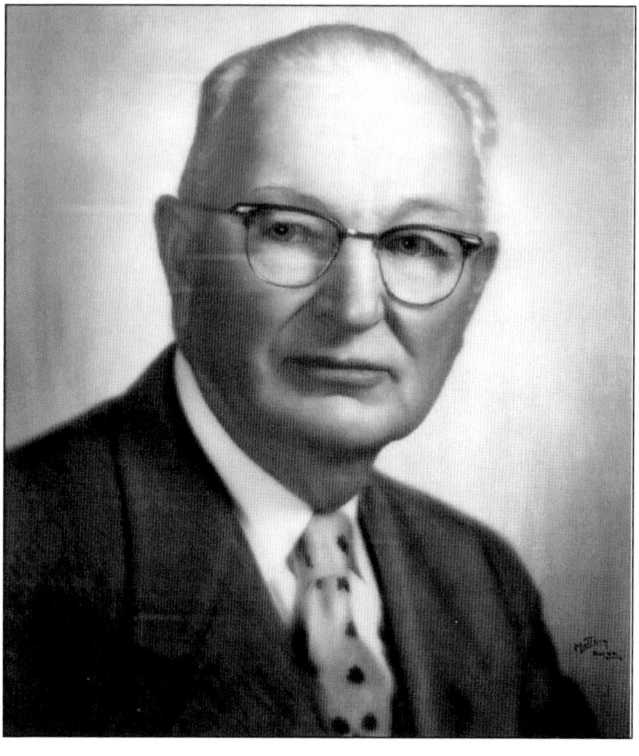

DR. WILLIS D. WEATHERFORD, SR. Dr. Weatherford was founder of YMCA Blue Ridge Assembly. (Swannanoa Valley Museum.)

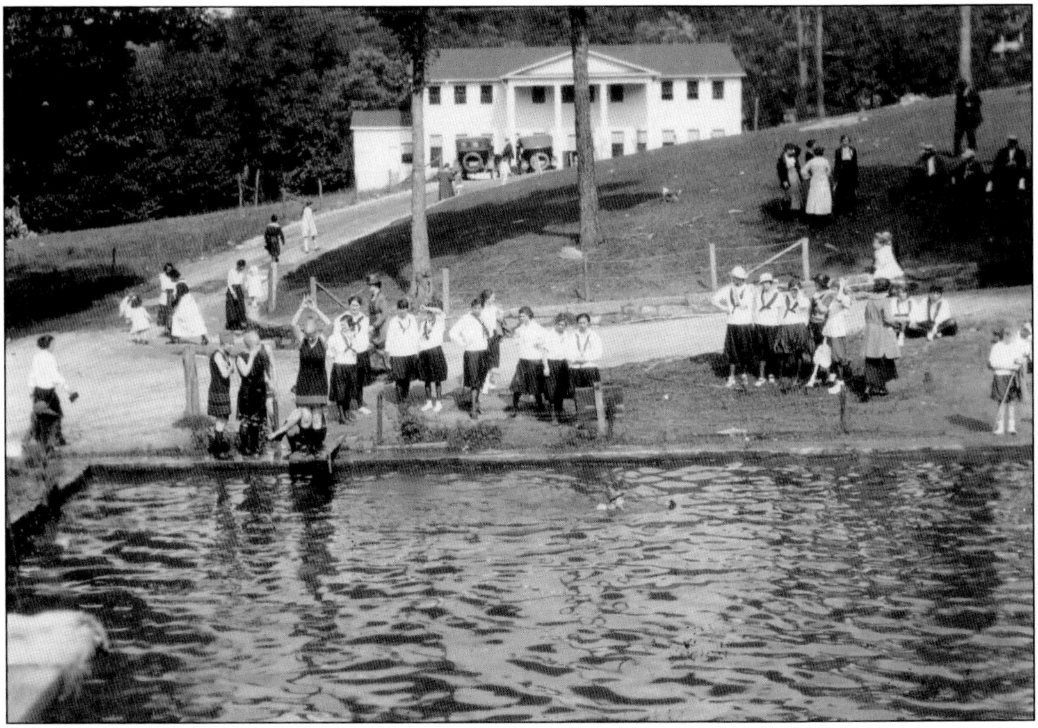

NOT JUST FOR BOYS. Blue Ridge Assembly served both the YMCA and YWCA. Shown here, a group of young women gathered by the swimming pool. College Hall is in the background, c. 1920. (Courtesy YMCA Blue Ridge Assembly.)

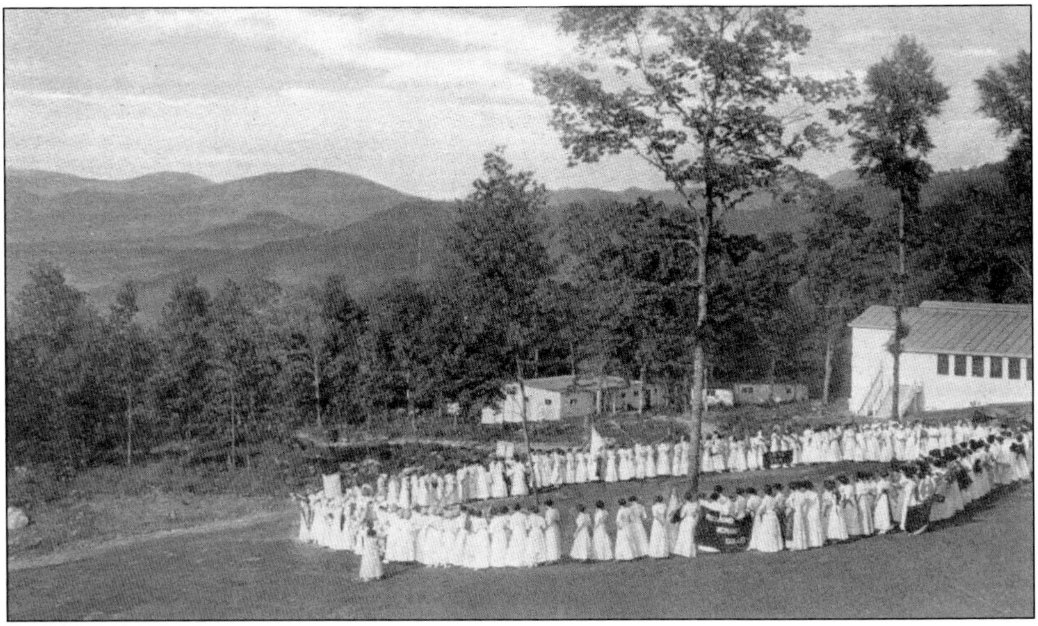

FORMAL CEREMONY. Young Women's Christian Association members form a circle on the grounds of YMCA Blue Ridge Assembly. (Swannanoa Valley Museum.)

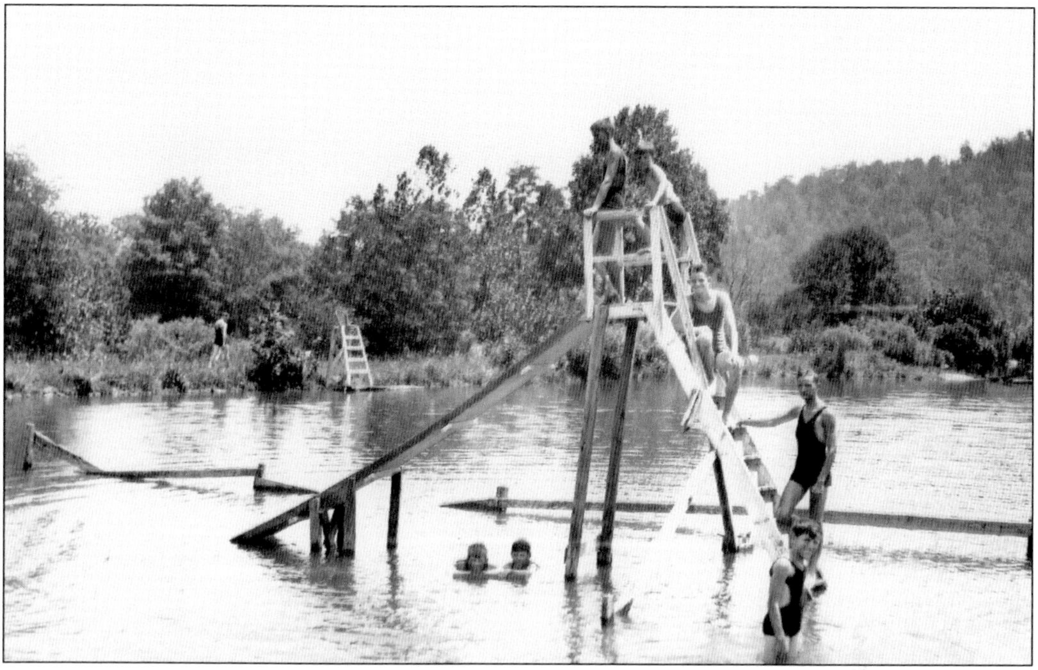

SWIMMING AT BLUE RIDGE ASSEMBLY. Young men enjoying a swim and a rustic slide in the lake at YMCA Blue Ridge Assembly, *c.* 1920. (Courtesy YMCA Blue Ridge Assembly.)

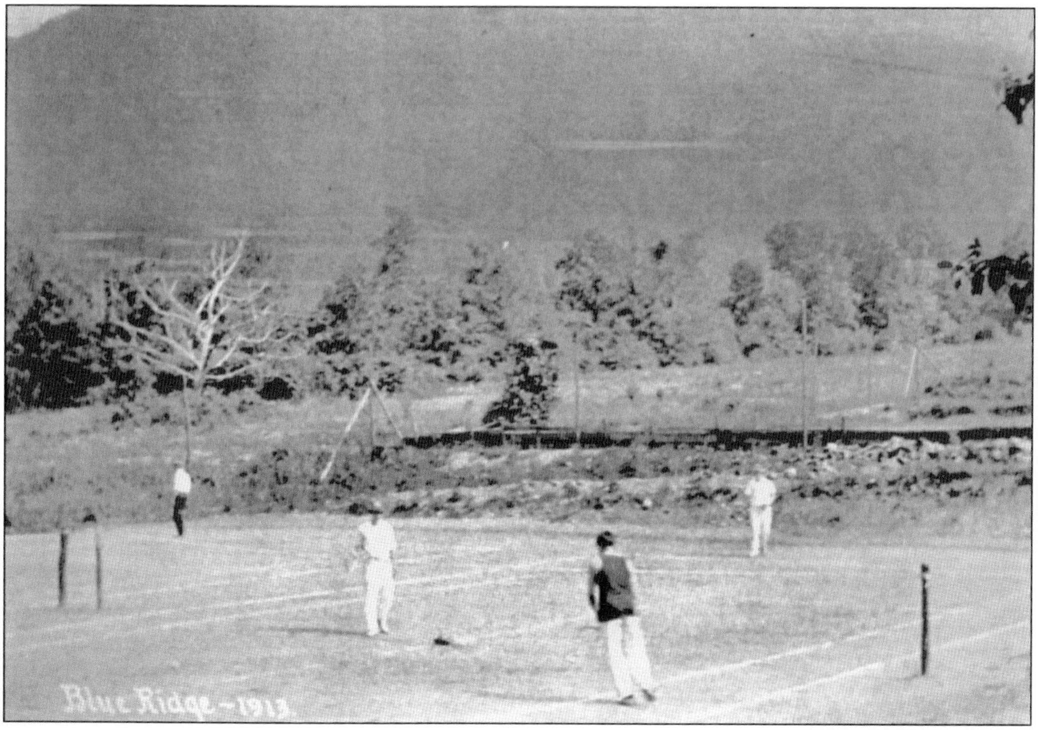

TENNIS ANYONE? Recreational opportunities abound for visitors to YMCA Blue Ridge Assembly. Here, conference-goers enjoy a game of tennis in 1913. (Courtesy Pack Memorial Library.)

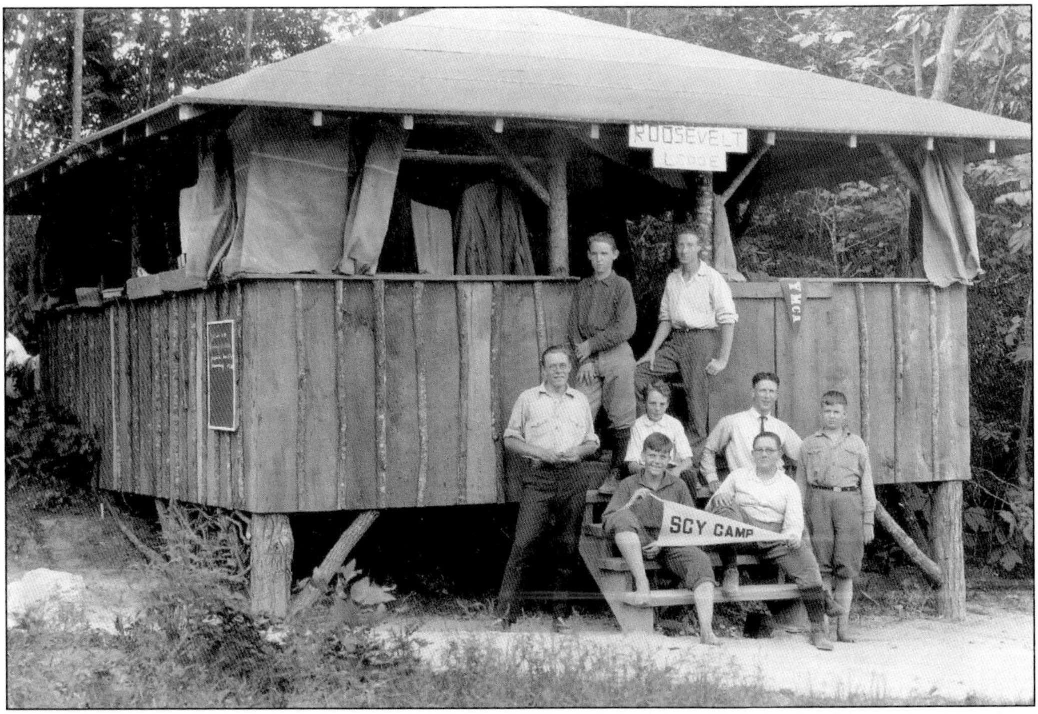

CABIN IN THE WOODS. Campers at SCY Camp, YMCA Blue Ridge Assembly are pictured in 1939. (Courtesy YMCA Blue Ridge Assembly.)

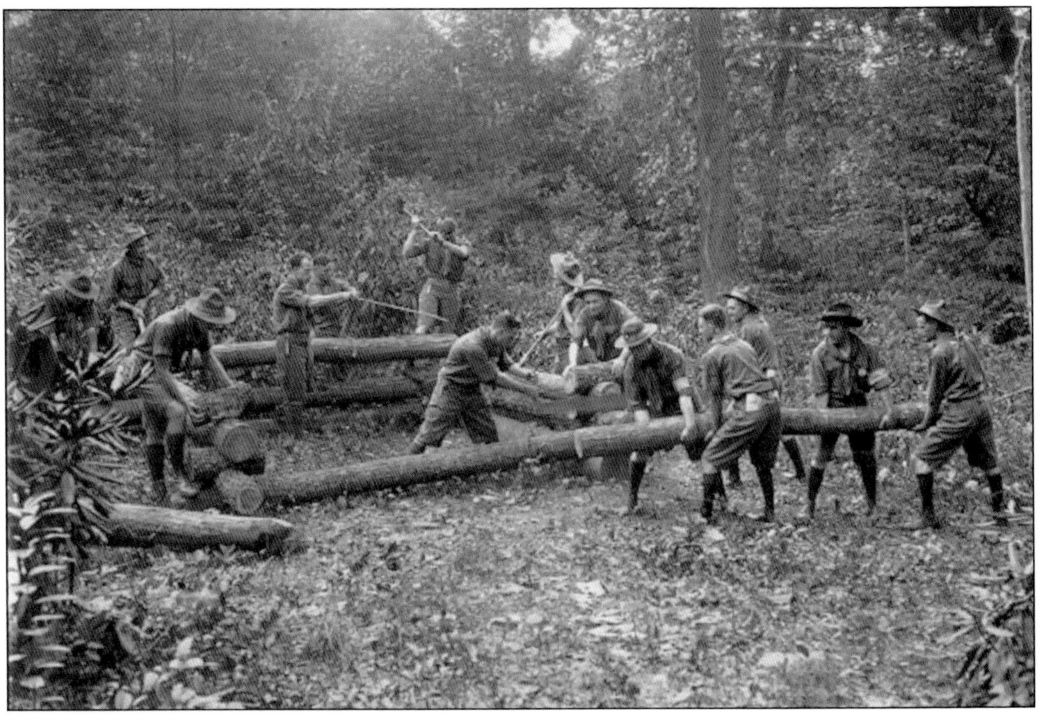

BOY SCOUTS AT BLUE RIDGE. Professional scouters build a log structure on the grounds of YMCA Blue Ridge Assembly in 1922. (Courtesy YMCA Blue Ridge Assembly.)

FIRE TOWER ON HIGH WINDY. North Carolina Forest Service Personnel had a panoramic view of the valley from an elevation of 4,280 feet. YMCA Blue Ridge Assembly is located in the cove below. (Courtesy YMCA Blue Ridge Assembly.)

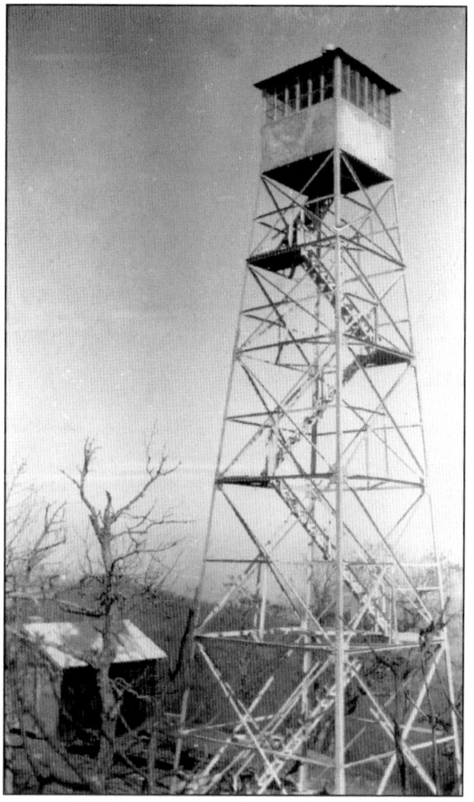

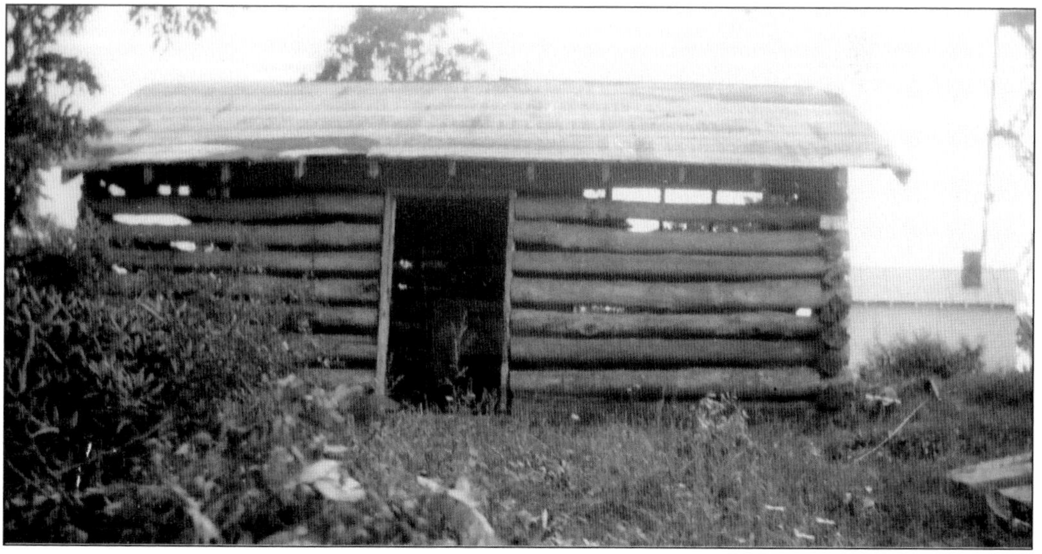

TACOA LODGE. This rustic cabin was built by YMCA Blue Ridge Assembly on the summit of High Windy for the enjoyment and protection of hikers. (Courtesy YMCA Blue Ridge Assembly.)

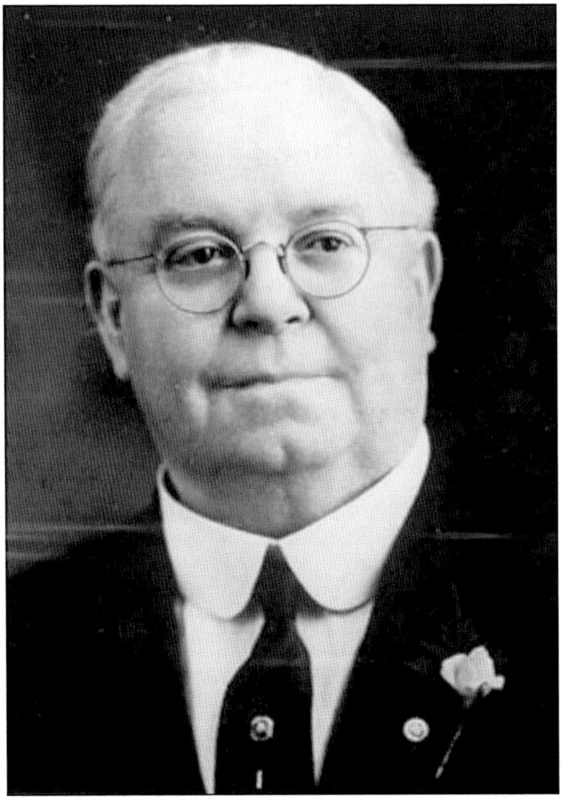

RIDGECREST LEADER. Dr. Bernard W. Spilman was the first general manager when a charter was granted to Ridgecrest Assembly in 1907. The first session was held in the summer of 1908. (Swannanoa Valley Museum.)

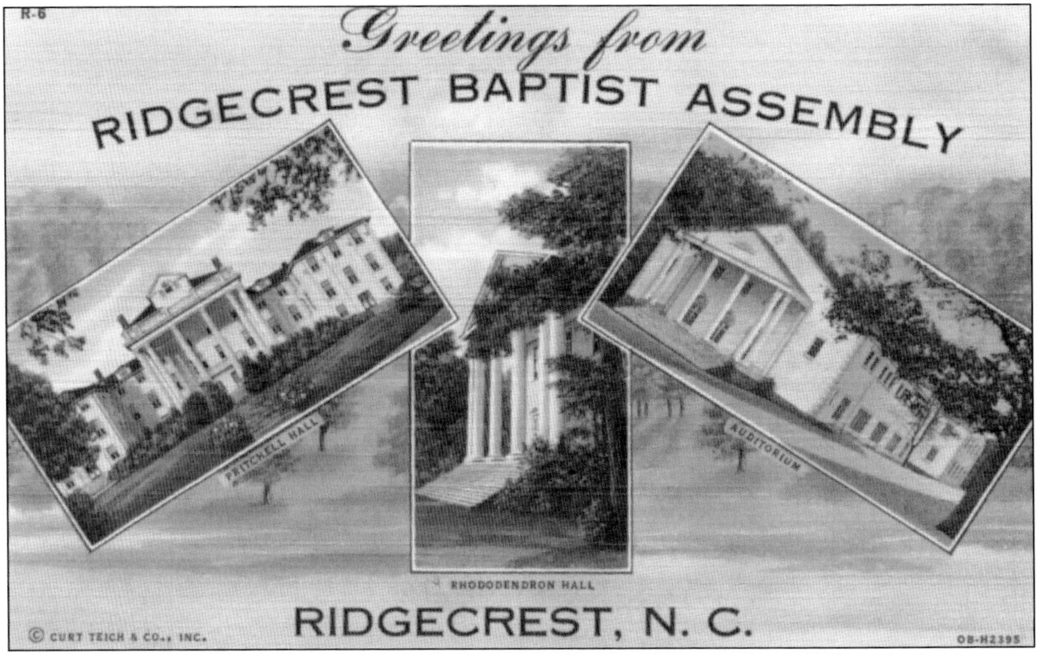

GREETINGS FROM RIDGECREST. At the eastern end of the Swannanoa Valley, the Ridgecrest Baptist Assembly draws thousands of visitors each year. Formed in 1907, the grounds cover 960 acres. (Swannanoa Valley Museum.)

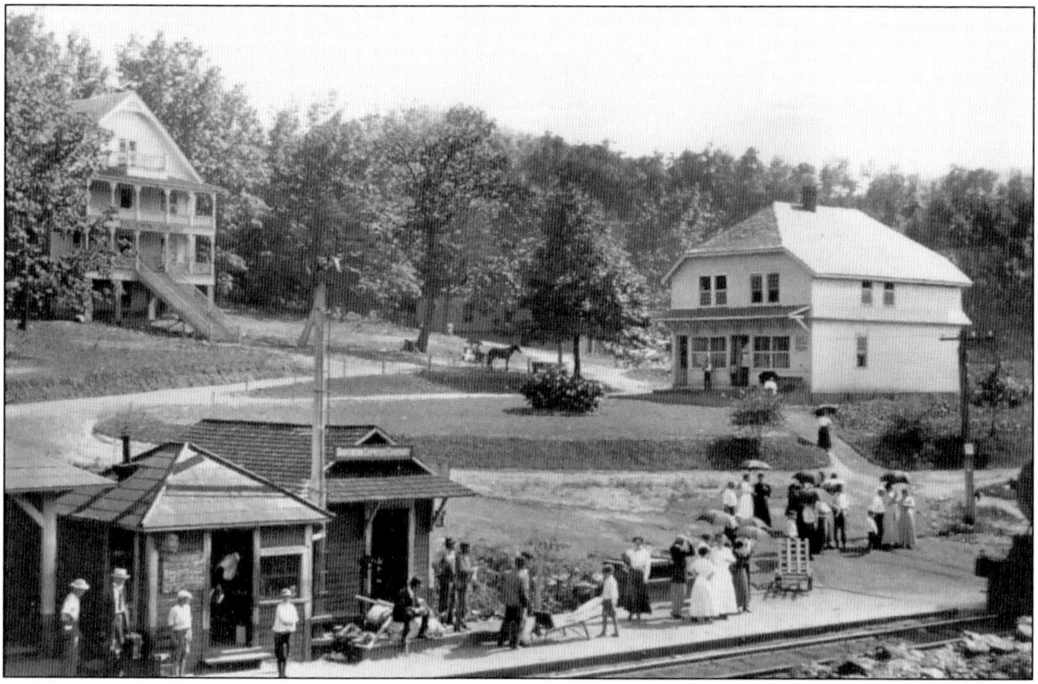

Arriving at Ridgecrest. The Southern Express Company served visitors as they arrived for their stay in the cool highlands of the Blue Ridge Mountains. (Swannanoa Valley Museum.)

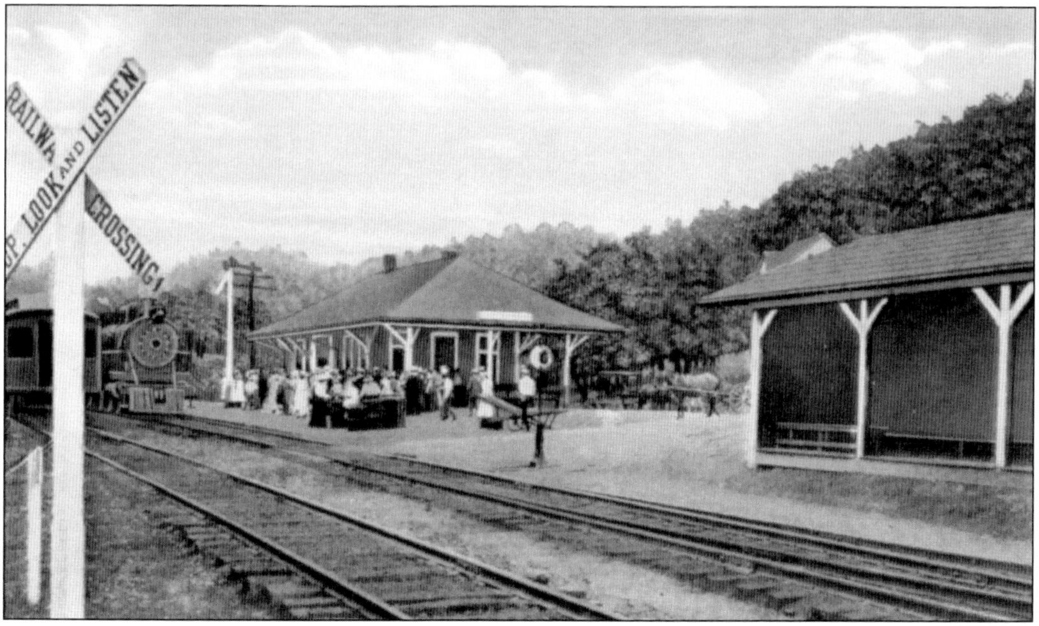

A Busy Station. The Ridgecrest depot was a busy place when conference-goers arrived and departed. (Swannanoa Valley Museum.)

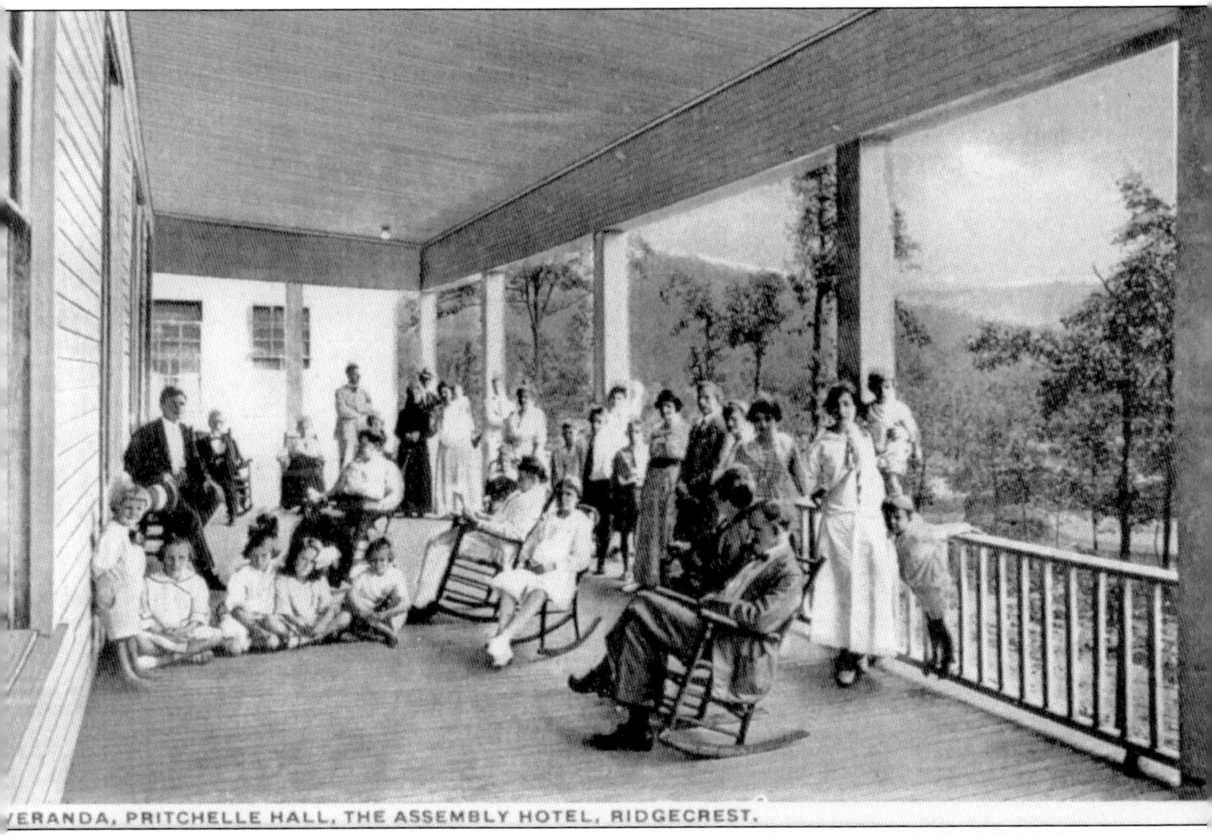

PRITCHELL HALL VISITORS. Conferees gather on the veranda of old Pritchell Hall, Ridgecrest, c. 1915. (Swannanoa Valley Museum.)

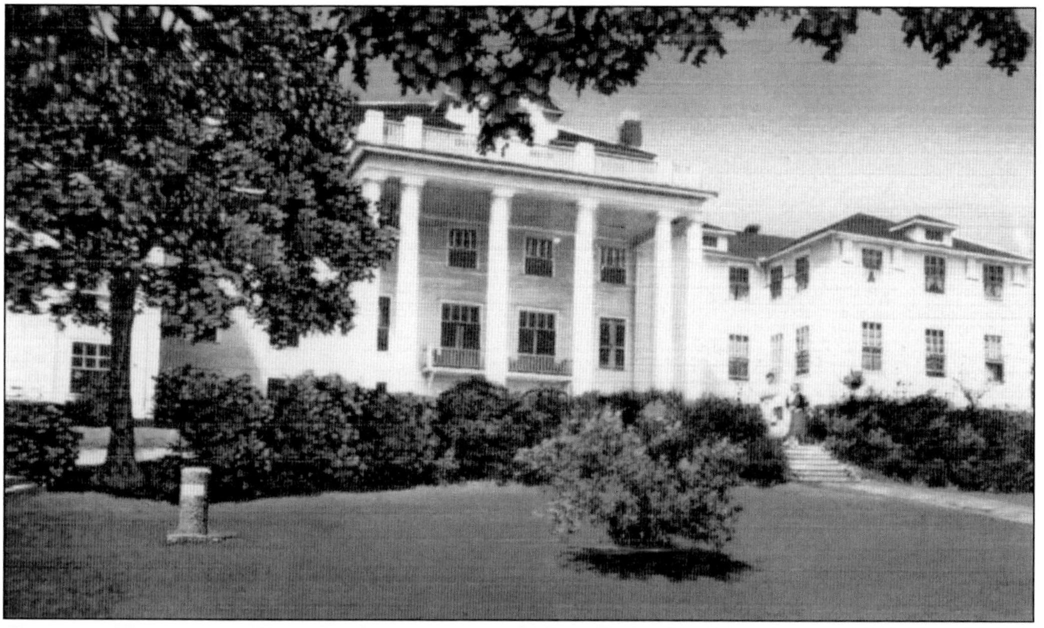

ORIGINAL PRITCHELL HALL. Built in 1914, Pritchell Hall was the main building of the conference center. It was named for Judge Jeter Pritchard and J.D. Elliot. (Swannanoa Valley Museum.)

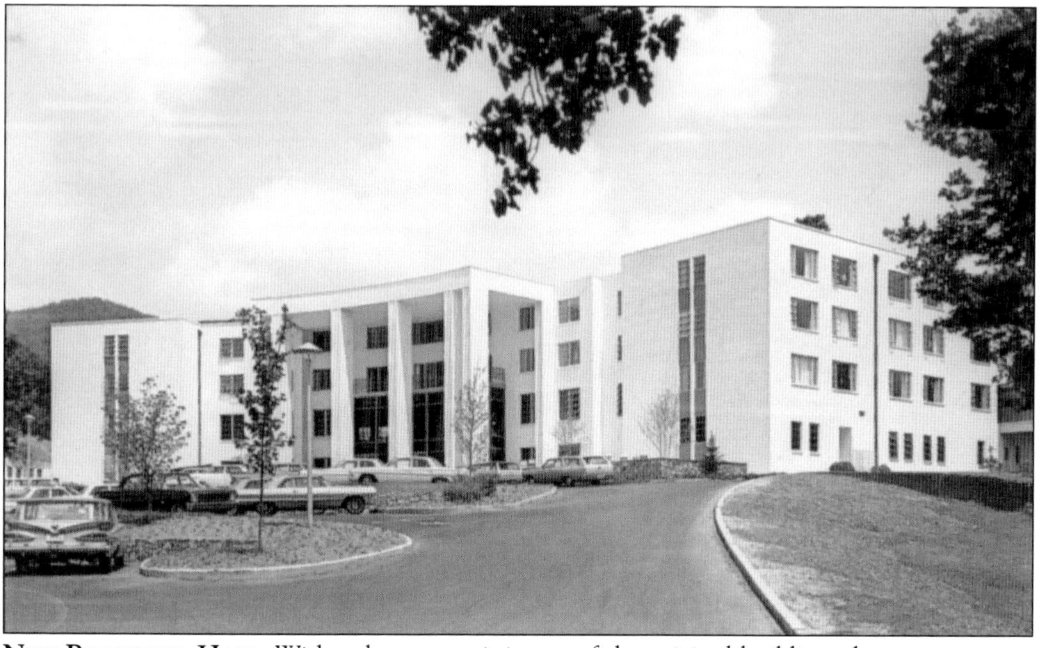

NEW PRITCHELL HALL. With columns reminiscent of the original building, the new structure was completed in the 1950s. (Swannanoa Valley Museum.)

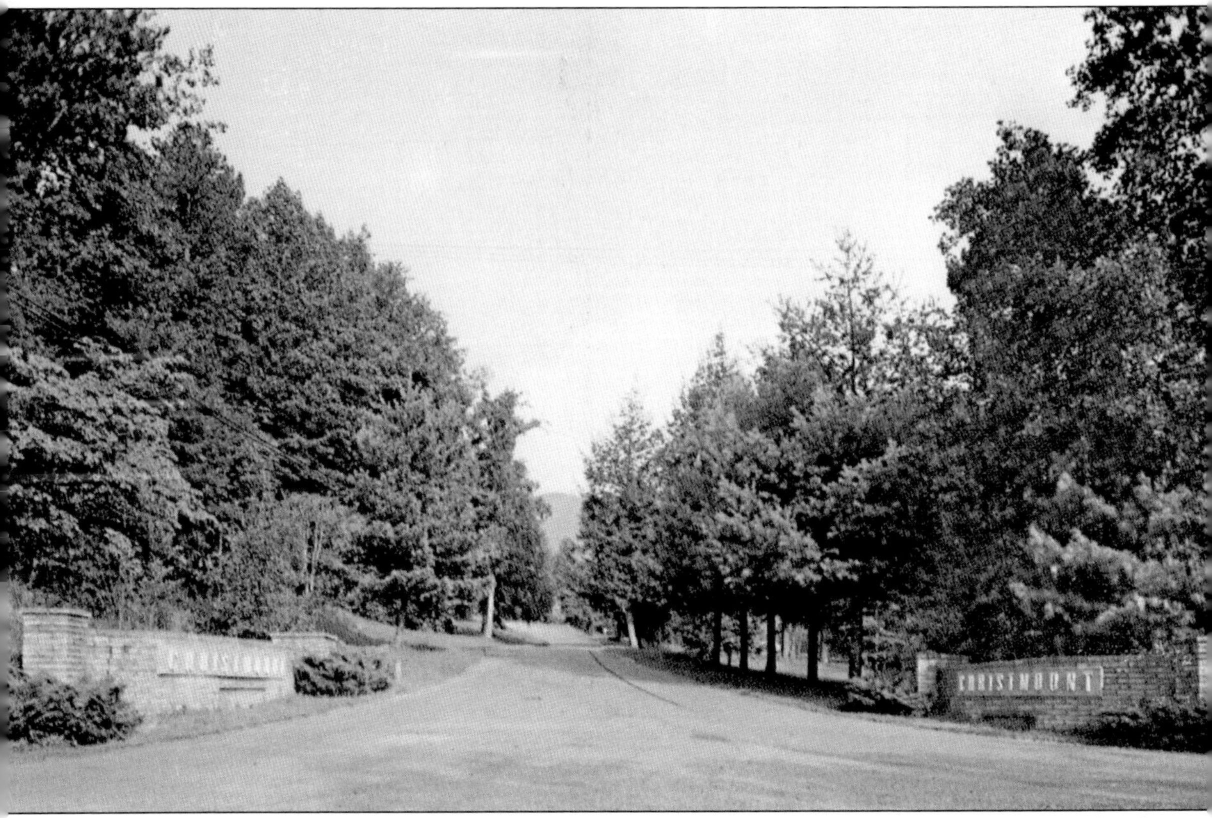

WELCOME TO CHRISTMOUNT. A contemporary entrance welcomes visitors to the grounds of Christmount Assembly. (Swannanoa Valley Museum.)

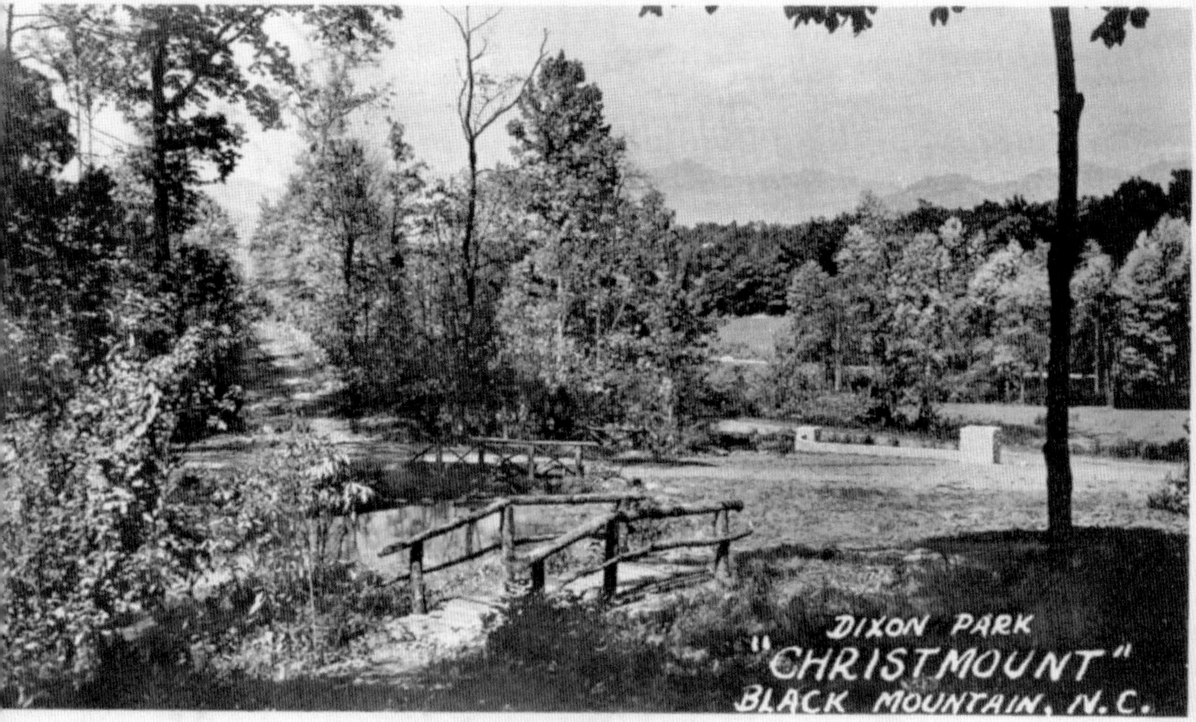

EARLY CHRISTMOUNT. Dixon Park, on the grounds of what was once the Guastavino Estate, is now part of Christmount. (Swannanoa Valley Museum.)

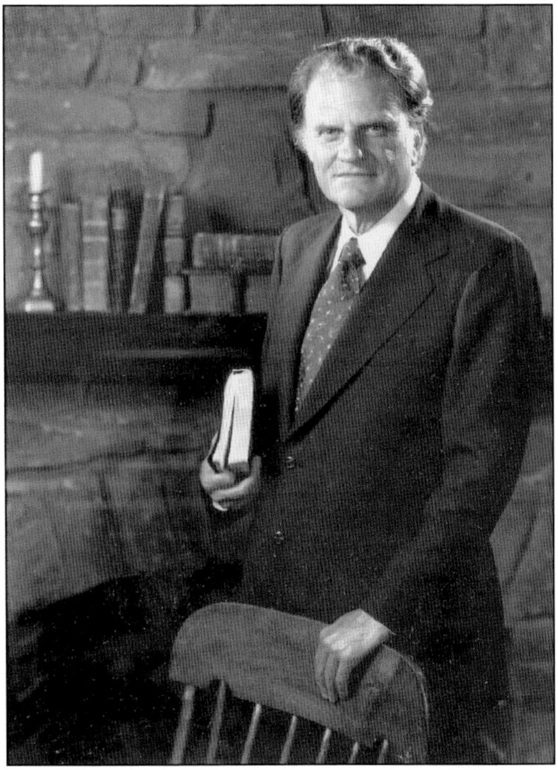

REV. BILLY GRAHAM. Perhaps the valley's most famous resident, Rev. Billy Graham, his wife Ruth, and their children moved to a rustic cabin high on a mountaintop just outside of Montreat. (Courtesy the Billy Graham Evangelistic Association.)

THE COVE. Also known as the "Billy Graham Training Center," The Cove is at the western end of the Swannanoa Valley. (Courtesy the Billy Graham Evangelistic Association.)

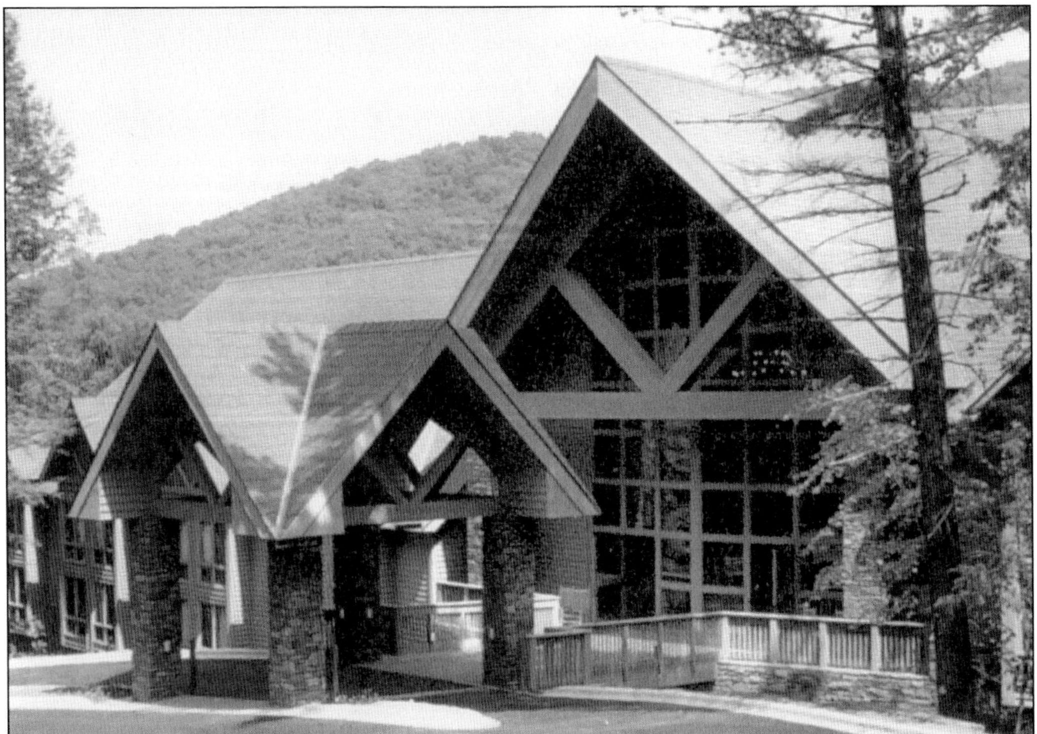

Five

CREATING COMMUNITIES

Many of the visitors to the Swannanoa Valley liked it so well they decided to return and settle permanently in its hills and coves. Communities grew, including North Fork, Ridgecrest, Broad River, Montreat, Black Mountain, Bee Tree, Grovemont, Swannanoa, and Riceville. Shown in this chapter are photos of the towns, homes, schools and churches, health care facilities, businesses, and industries that make up the valley community.

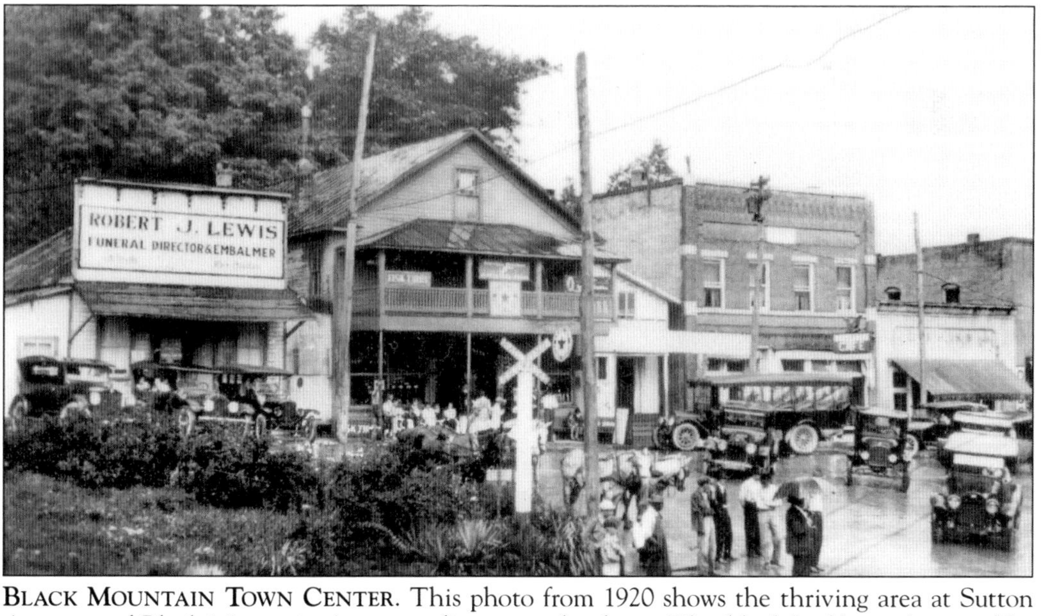

BLACK MOUNTAIN TOWN CENTER. This photo from 1920 shows the thriving area at Sutton Avenue and Black Mountain Avenue, adjacent to the depot. This block had been destroyed by fire in 1912. (Swannanoa Valley Museum.)

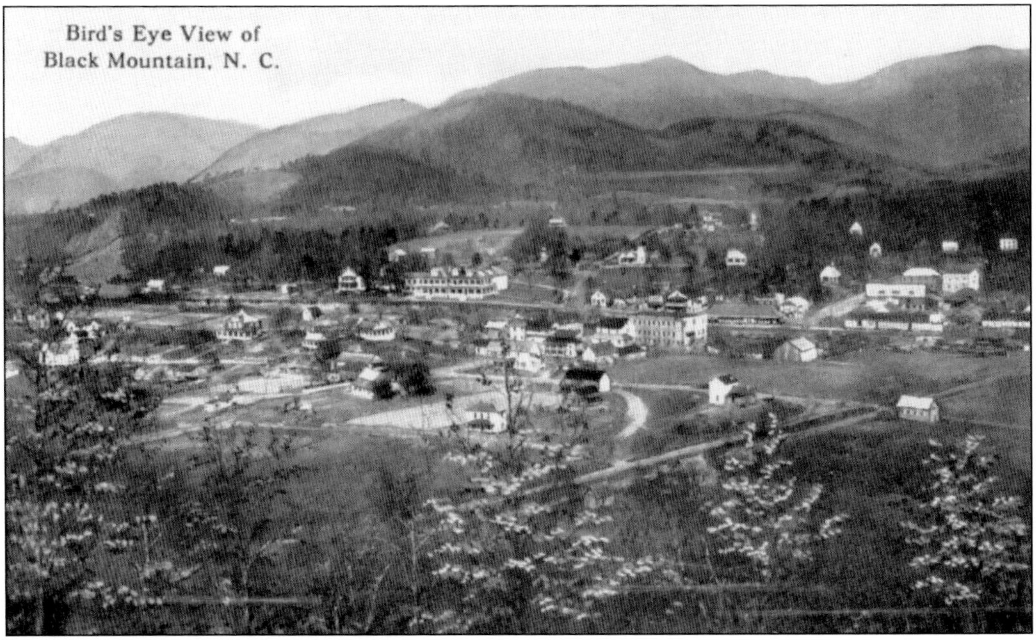

TOWN OF BLACK MOUNTAIN. Before the railroad the town was known as Grey Eagle, but changed its name when the Southern Railroad named its depot Black Mountain. The town was incorporated in 1893. (Swannanoa Valley Museum.)

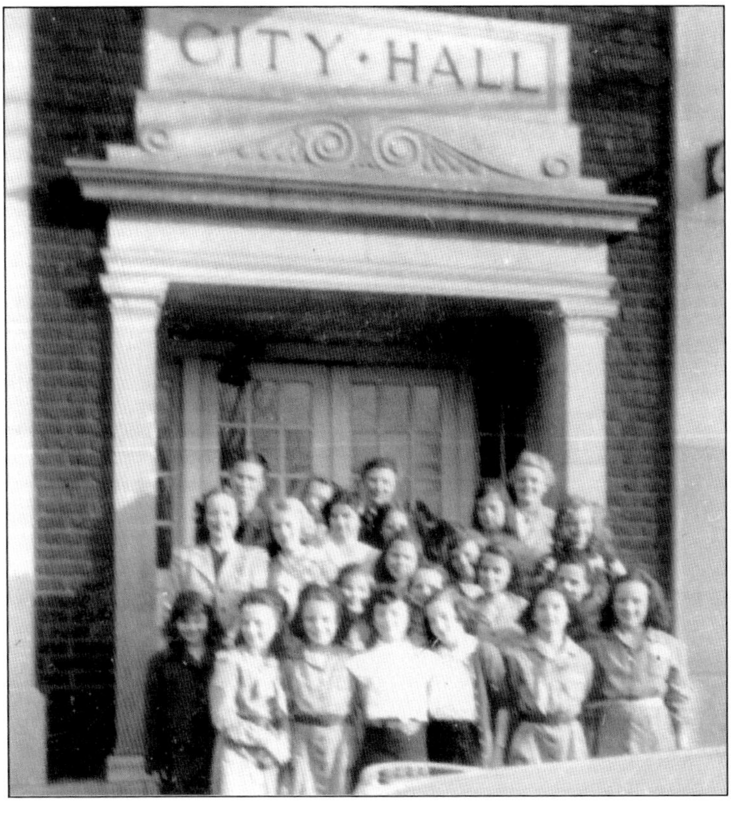

GIRL SCOUTS. A troop of Girl Scouts poses on the front steps of the Black Mountain City Hall building in 1949. When the new town administration buildings were constructed, both city hall and the fire house were abandoned for some years. City hall has been restored and is now the Black Mountain Center for the Arts. The fire house, built in 1921, is home to the Swannanoa Valley Museum. (Courtesy Mary Elizabeth Tyson.)

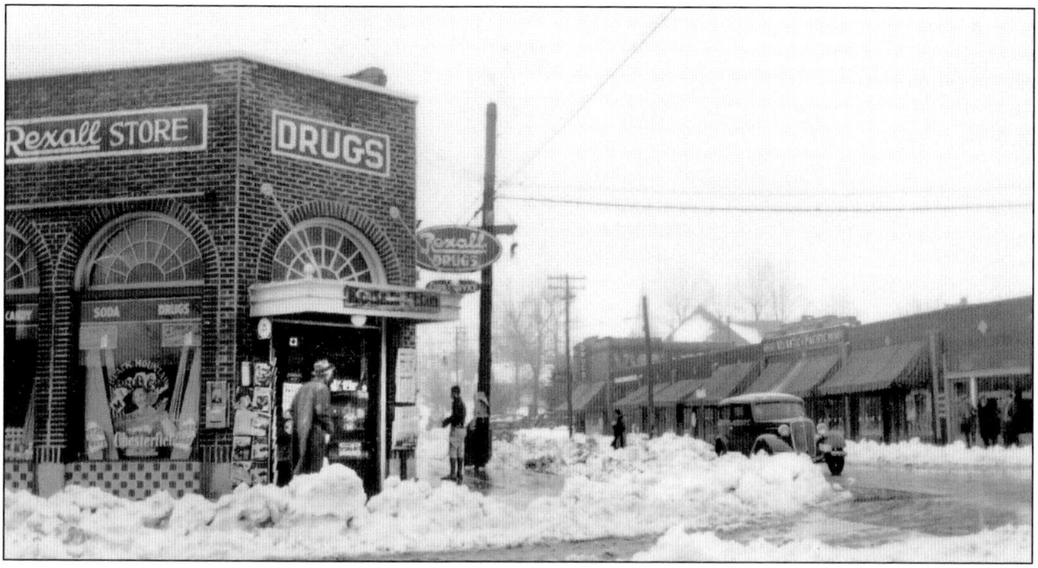

SNOWY TOWN SCENE. Taken at the corner of Broadway and State Streets in Black Mountain, looking west, this snapshot shows the results of a substantial snowstorm in the valley. (Swannanoa Valley Museum.)

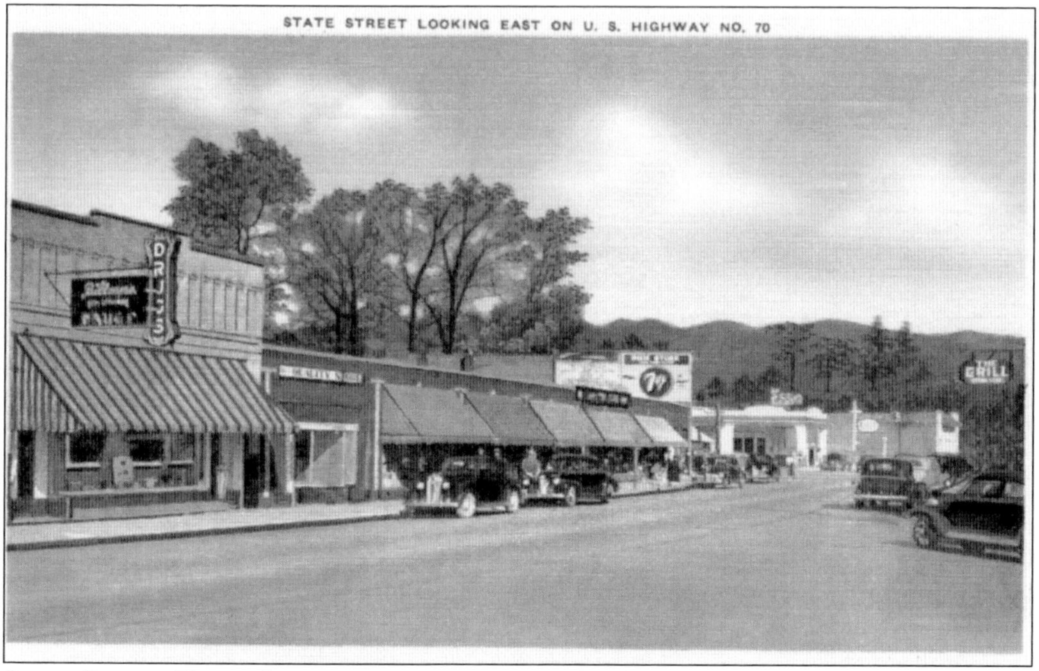

STATE STREET, BLACK MOUNTAIN. State Street is also the main state highway through Black Mountain, first known as Highway 10, and later changed to Highway 70. It is now the town's business center. (Swannanoa Valley Museum.)

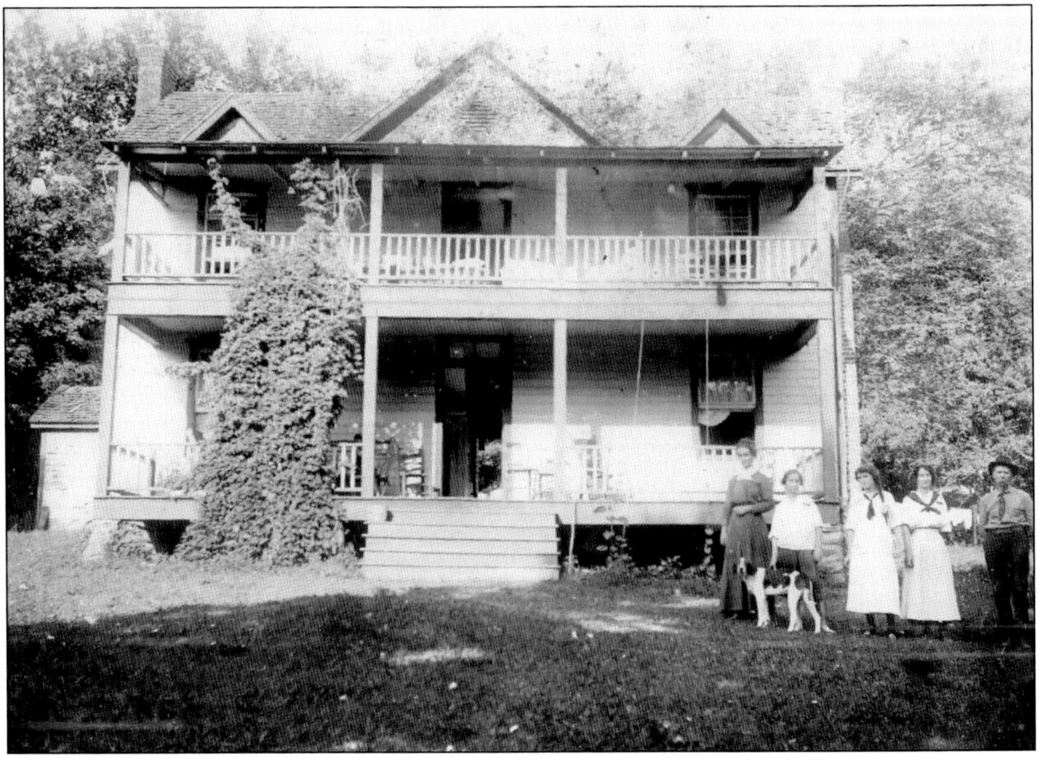

WILLIAM HENRY "CHAMP" AND ELSIE BURNETT HOUSE. It was home to the Burnett family in 1920 when this photo was taken. (Swannanoa Valley Museum.)

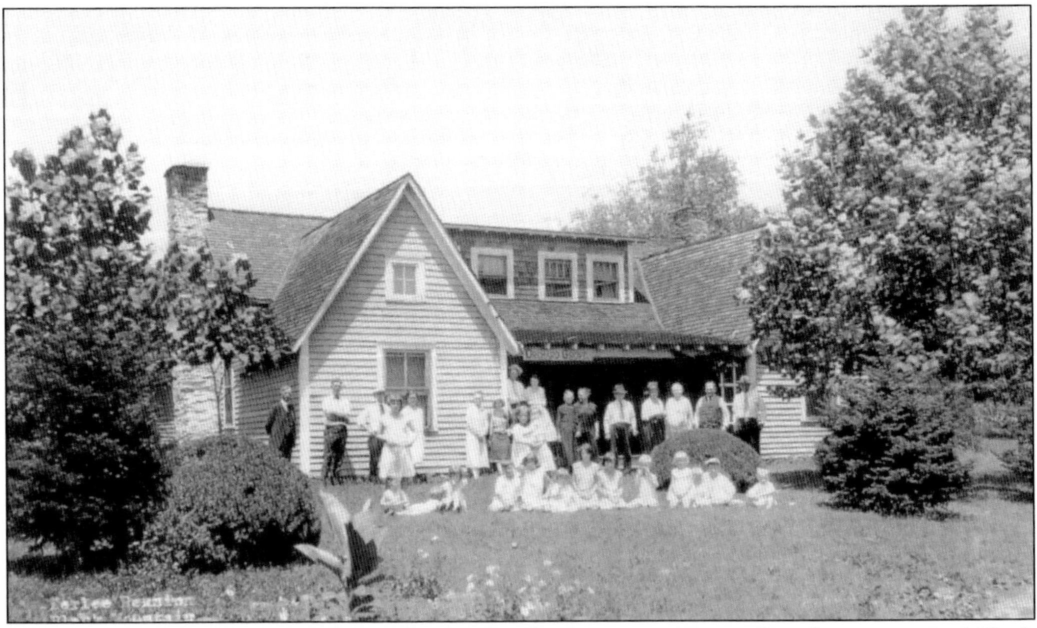

ORCHARD GROVE. Home to the Kerlee family, this house was located at the east end of Black Mountain. It was once the post office. The photo is of the Kerlee Family Reunion, July 20, 1930. (Hemphill Collection, Swannanoa Valley Museum.)

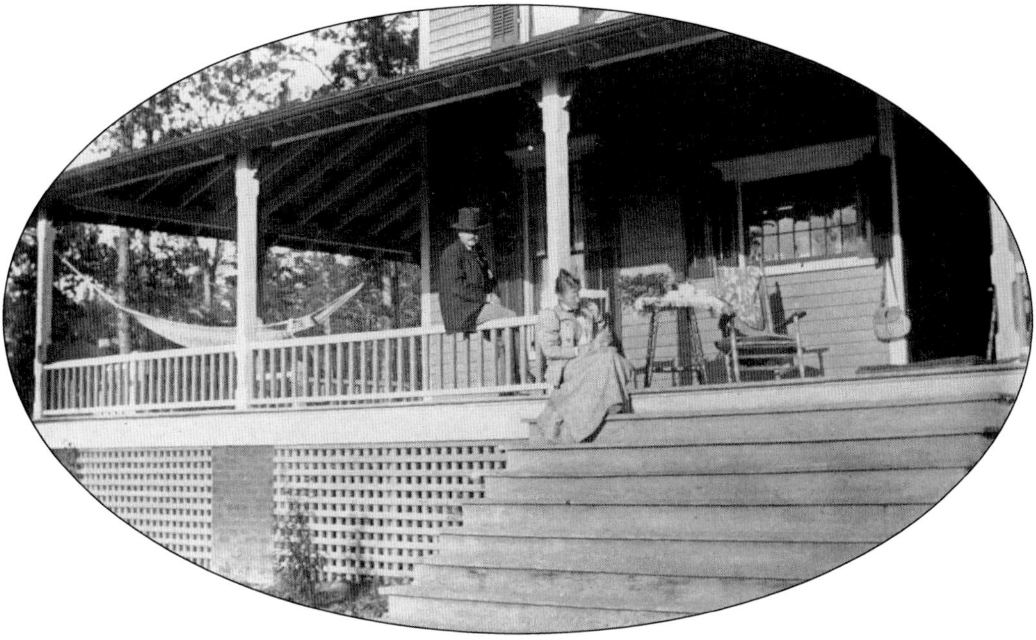

VANCE HOUSE. A cyanotype image taken by Gertrude Sprague in 1900 shows the Black Mountain home of Charles Vance, son of Sen. and Mrs. Zebulon Vance. The home is still located on Sunset Mountain. (Swannanoa Valley Museum.)

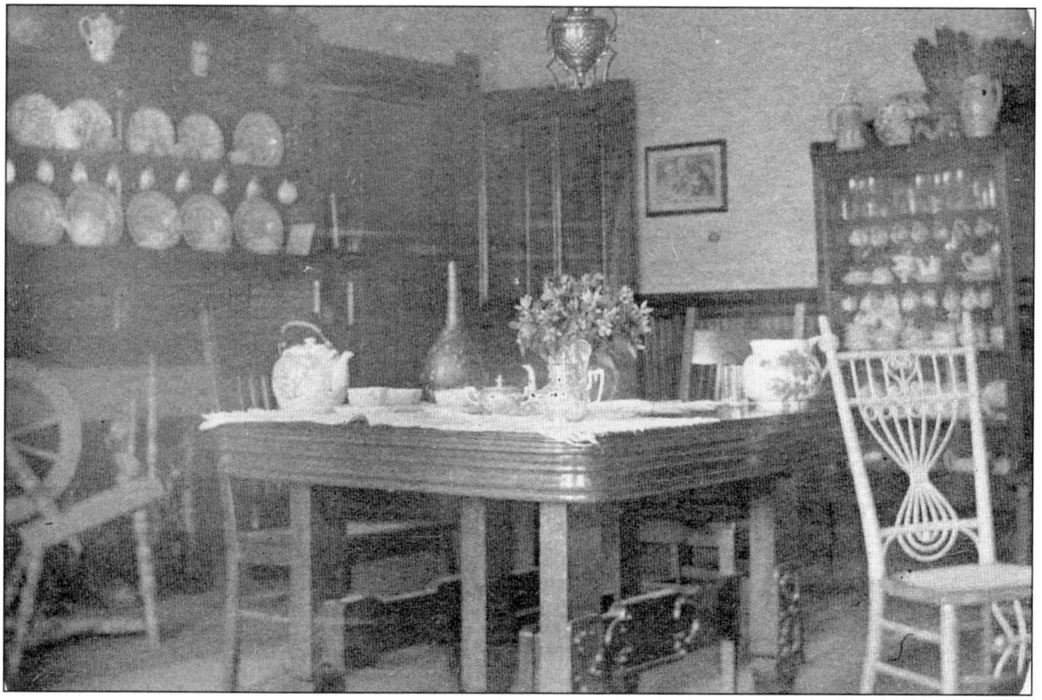

VANCE DINING ROOM. Gertrude Sprague captured this rare image of the interior of the Vance House while compiling her cyanotypes of life in the valley, c. 1900. (Swannanoa Valley Museum.)

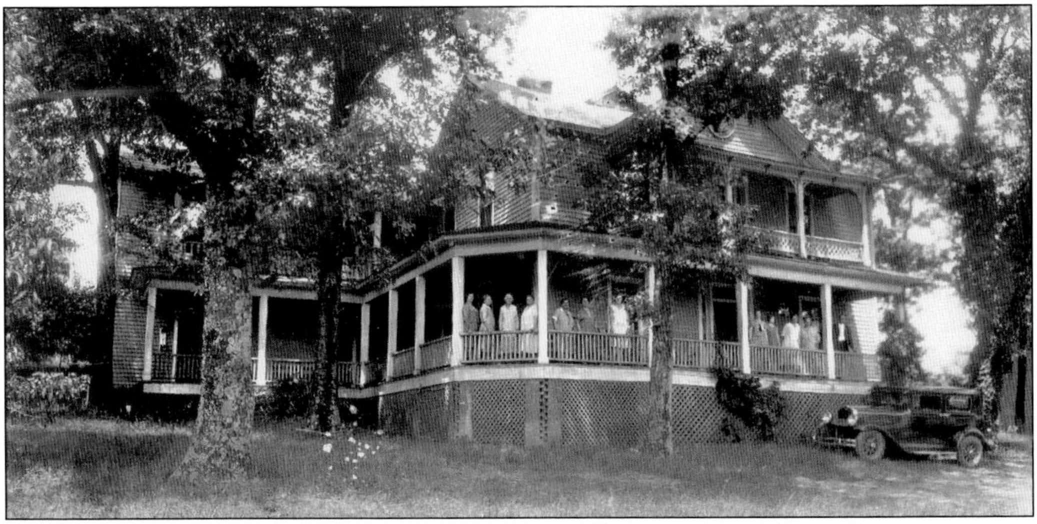

CAUBLE HOUSE. Known as the "Cauble House" in 1904, this home, located across State Street from the Monte Vista Hotel, was the "Washington House" in 1894. (Swannanoa Valley Museum.)

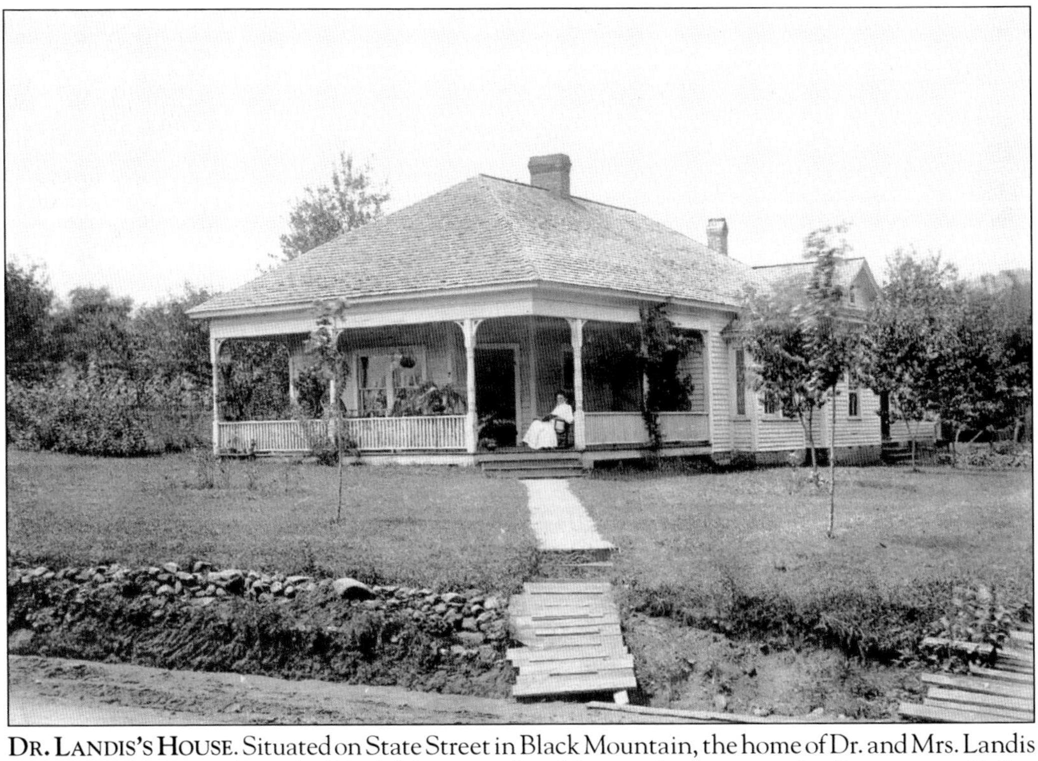

DR. LANDIS'S HOUSE. Situated on State Street in Black Mountain, the home of Dr. and Mrs. Landis was across the street from the Black Mountain Fire House, which is now the Swannanoa Valley Museum. (Swannanoa Valley Museum.)

MOUNTAIN HOUSE. Built in 1851 by William Patton, the Mountain House was on the way to Mt. Mitchell's summit. (Engraving from *Harper's* magazine.)

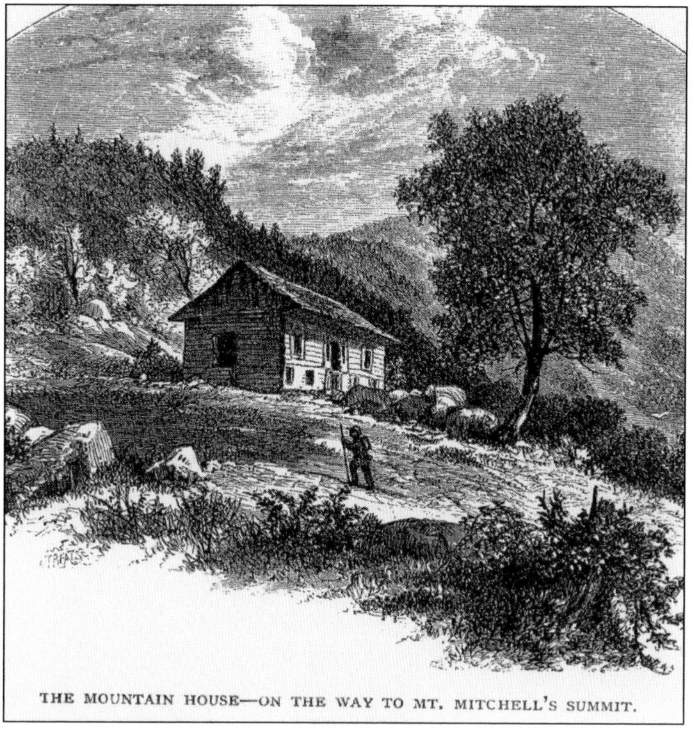

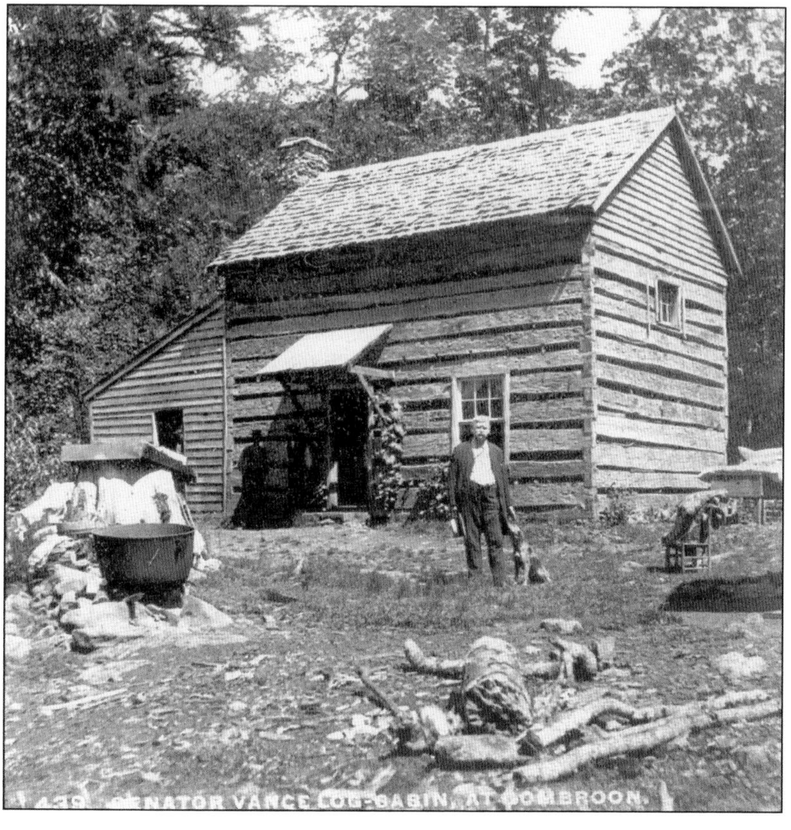

SENATOR ZEBULON VANCE. The senator stands in front of a log cabin on his estate, Gombroon, prior to building the huge, Victorian mansion by that name in 1880. The cabin later became known as the McGinnis cabin. (Courtesy Pack Memorial Library.)

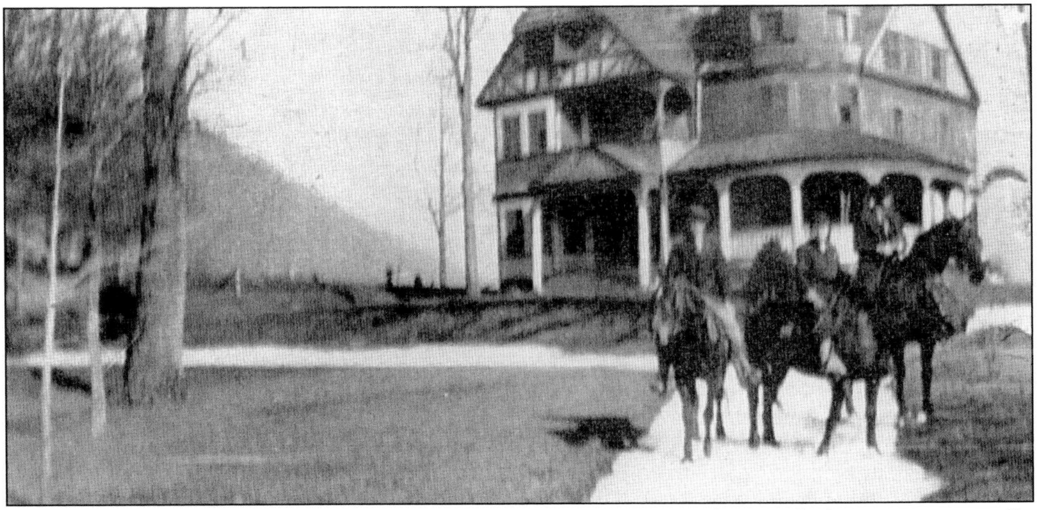

GOMBROON VISIT. The view of the elegant North Fork home of Sen. and Mrs. Zebulon Vance is partially obstructed in this casual pre-1915 photo. (Parker Collection, courtesy Robert Goodson.)

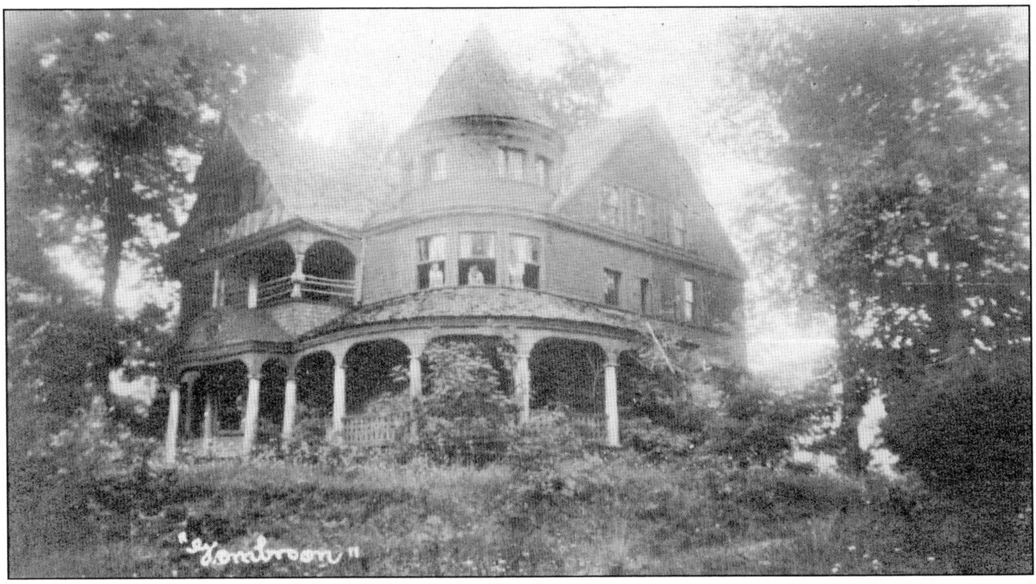

GOMBROON. Built by the second wife of Senator Vance, Florence S. Martin, Gombroon was sited high in the North Fork Valley. After the senator's death, Mrs. Vance returned to Washington, leaving the house deserted. In this ghostly photo, curiosity-seekers can be seen in the upper windows of the derelict mansion some time after 1915. (Courtesy Robert Goodson.)

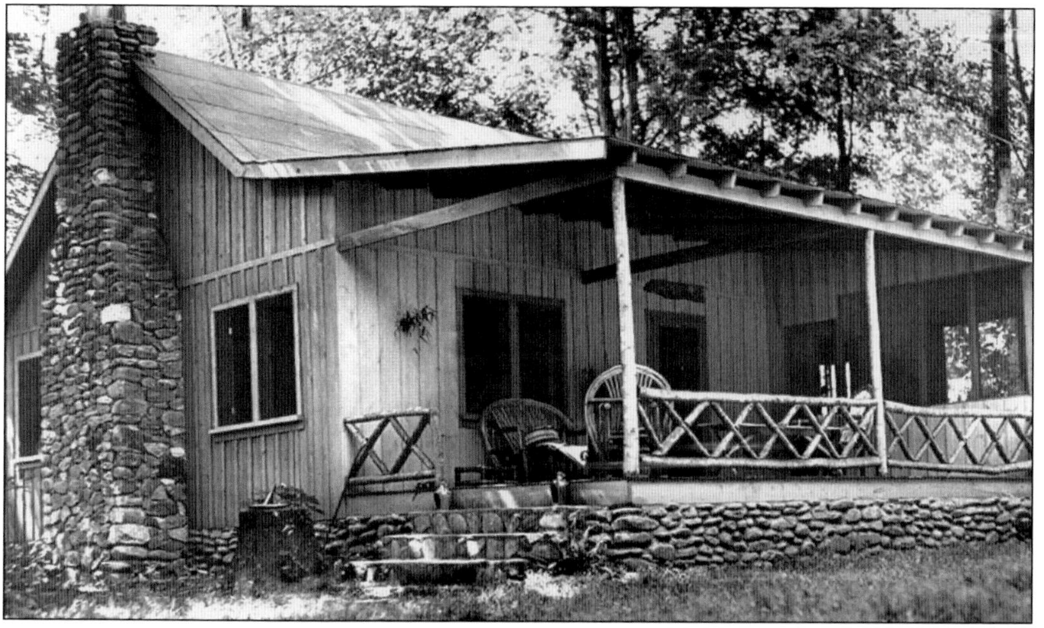

FORKLIFF. This rustic North Fork home belonged to Adm. and Mrs. Clifford Crawford, who retired here after his distinguished naval career. A 1915 graduate of the Naval Academy, Crawford rose to the position of Commander Submarines Atlantic. The house is used today as an information center for the Laurel Ridge community. (Swannanoa Valley Museum.)

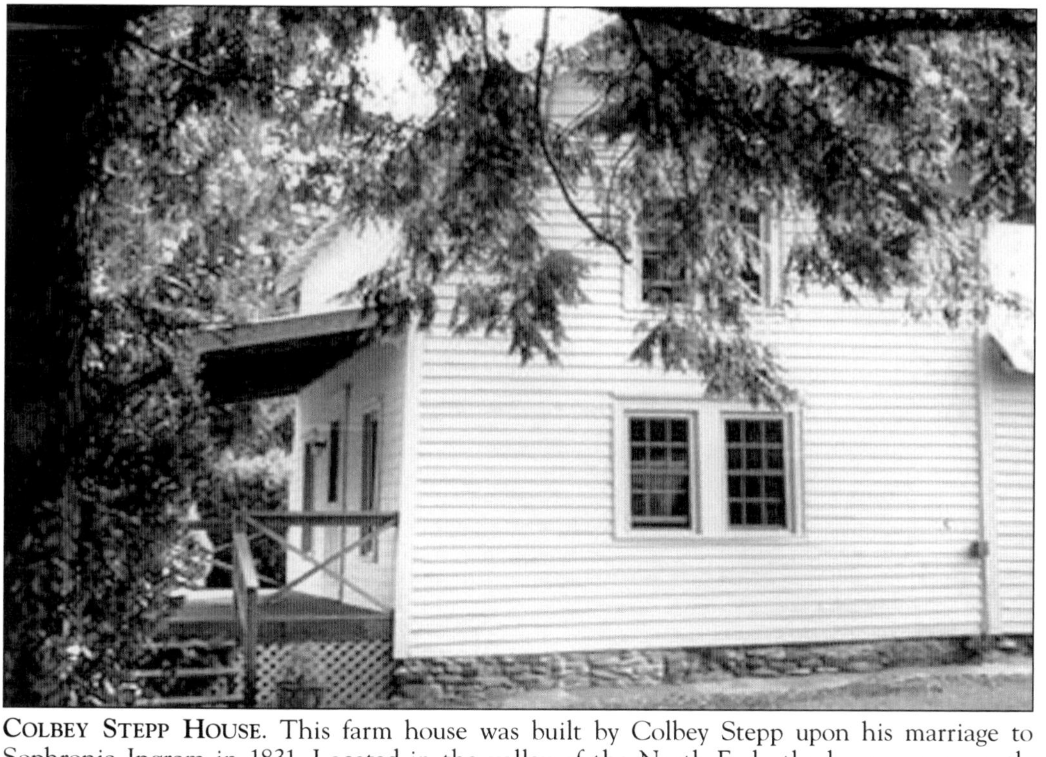

COLBEY STEPP HOUSE. This farm house was built by Colbey Stepp upon his marriage to Sophronia Ingram in 1831. Located in the valley of the North Fork, the house was recently restored by his descendant, Robert Goodson. (Courtesy Robert Goodson.)

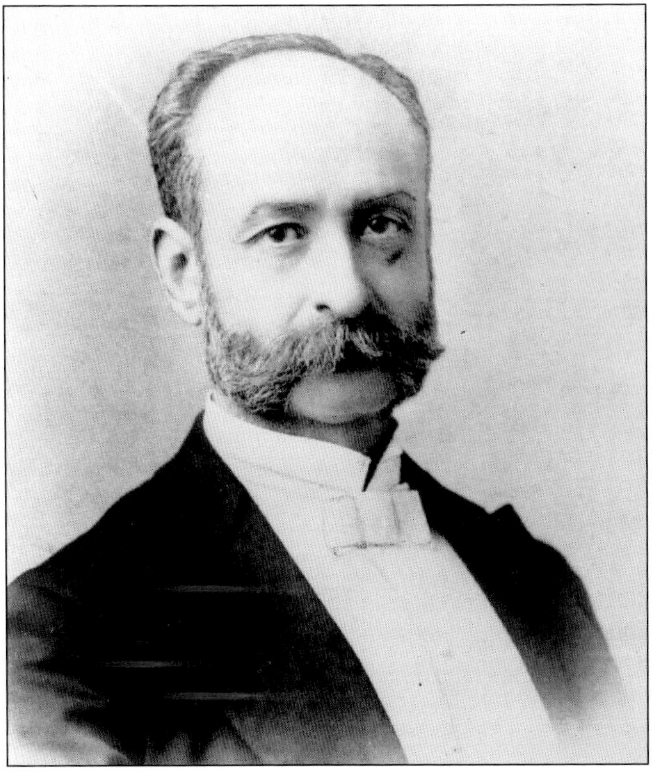

RAPHAEL GUASTAVINO II. A Spanish architect and builder who came to western North Carolina to work on the Vanderbilt mansion, Biltmore House, Guastavino had improved a traditional way of constructing domes and vaults, using thin layers of tile in quick-setting mortar to form decorative and fireproof vaulting. His work is noted worldwide and may be seen locally at Asheville's Basilica of St. Lawrence. (Courtesy Pack Memorial Library.)

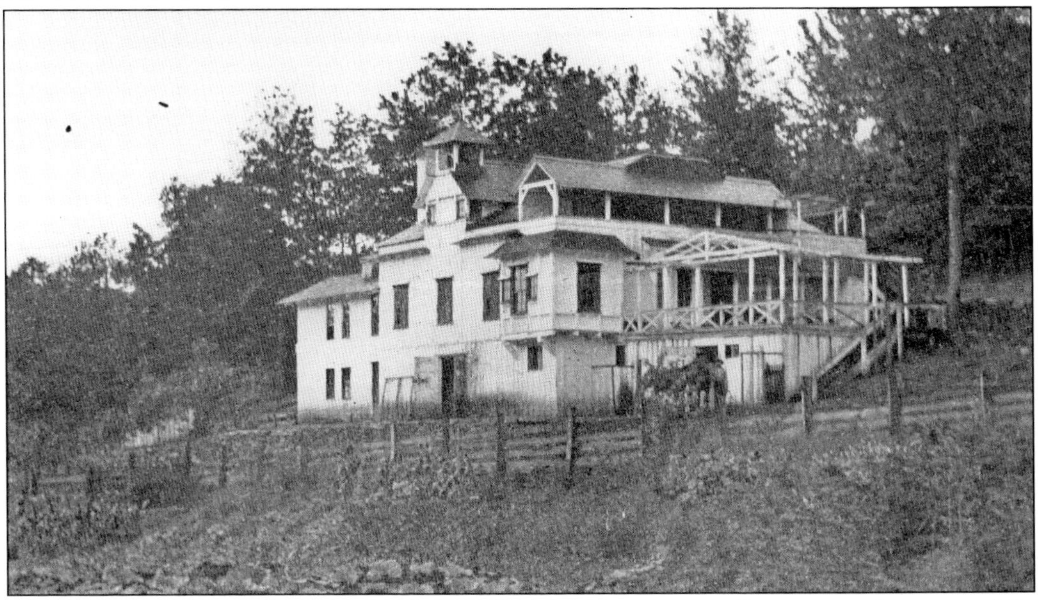

THE SPANISH CASTLE. Spanish architect Raphael Guastavino II came to the area while working on Biltmore House. Like so many others, he was taken with the Swannanoa Valley and built a home here. His estate, which is now home to the Christmount Assembly, was called "Rhododendron," but locals nicknamed it the "Spanish Castle." This cyanotype image was taken by Gertrude Sprague, *c.* 1900. Here the house is uncompleted, with the living quarters above the ground-level barn. (Swannanoa Valley Museum.)

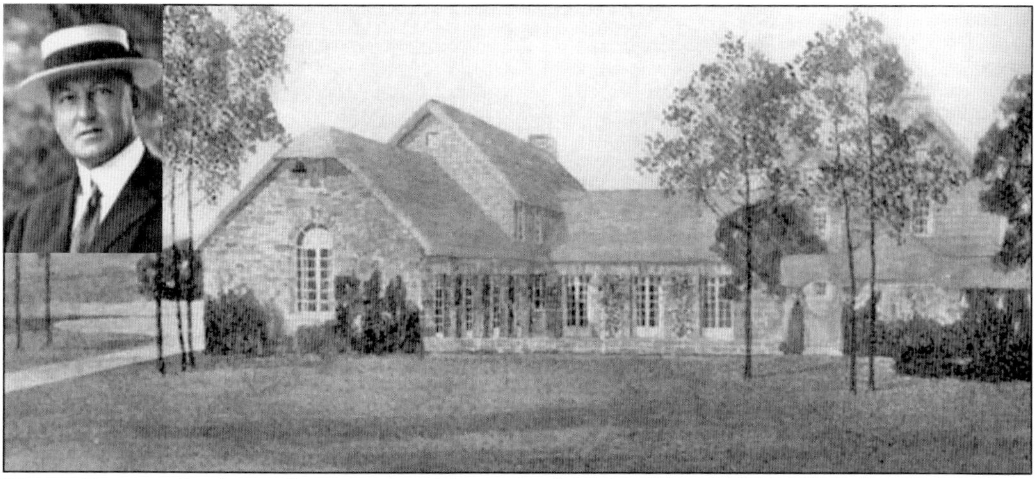

TERRY ESTATE. In the early 1920s Franklin Terry (inset), then an executive with the National Electric Lamp Association, later to become General Electric, passed through the valley and found it a perfect setting for a country home. He built the second largest home in western North Carolina, and called it "InTheOaks." (Postcard courtesy Don Talley; Terry photograph courtesy Montreat College.)

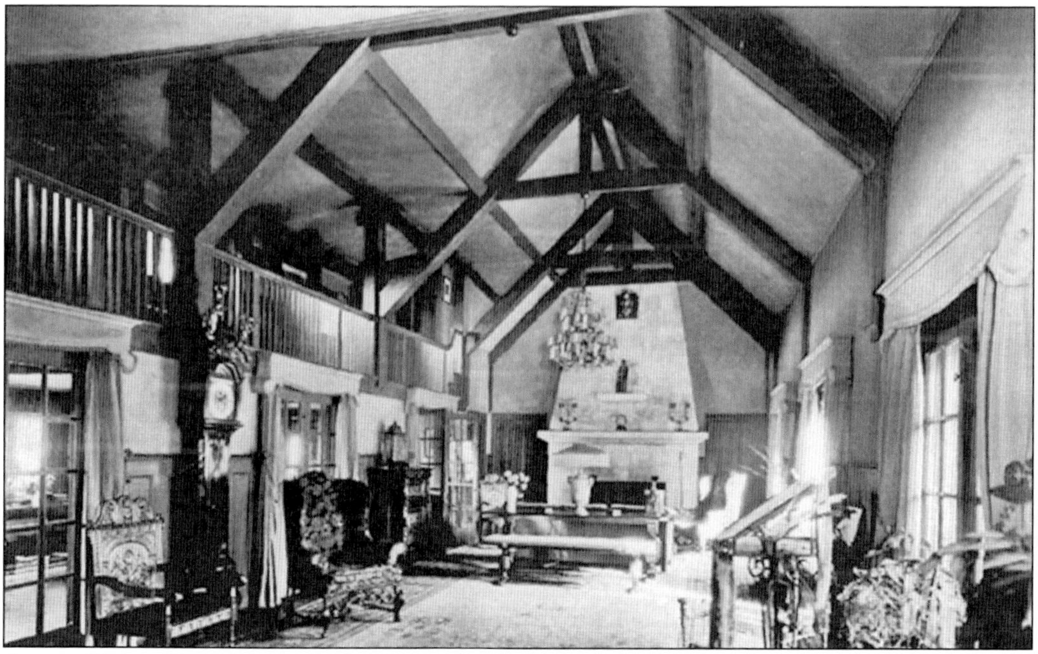

GREAT HALL. The interior of the manor house features a "Great Hall," with two-story ceilings and a gallery above a large stone fireplace. InTheOaks was deeded to the Episcopal Archdiocese upon the death of Mrs. Lillian Terry, and was recently purchased by Montreat College as an extension of its campus. (Courtesy Montreat College.)

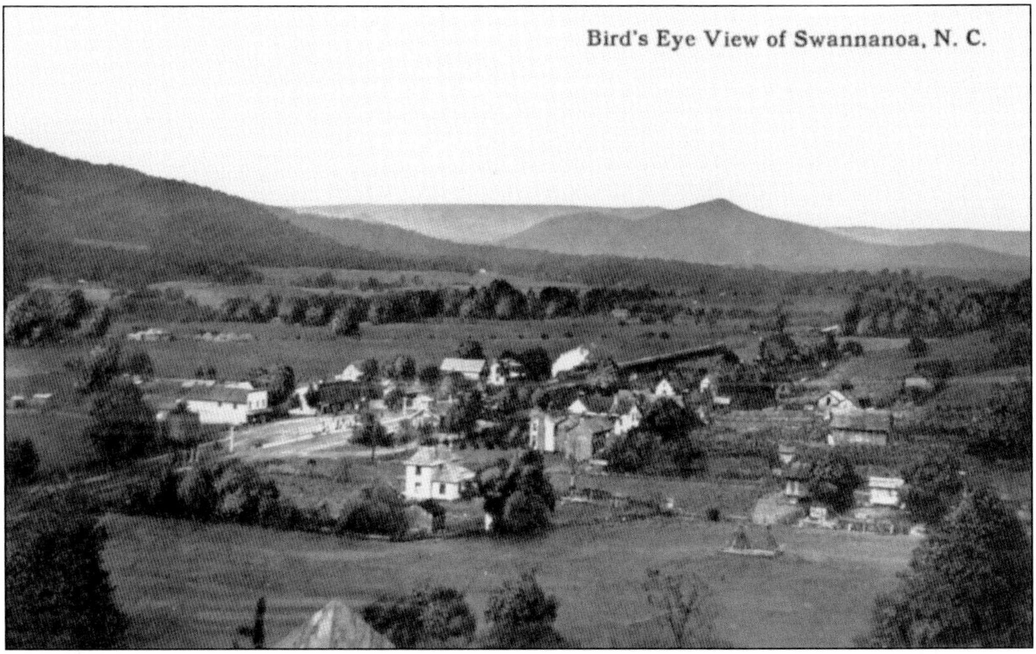

VILLAGE OF SWANNANOA. The center of a more rural community than Black Mountain, Swannanoa has never become an incorporated town. It has been the hub of commerce for a large area, especially after the Beacon Manufacturing Plant moved to Swannanoa in 1925. (Swannanoa Valley Museum.)

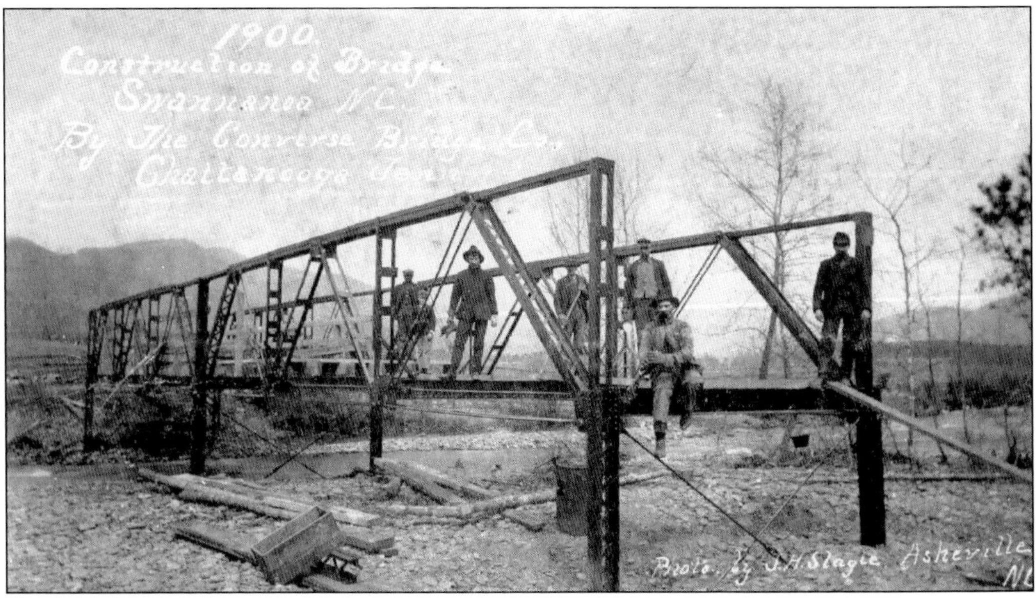

BRIDGE IN SWANNANOA. One of the earliest bridges across the Swannanoa River was built in Swannanoa in 1900 by the Converse Bridge Co. of Chattanooga, Tennessee, as is inscribed on this photo. (Swannanoa Valley Museum.)

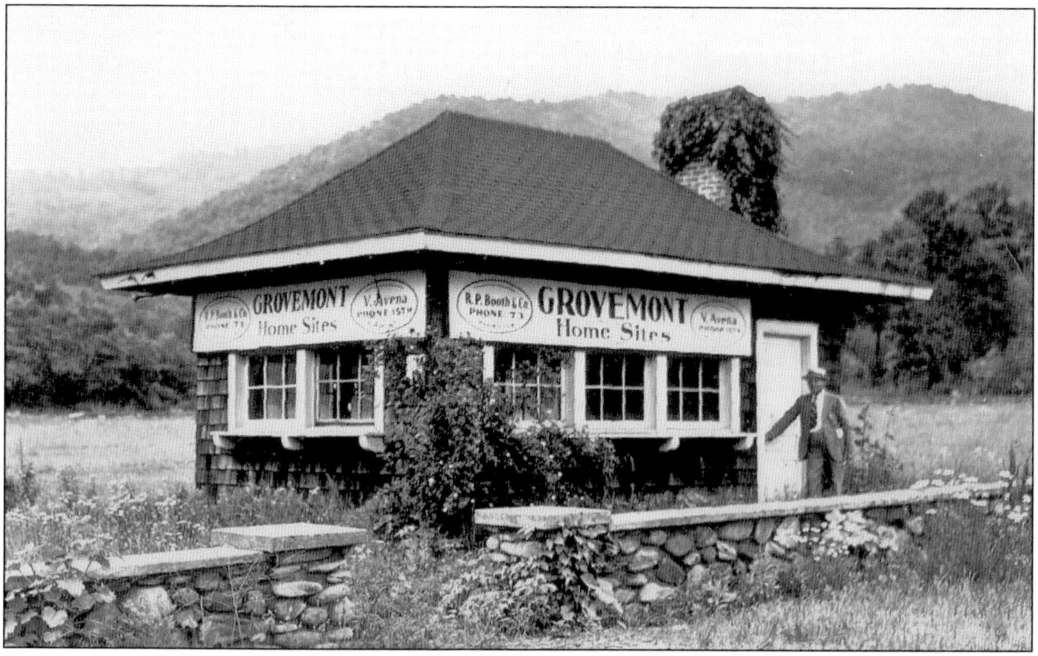

GROVEMONT REAL ESTATE OFFICE. Developer E.W. Grove, builder of the Grove Park Inn and the Grove Arcade in Asheville, designed one of the earliest planned communities, Grovemont, to be built in Swannanoa. He also developed a country club facility at Lake Eden, but he died before it could be completed. (Swannanoa Valley Museum.)

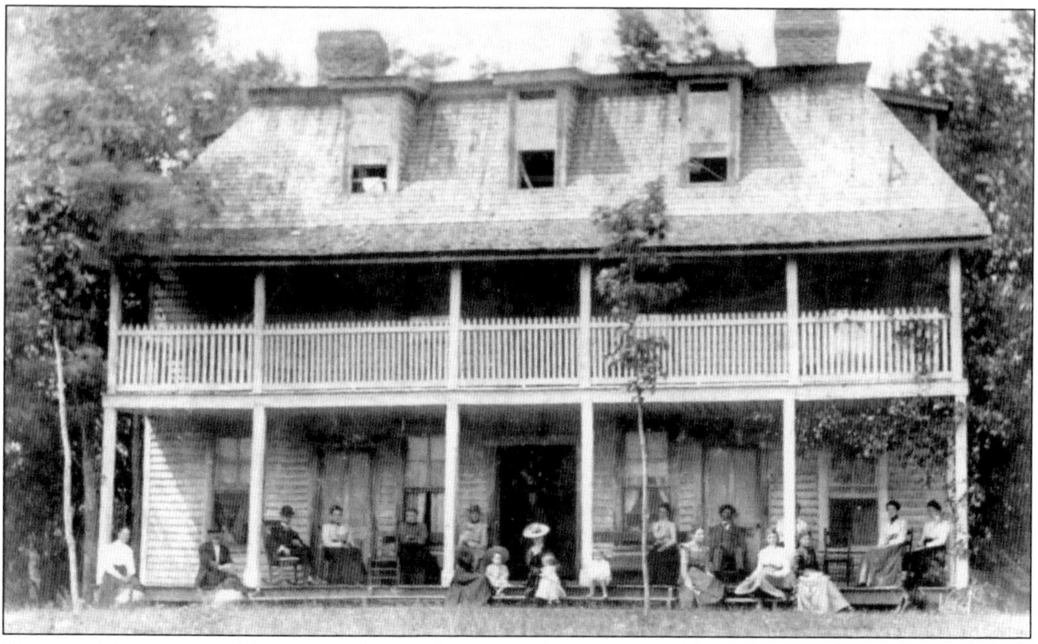

PATTON BOARDING HOUSE. In the early years of tourism, many valley residents opened their homes to visitors, and some, like Squire Patton, built large boarding houses. This home on Patton Hill Road is c. 1890. (Swannanoa Valley Museum.)

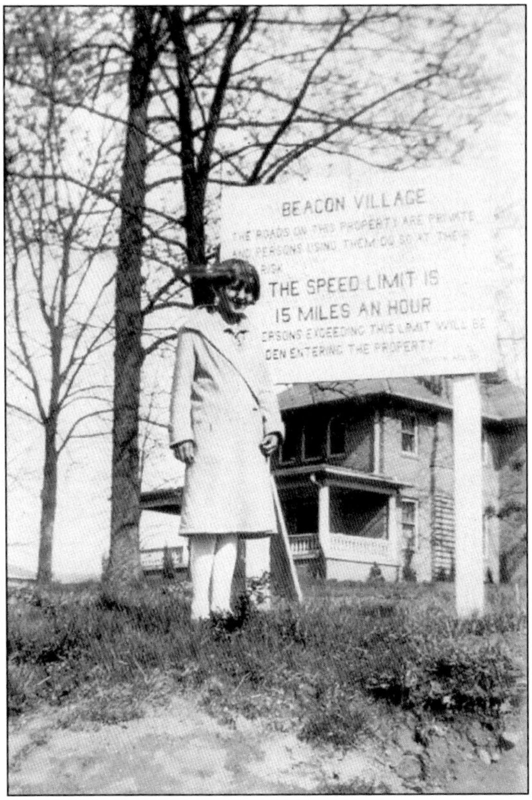

BEACON VILLAGE HOME. Beacon Village was built as rental housing for the employees of Beacon Manufacturing in Swannanoa. The homes were sold to resident employees in the 1950s. This sign warns that the roads are private property. (Courtesy Pack Memorial Library.)

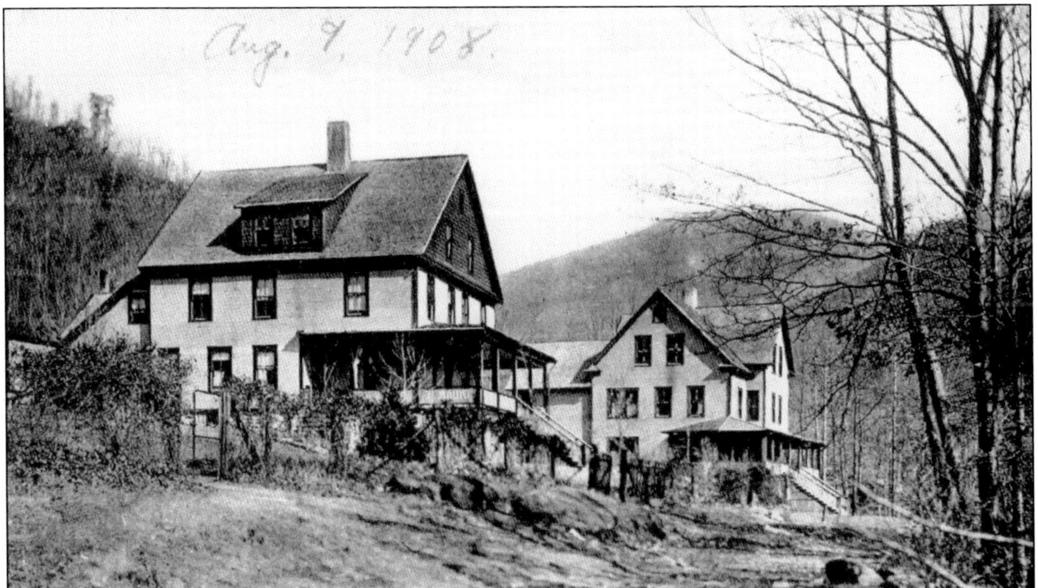

EARLY MONTREAT HOUSES. Although the first "accommodations" in Montreat were tents, parcels of land were later sold and permanent houses were built. These are *c.* 1908 (Swannanoa Valley Museum.)

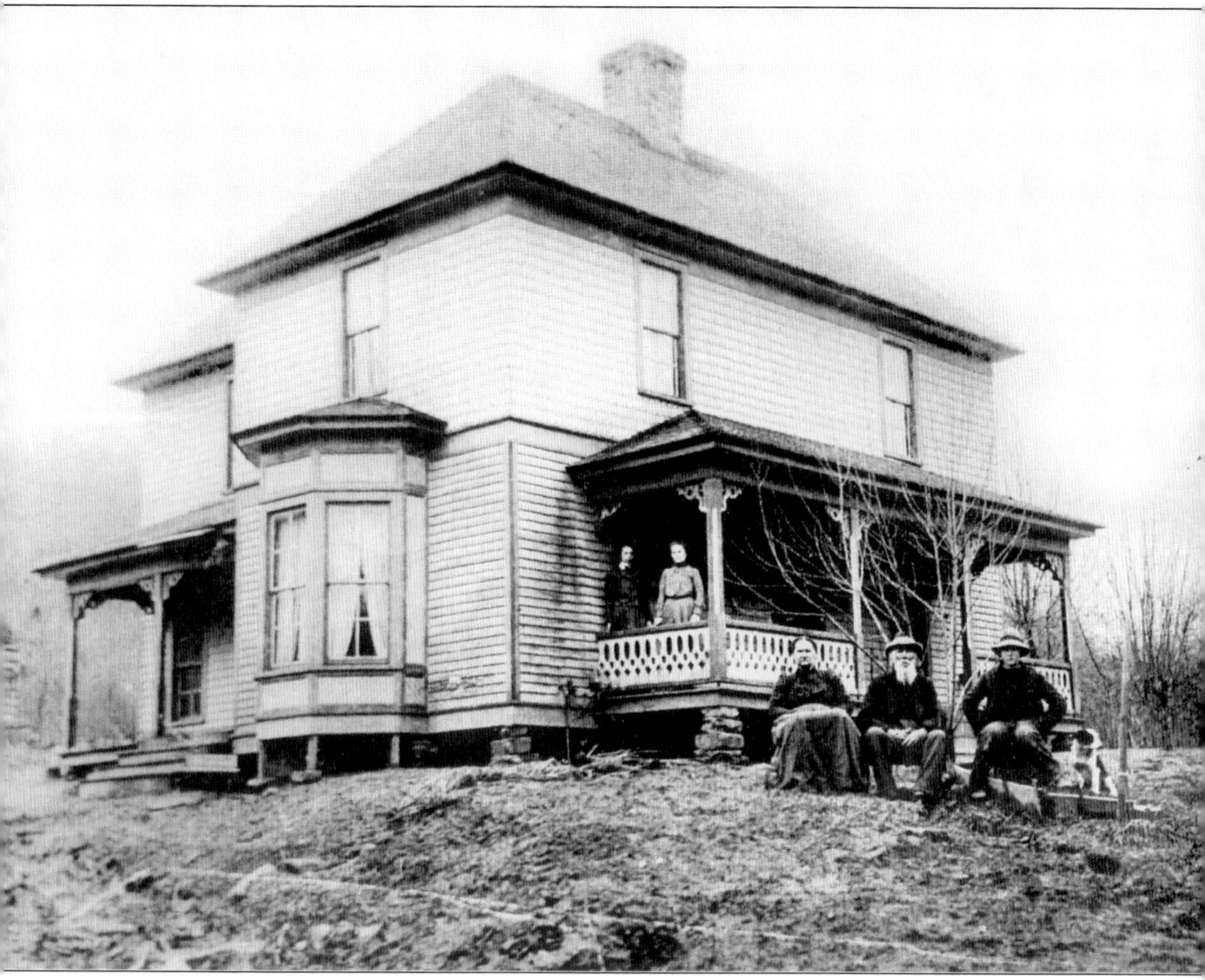

MAE GILLIAM'S HOUSE. Aunt Mae Gilliam lived in this house in Broad River until it burned around 1940. Mae was the librarian for the Broad River community. (Courtesy Joan Allison Hyatt.)

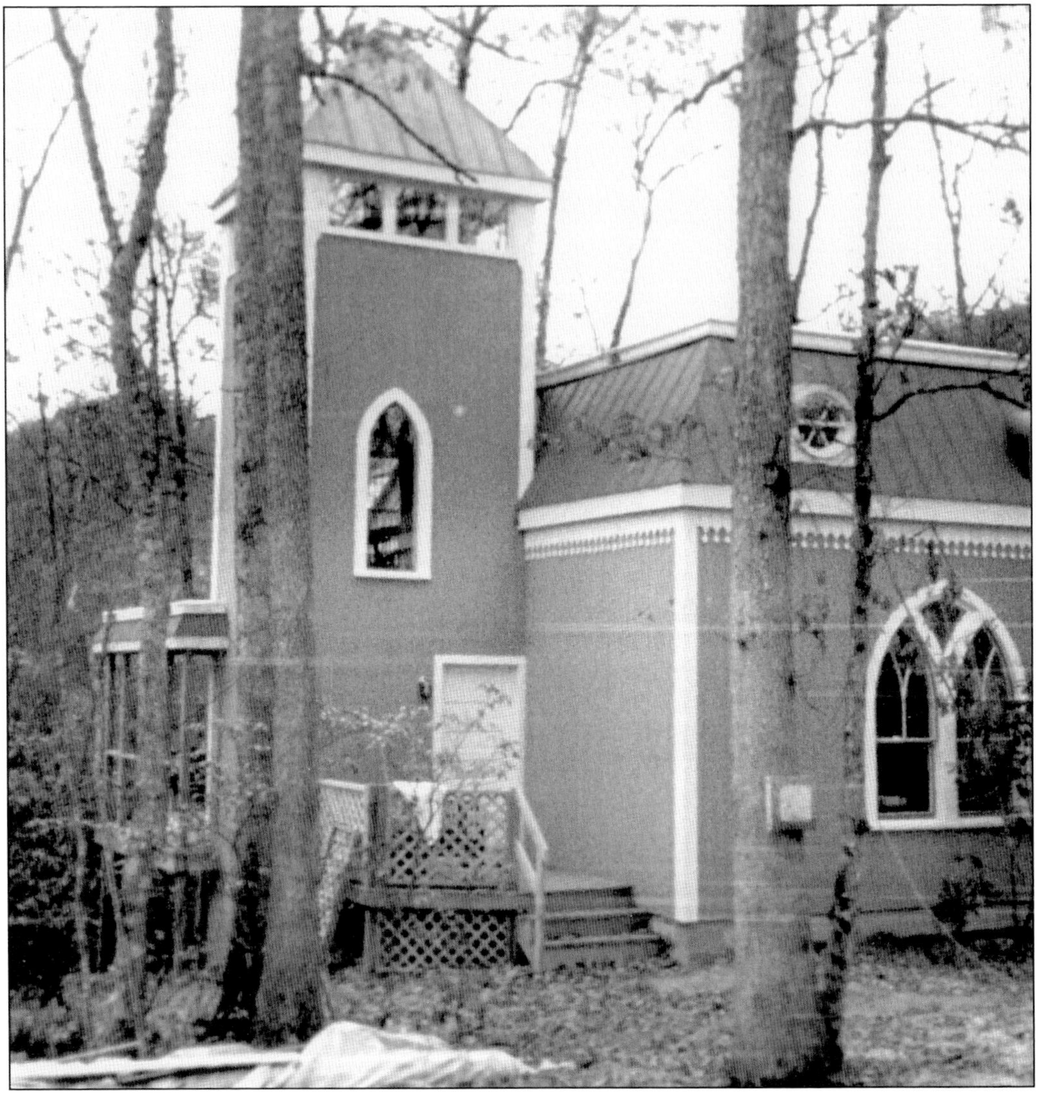

FANCIFUL WOODLAND HOME. Built in the 1970s by Kay Green, this home features many unusual architectural elements that were salvaged from the old First Presbyterian Church in Black Mountain, which was built by W.C. Green, Kay's grandfather. When the church was replaced, Kay was given her choice of materials for the house. (Courtesy Mary Elizabeth Tyson.)

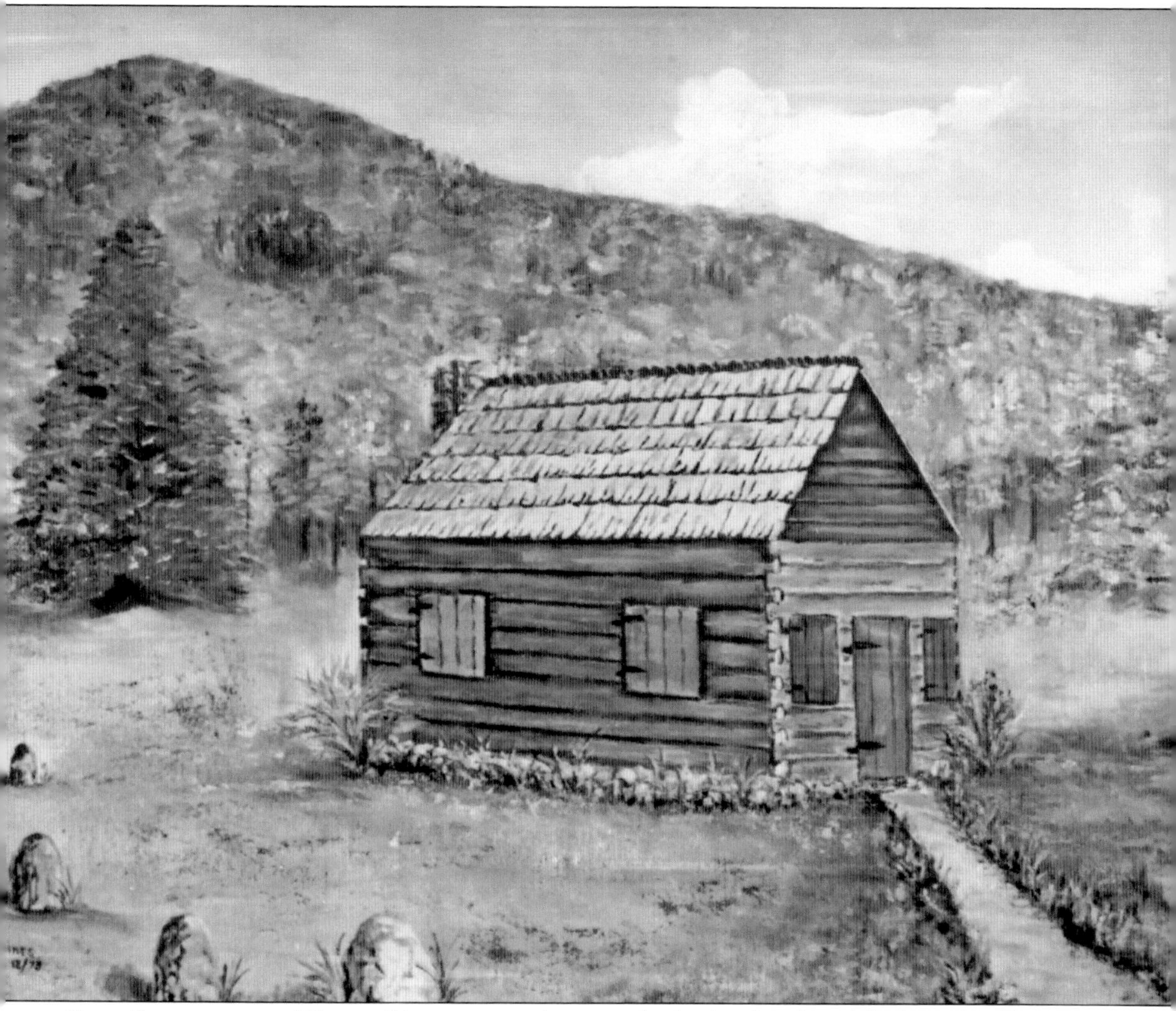

FIRST SCHOOLHOUSE. The small log structure that served as both a church and the first schoolhouse in Black Mountain, *c.* 1837, was located where the Tabernacle Church now stands. The painting, by Martha Raines, is owned by the Tabernacle Church. (Swannanoa Valley Museum.)

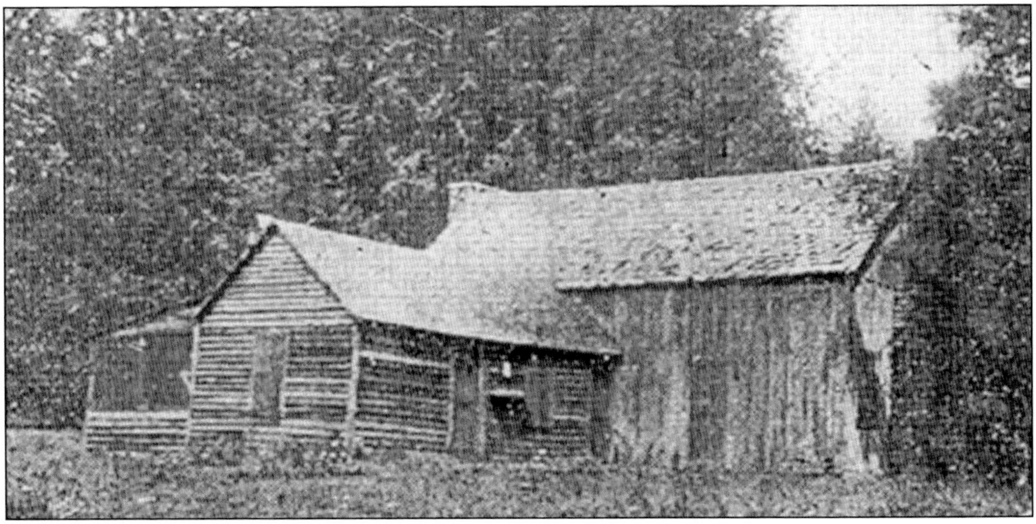

BAILEY LAW SCHOOL. In 1859, lawyer John Lancaster Bailey (pictured below, left) established a law school in this log building located in the North Fork Valley, near the intake of the present-day Asheville Watershed. The school remained open at this site until 1861. After the Civil War, Bailey reopened his school in Asheville. The school building is seen below to the right as it appeared *c.* 1960 (Above courtesy Joyce Parris; below right courtesy of June Glenn Collection.)

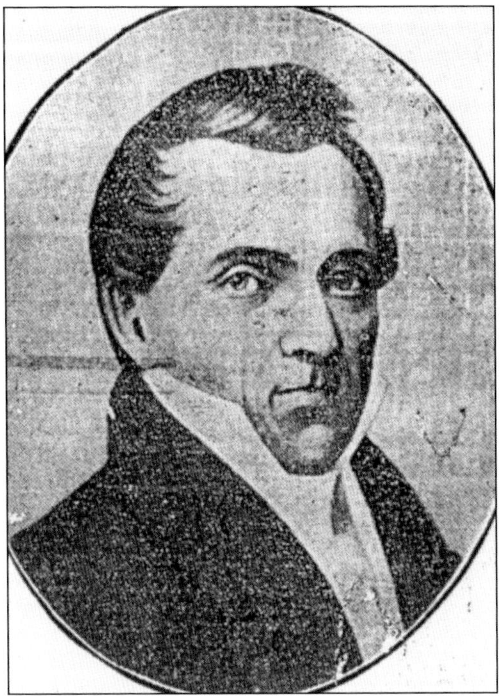

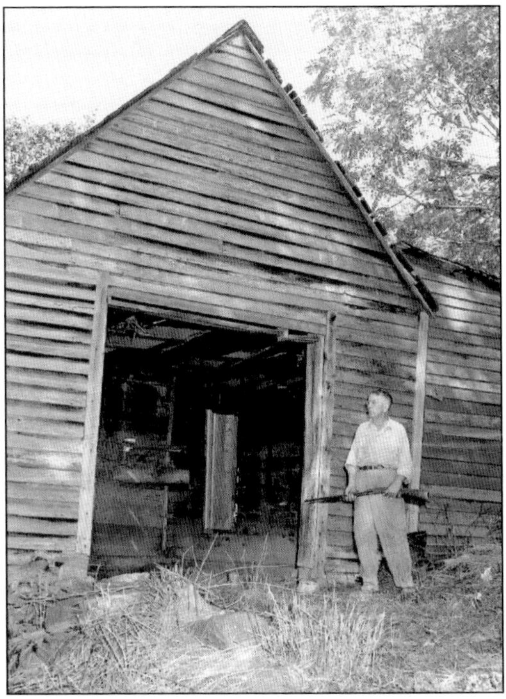

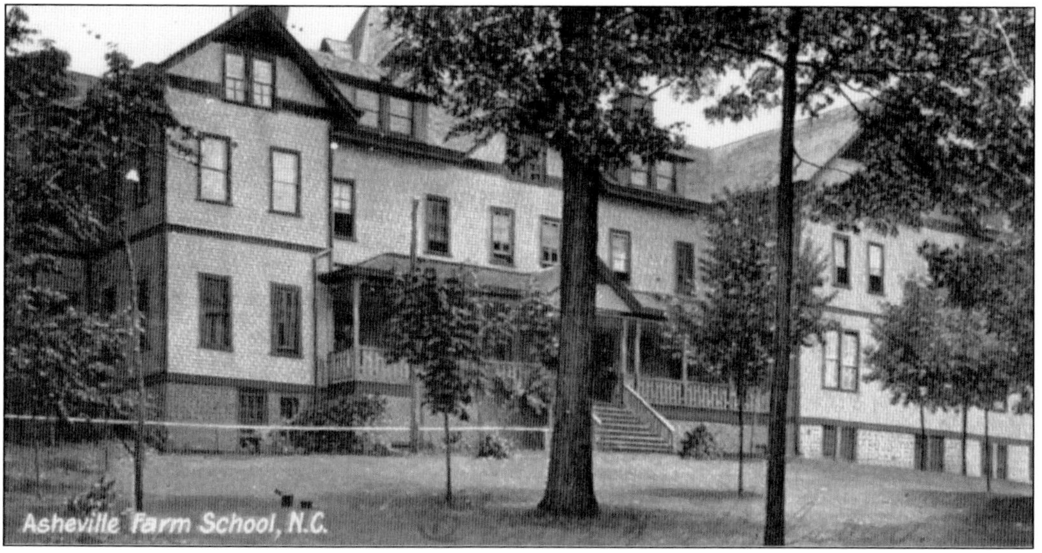

ASHEVILLE FARM SCHOOL, C. 1897. Established in 1894 by the United Presbyterian Church as a boarding school for Appalachian boys, the Asheville Farm School taught agricultural sciences. The school later became Warren Wilson College. (Swannanoa Valley Museum.)

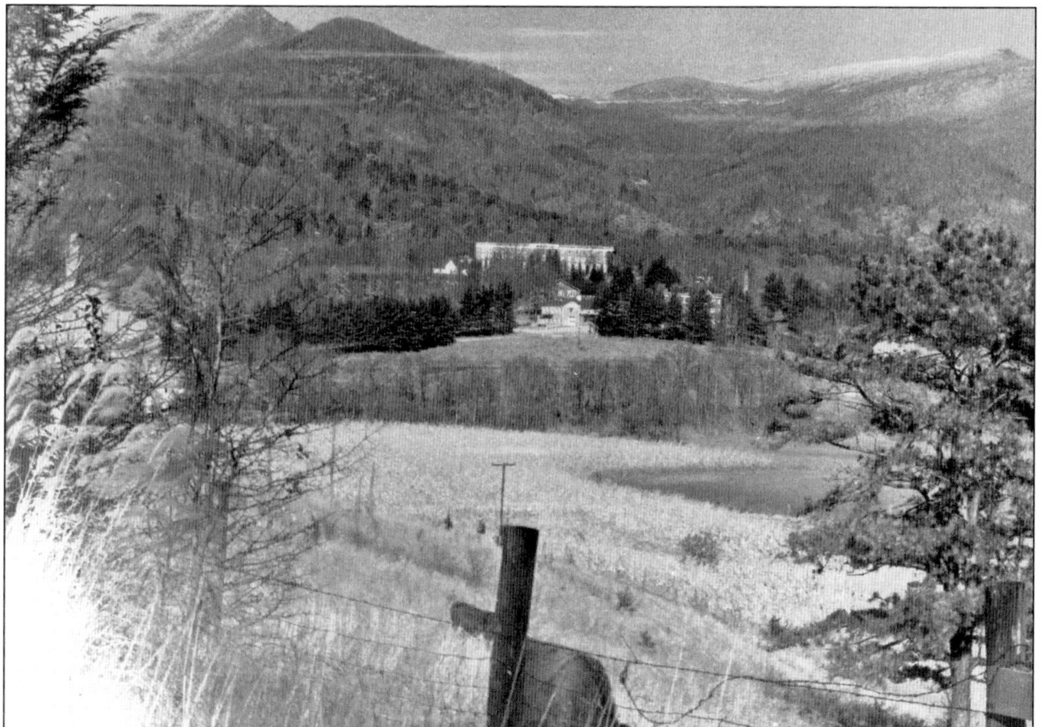

WARREN WILSON COLLEGE. In 1972, the Presbyterian Board of National Missions deeded over the property to the college board of trustees. Warren Wilson's Swannanoa Valley location is ideal for its renowned agricultural programs. The curricula has expanded to include many liberal arts studies as well. (Noah Collection, courtesy David Rozzell.)

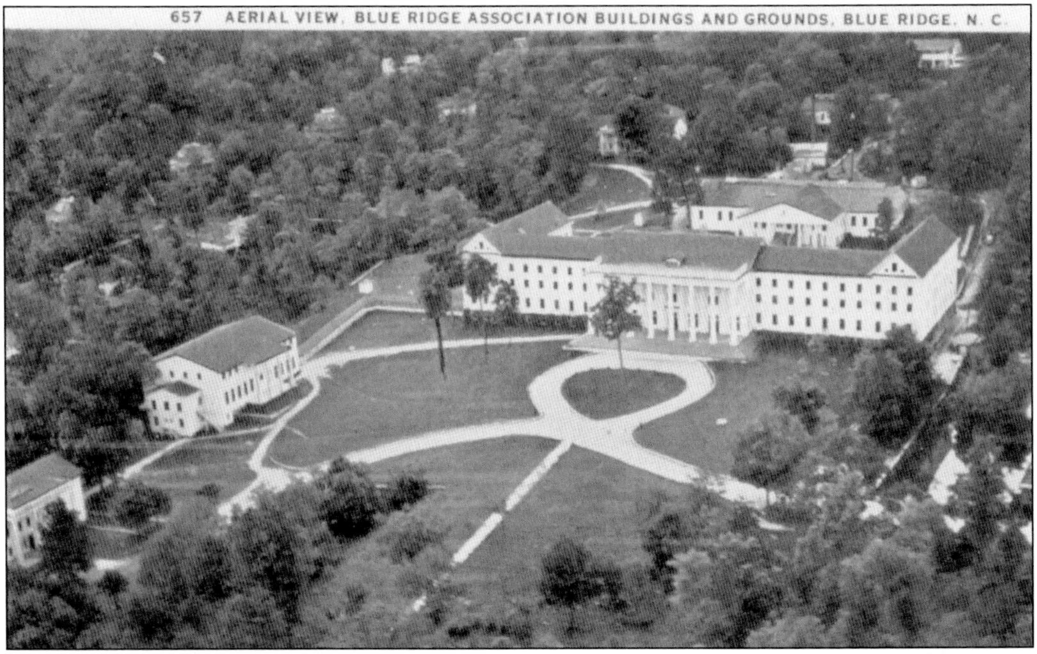

FIRST CAMPUS OF BLACK MOUNTAIN COLLEGE. In the early years, students at Black Mountain College met in Robert E. Lee Hall at Blue Ridge Assembly, shown in this aerial view. (Courtesy Don Talley.)

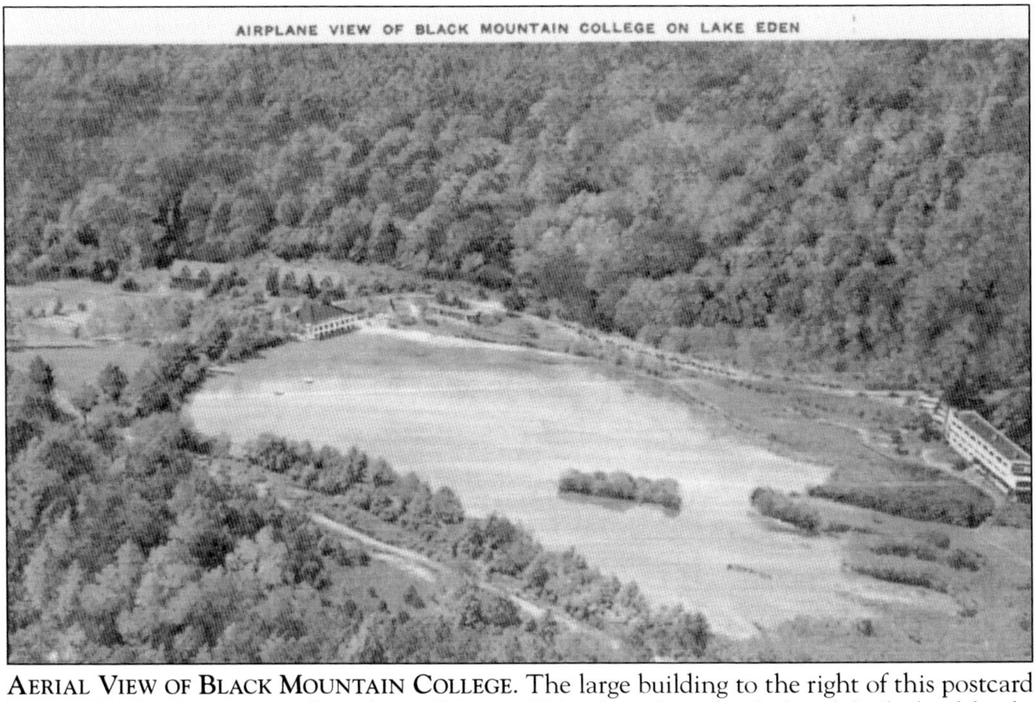

AERIAL VIEW OF BLACK MOUNTAIN COLLEGE. The large building to the right of this postcard housed Black Mountain College from 1941 to 1956, when the school closed for lack of funds. (Courtesy Don Talley.)

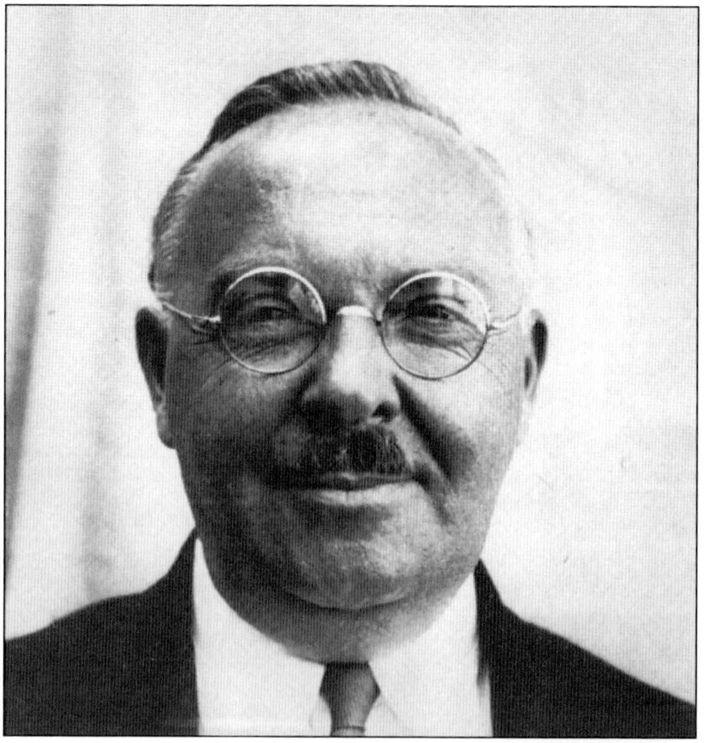

JOHN ANDREW RICE. A forward-thinking and somewhat rogue educator, Rice left Rollins College in Florida to found Black Mountain College, which proved to be a dynamic experiment in education. The institution attained world fame during its operation between 1933 and 1956. Its extensive arts curriculum attracted many European teachers, especially those who left Germany when the Nazis closed the Bauhaus.

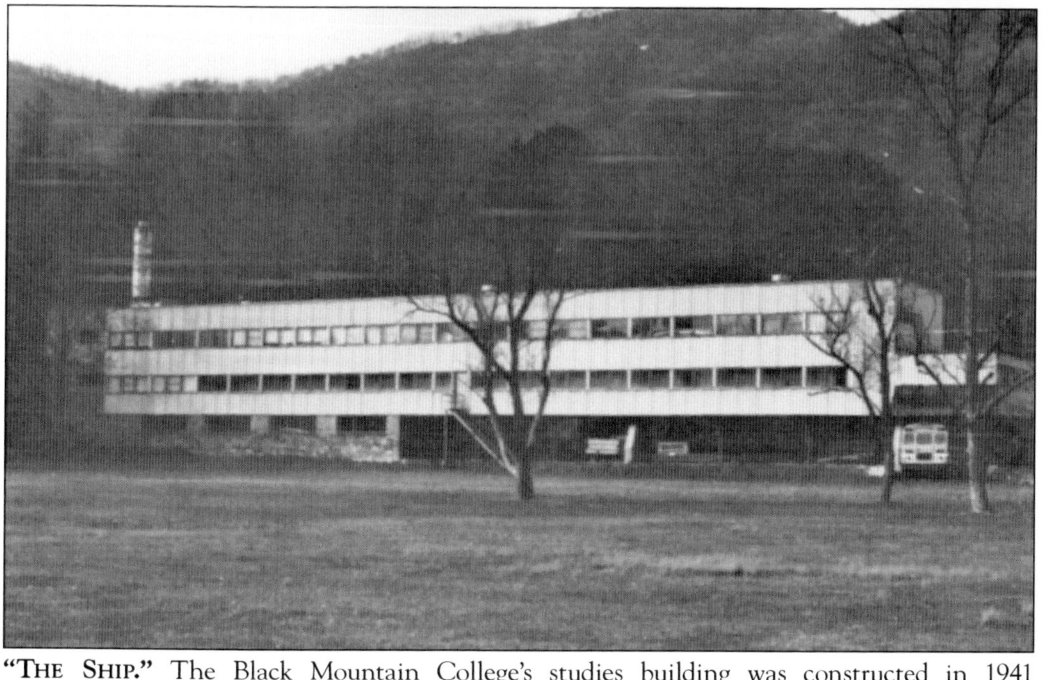

"THE SHIP." The Black Mountain College's studies building was constructed in 1941 at Lake Eden on the site of a proposed country club development of E.W. Grove. Of three planned wings designed by A.L. Kocher, the students and faculty only built one. The building remains standing, but as part of a private boys' camp it is not available to the public. (Swannanoa Valley Museum.)

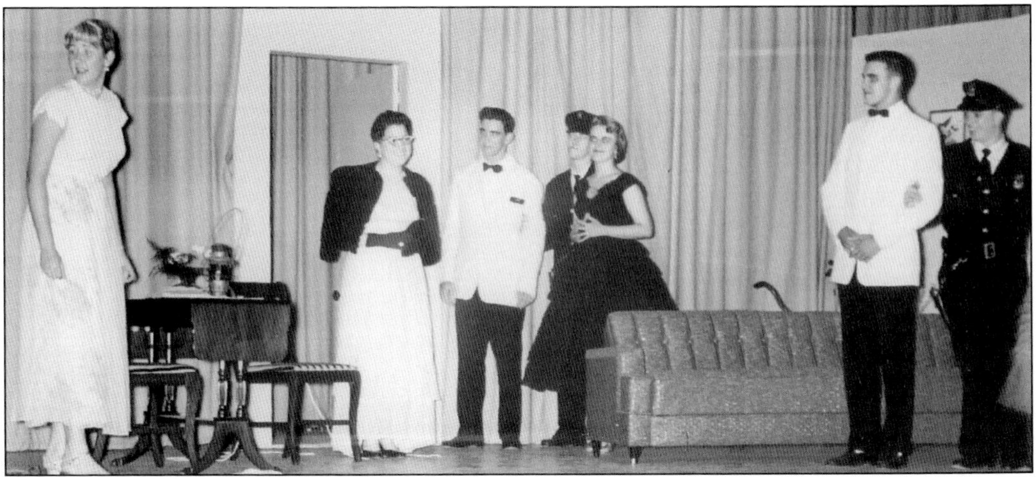

OWEN HIGH SCHOOL PLAY. Students at Owen High School perform in a school production in 1958. (Courtesy Mary Elizabeth Tyson.)

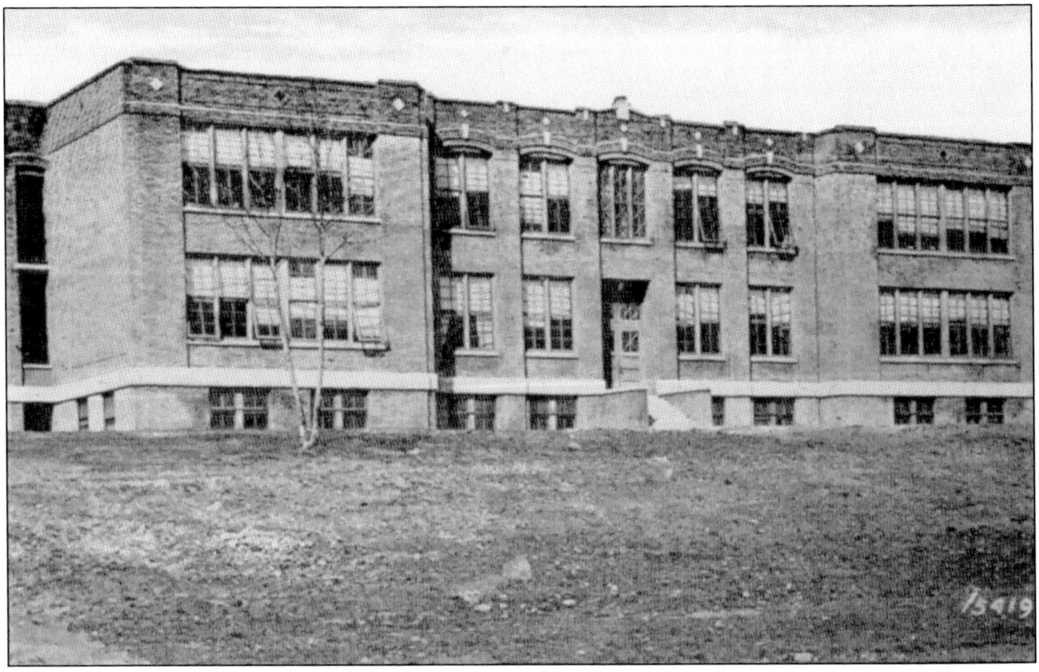

BLACK MOUNTAIN HIGH SCHOOL, C. 1919. After the consolidation of the two valley high schools into Owen High, in 1955, this building was torn down and a new elementary school was contructed on the site. (Swannanoa Valley Museum.)

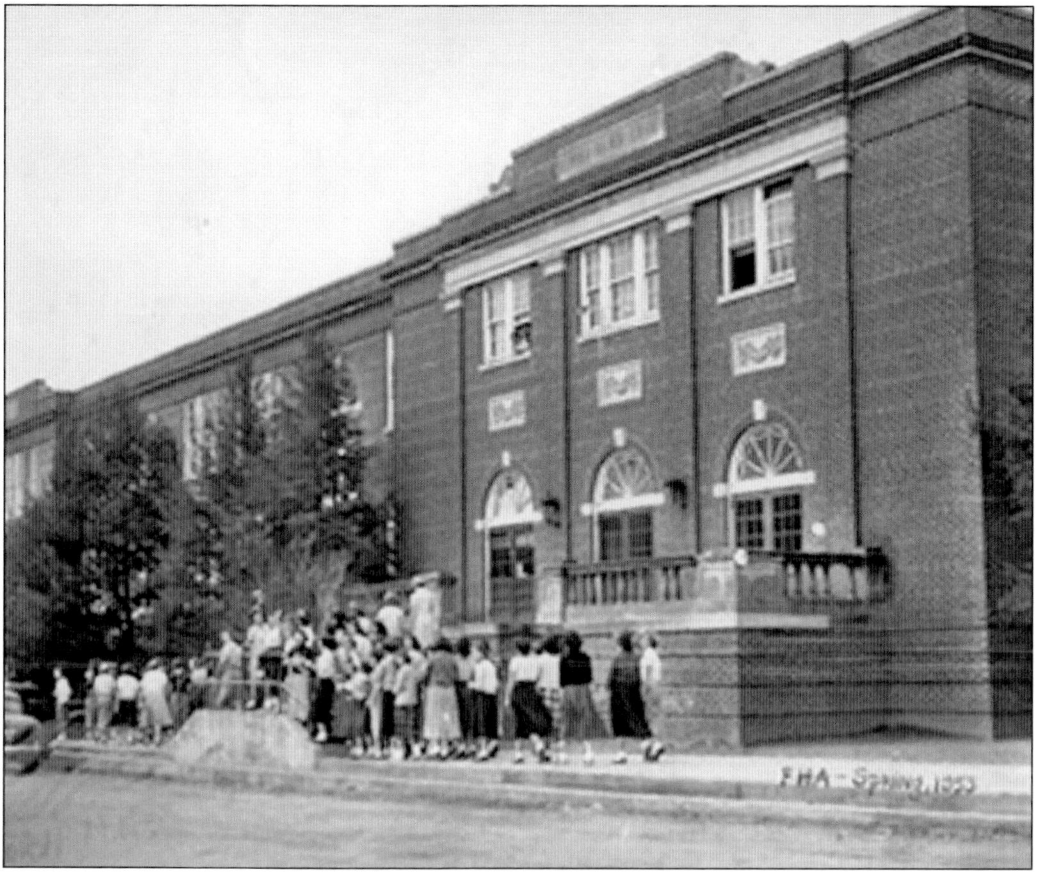

SWANNANOA HIGH SCHOOL, 1953. This is now the campus of the Buncombe Community School East in Swannanoa. (Swannanoa Valley Museum.)

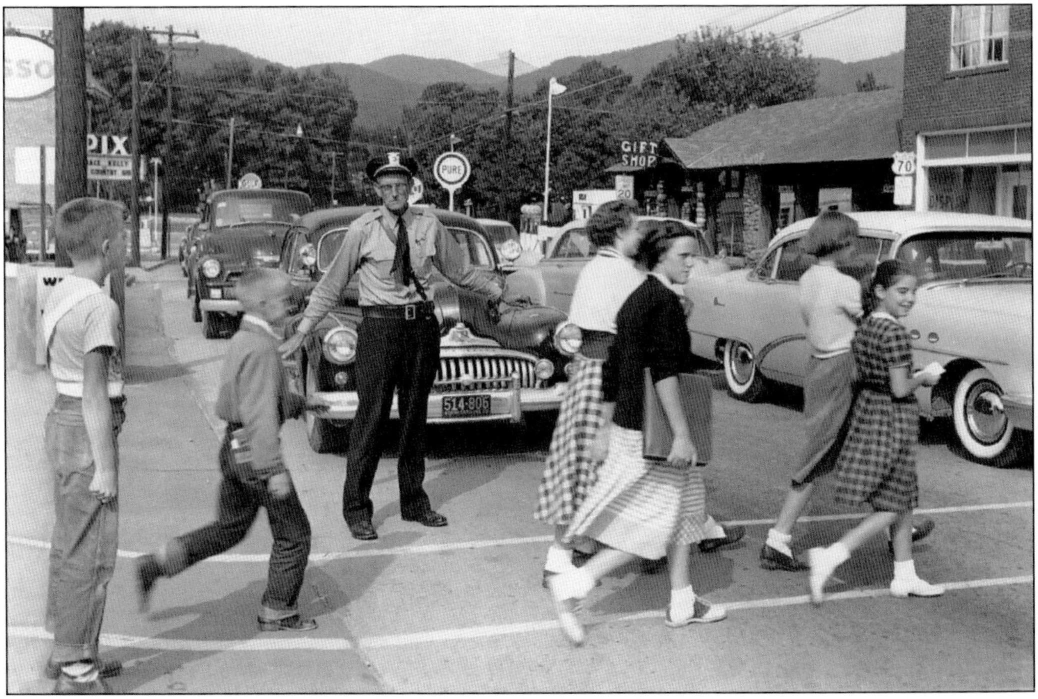

SCHOOL CROSSING. Police officer Lawt Allen guards school kids crossing State Road 70 in Black Mountain, *c.* 1955. (Swannanoa Valley Museum.)

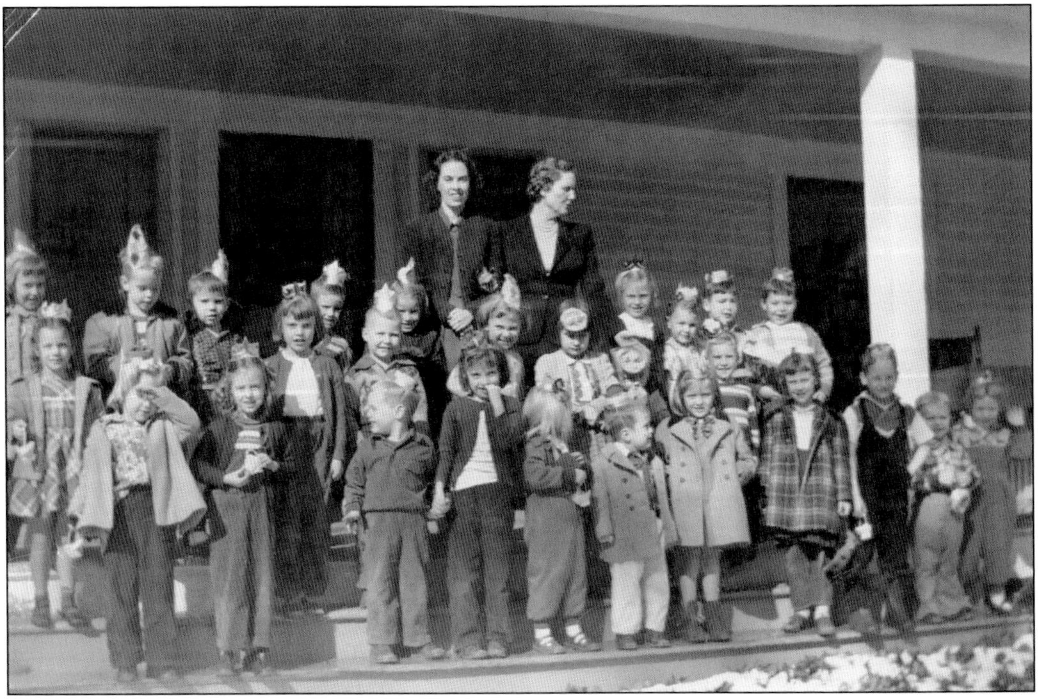

KINDERGARTEN KIDS. Black Mountain Kindergarten students and teachers are pictured in 1951. (Courtesy Cheryl Burgess Edwards Collection.)

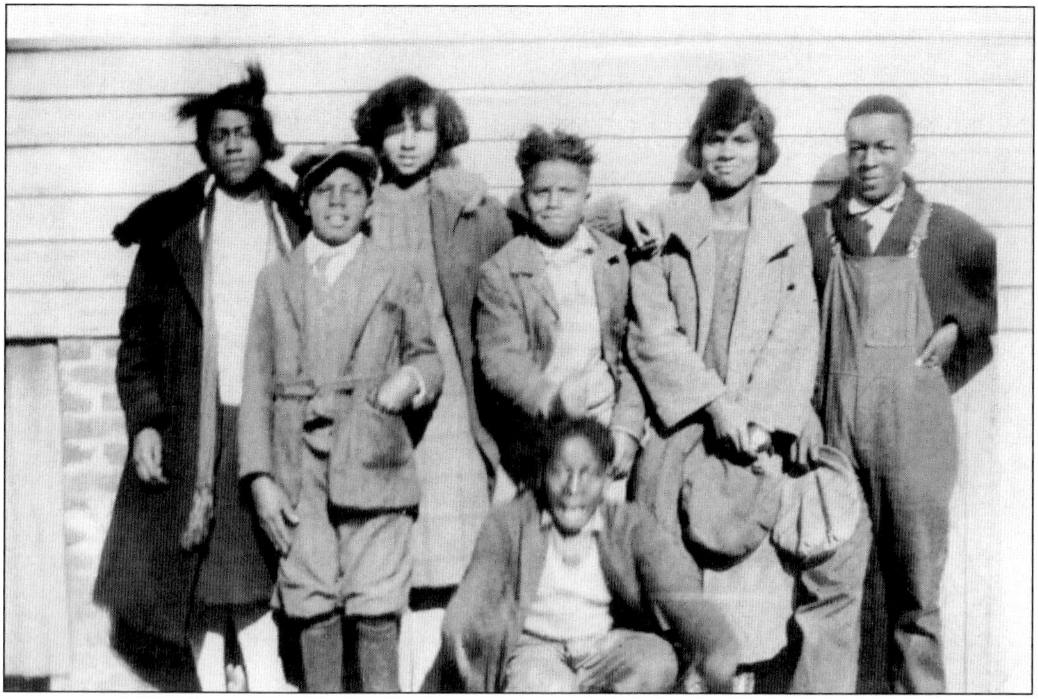

SMILE FOR THE CAMERA. Charles Daugherty, front and center, clowns for the camera in this 1945 photo with a group of elementary school children. The pre-integration school was located on Cragmont Road. (Swannanoa Valley Museum.)

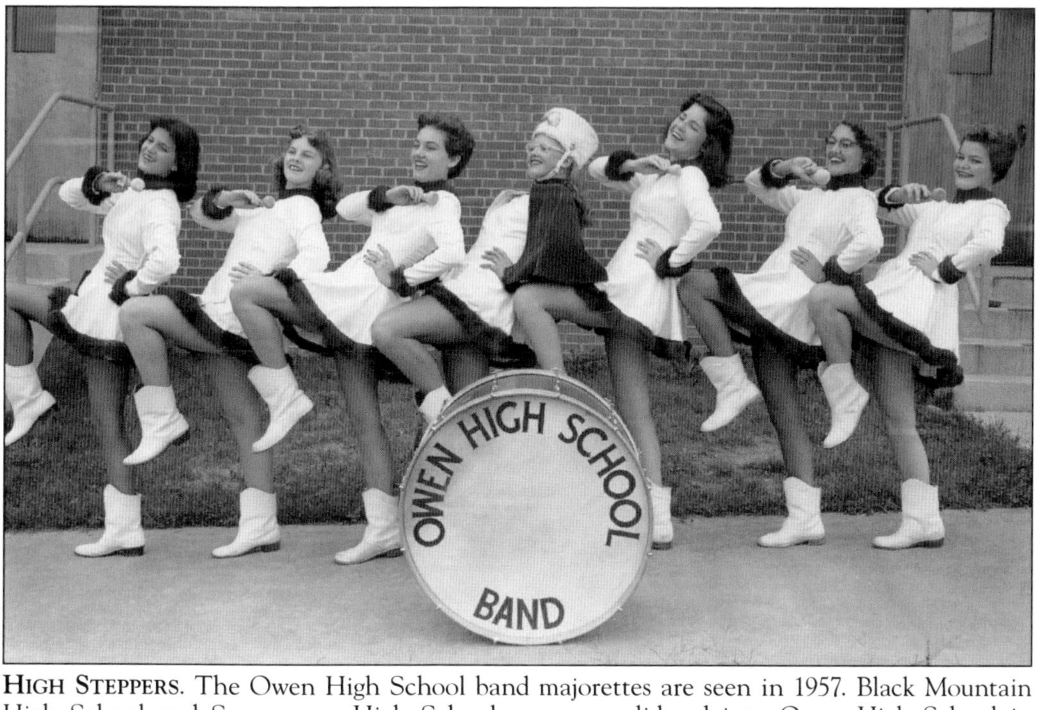

HIGH STEPPERS. The Owen High School band majorettes are seen in 1957. Black Mountain High School and Swannanoa High School were consolidated into Owen High School in January 1955. (Swannanoa Valley Museum.)

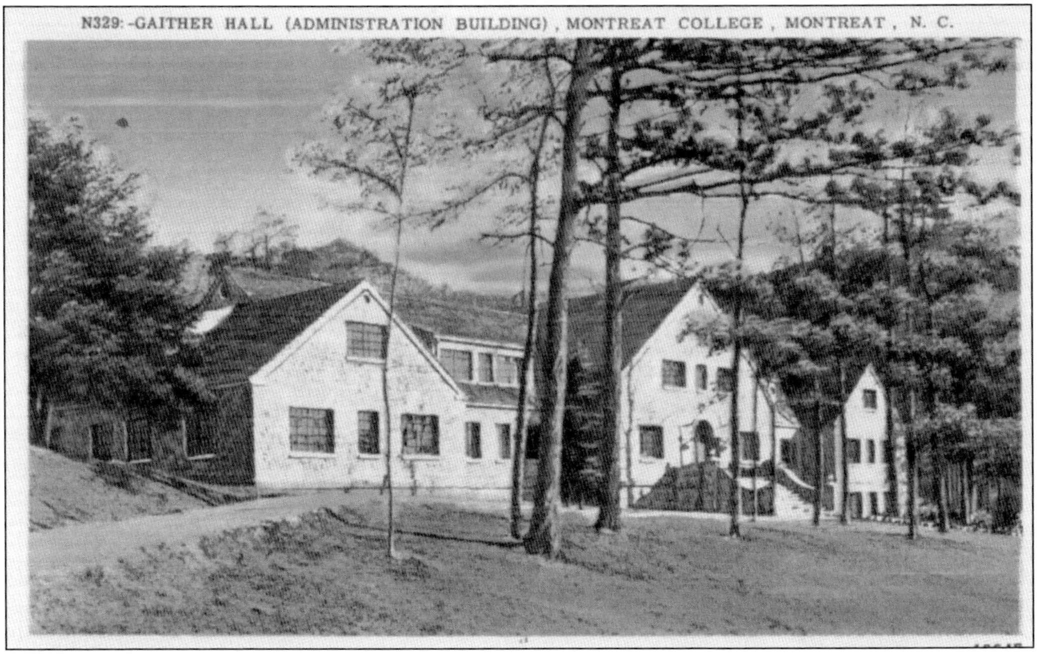

MONTREAT COLLEGE. Named in memory of Sadie K. Gaither, Gaither Hall is in the center of the campus of Montreat College and serves as its administrative building. (Courtesy Don Talley.)

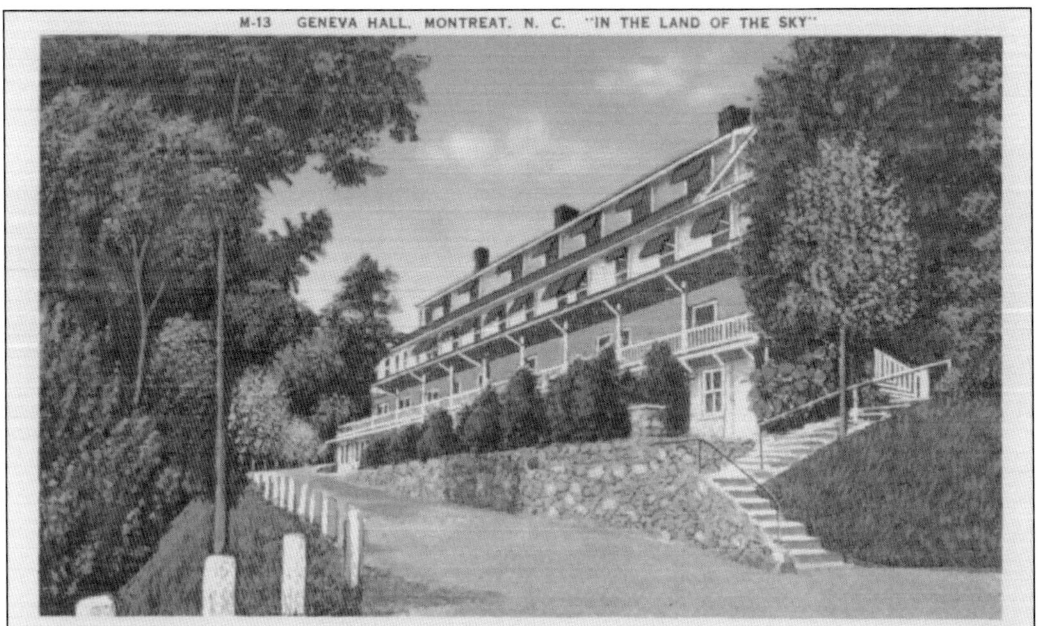

GENEVA HALL. No longer standing, this was once a residential facility at Montreat College. (Courtesy Don Talley.)

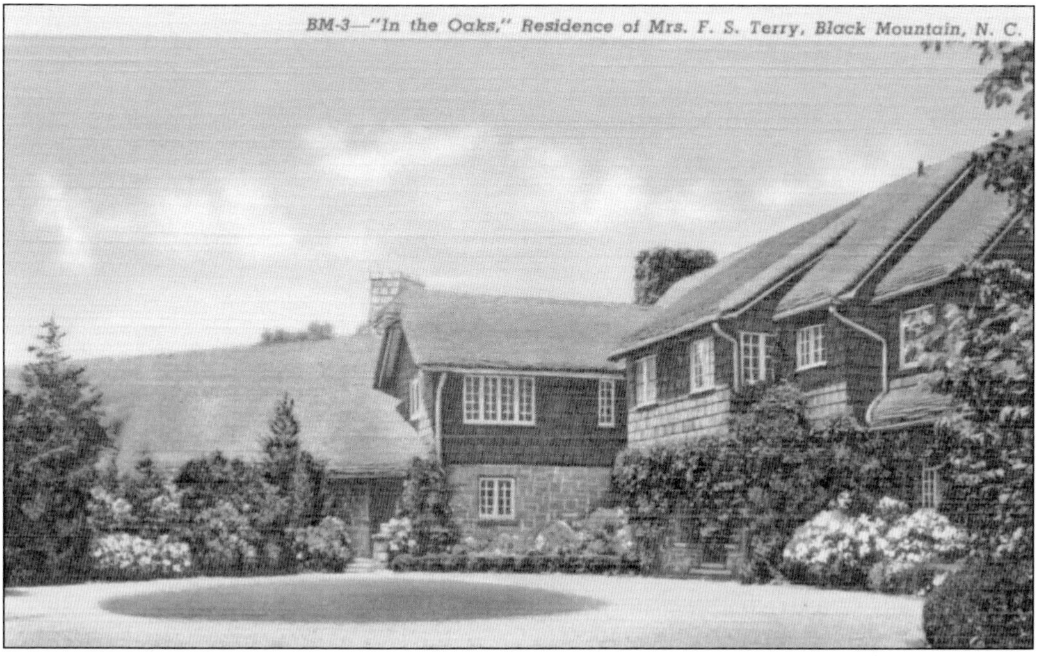

SECOND MONTREAT CAMPUS. In 2002, Montreat College purchased the old Terry Estate, In The Oaks, and is using the buildings and grounds as its Black Mountain campus. (Courtesy Don Talley.)

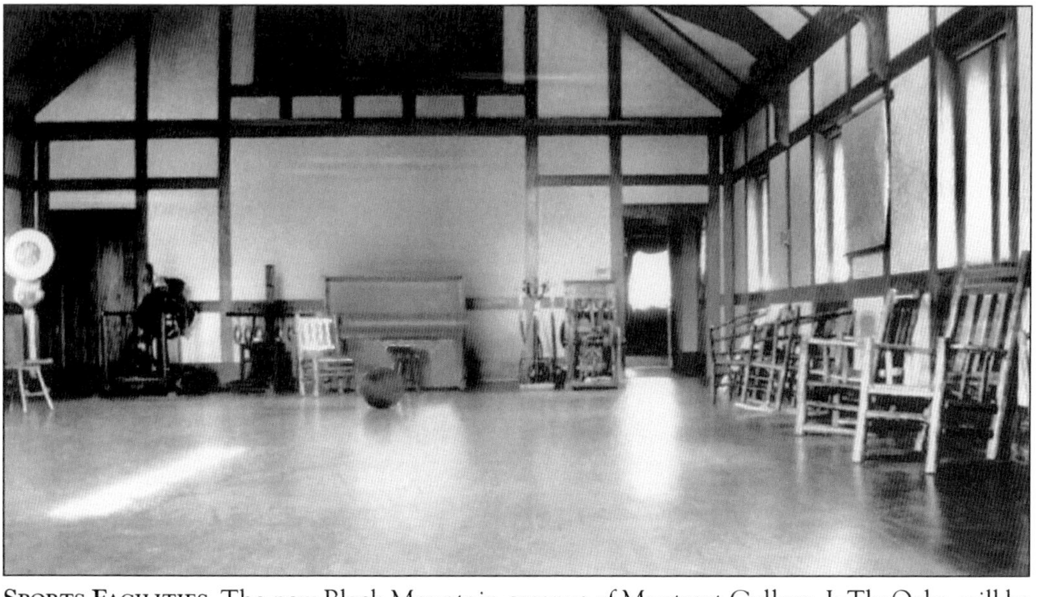

SPORTS FACILITIES. The new Black Mountain campus of Montreat College, InTheOaks, will be partially used for sports. A 1924 addition to the original Terry Estate added this ballroom, later used as a gymnasium with a swimming pool on the floor beneath. (Courtesy Montreat College.)

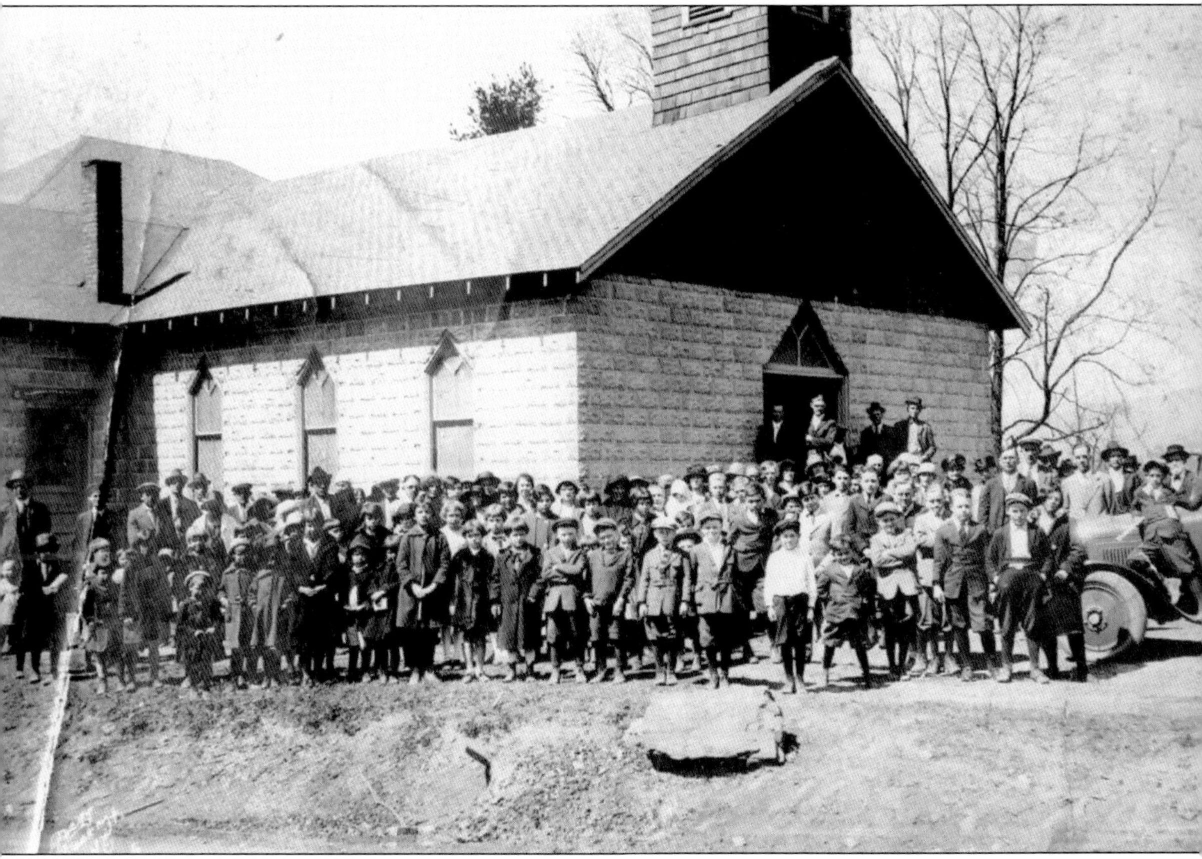

SWANNANOA FIRST BAPTIST CHURCH. The congregation is pictured in 1922. (Swannanoa Valley Museum.)

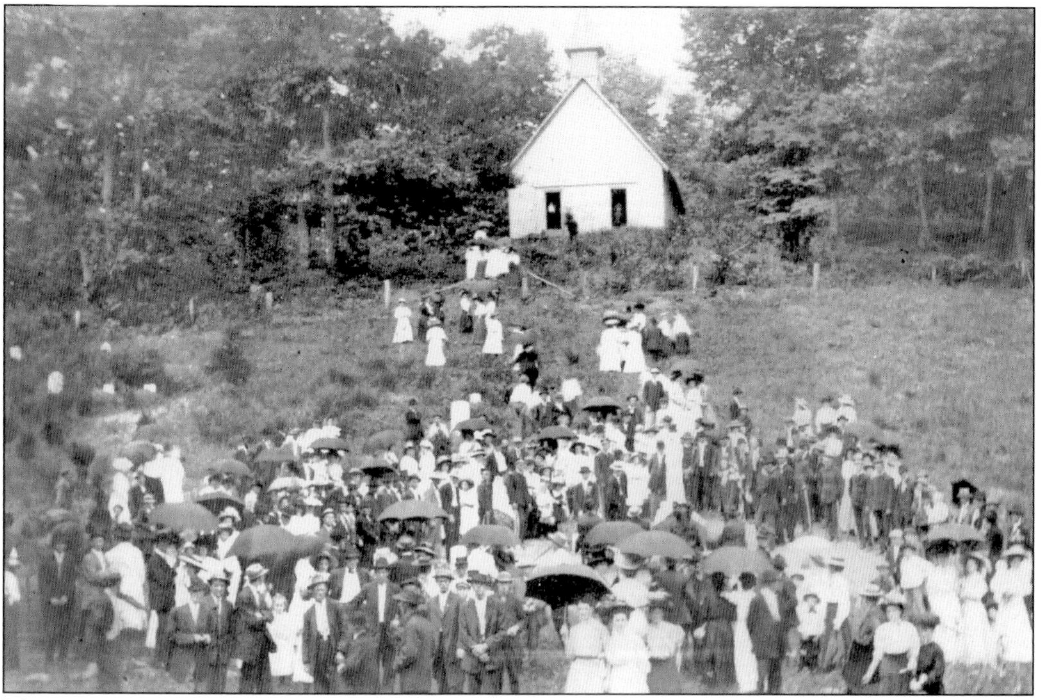

MOUNTAIN VIEW BAPTIST CHURCH. A rainy Sunday scene is captured at this historic North Fork church. This site is now under water, in the Asheville Watershed's North Fork Reservoir. A new church was built in 1951, high on a nearby hillside overlooking the lake. (Swannanoa Valley Museum.)

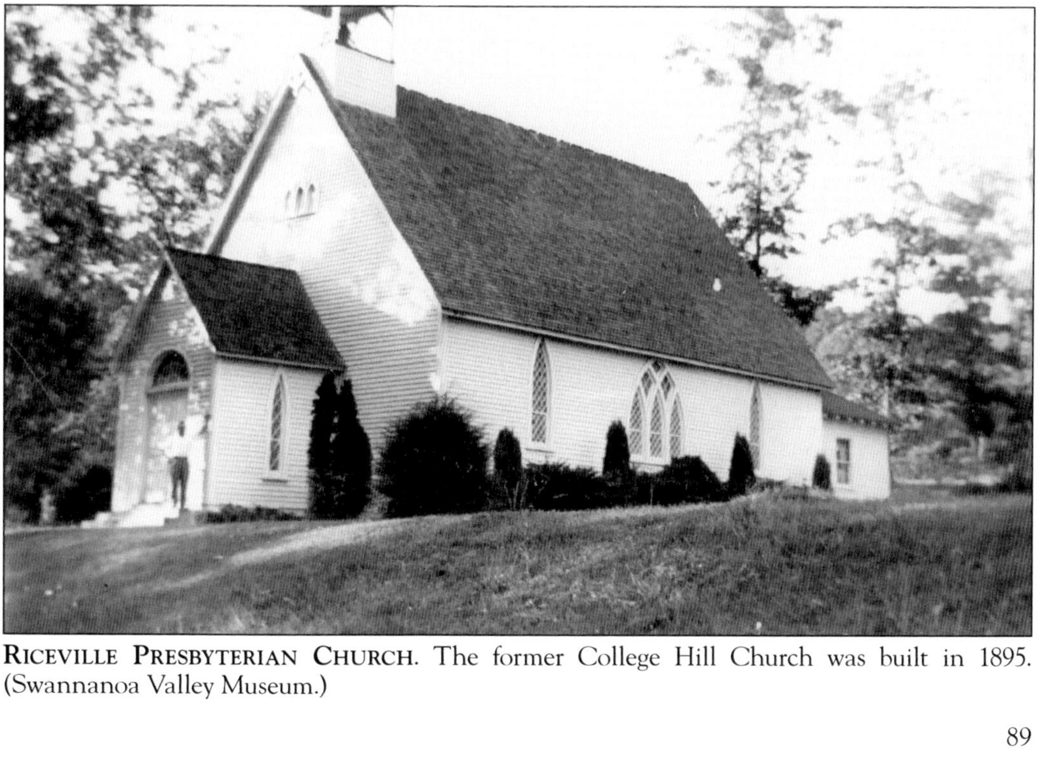

RICEVILLE PRESBYTERIAN CHURCH. The former College Hill Church was built in 1895. (Swannanoa Valley Museum.)

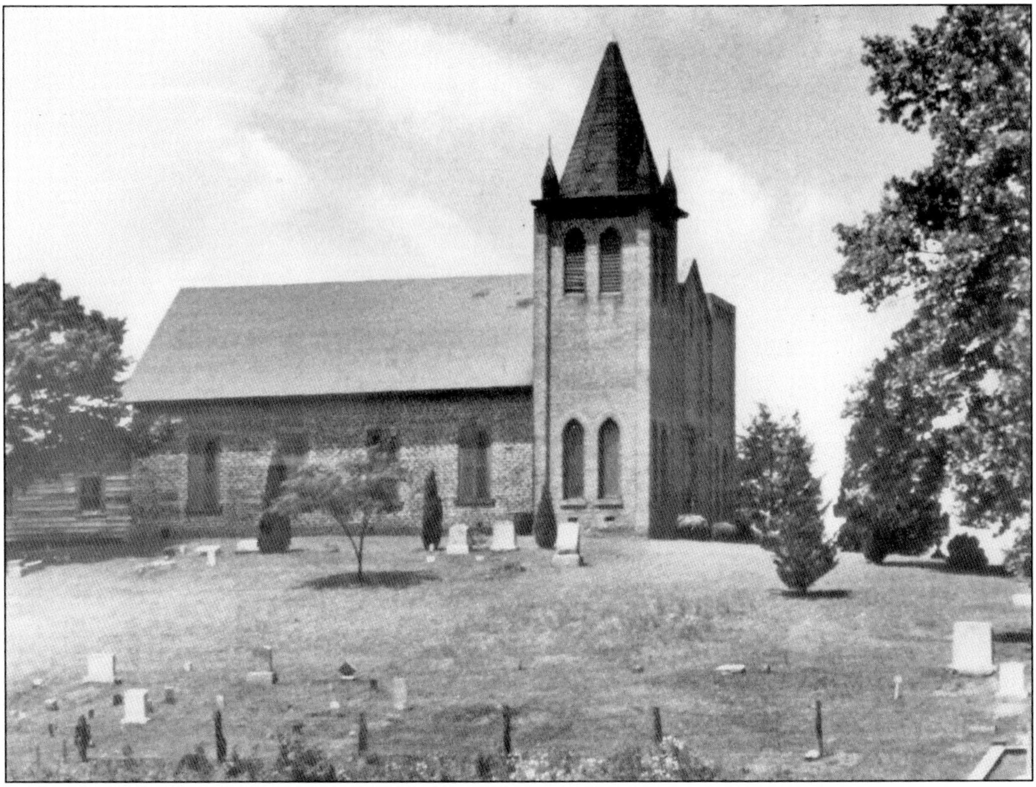

PINEY GROVE PRESBYTERIAN. Constructed in 1880 by church members using hand-made bricks, this was one of the valley's historic churches. It was used continually for 82 years before being replaced on the original site. Many of the area's early settlers, as well as their descendants, are buried in this churchyard. The church is now the First Presbyterian Church of Swannanoa. (Swannanoa Valley Museum.)

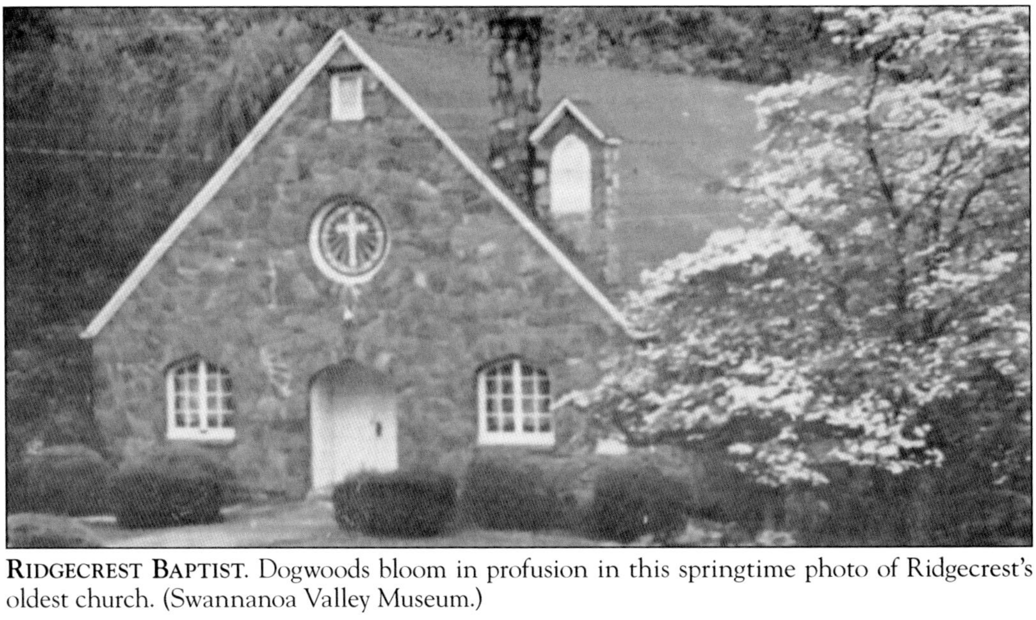

RIDGECREST BAPTIST. Dogwoods bloom in profusion in this springtime photo of Ridgecrest's oldest church. (Swannanoa Valley Museum.)

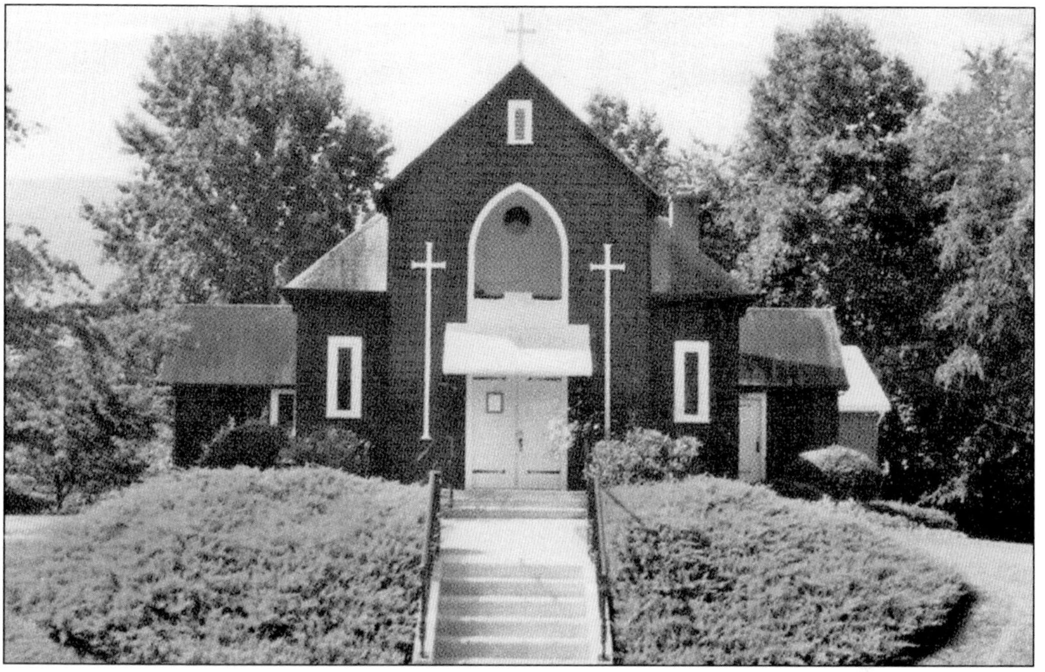

ST. MARY MARGARET CATHOLIC CHURCH. Built on land purchased from the E.W. Grove estate in 1936, the church was dedicated in October 1936. The diocese encompasses four townships in East Buncombe County. (Swannanoa Valley Museum.)

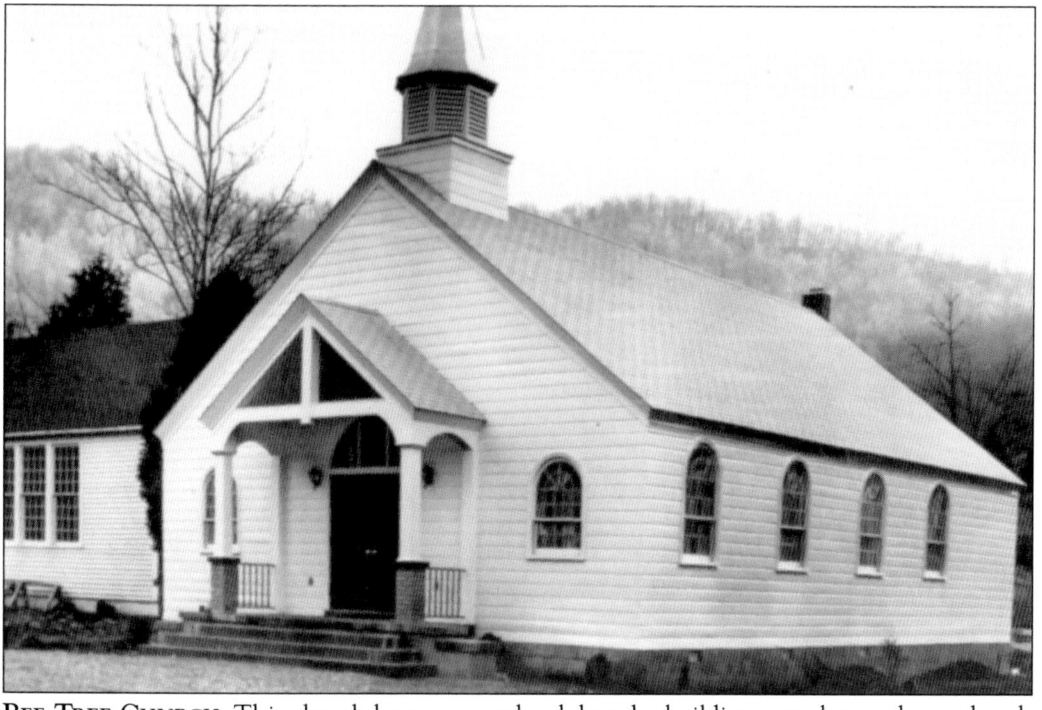

BEE TREE CHURCH. This church began as a school, but the building was also used as a church since its construction in 1903. When schools were consolidated in 1920, the building was purchased for the Bee Tree Christian Church.

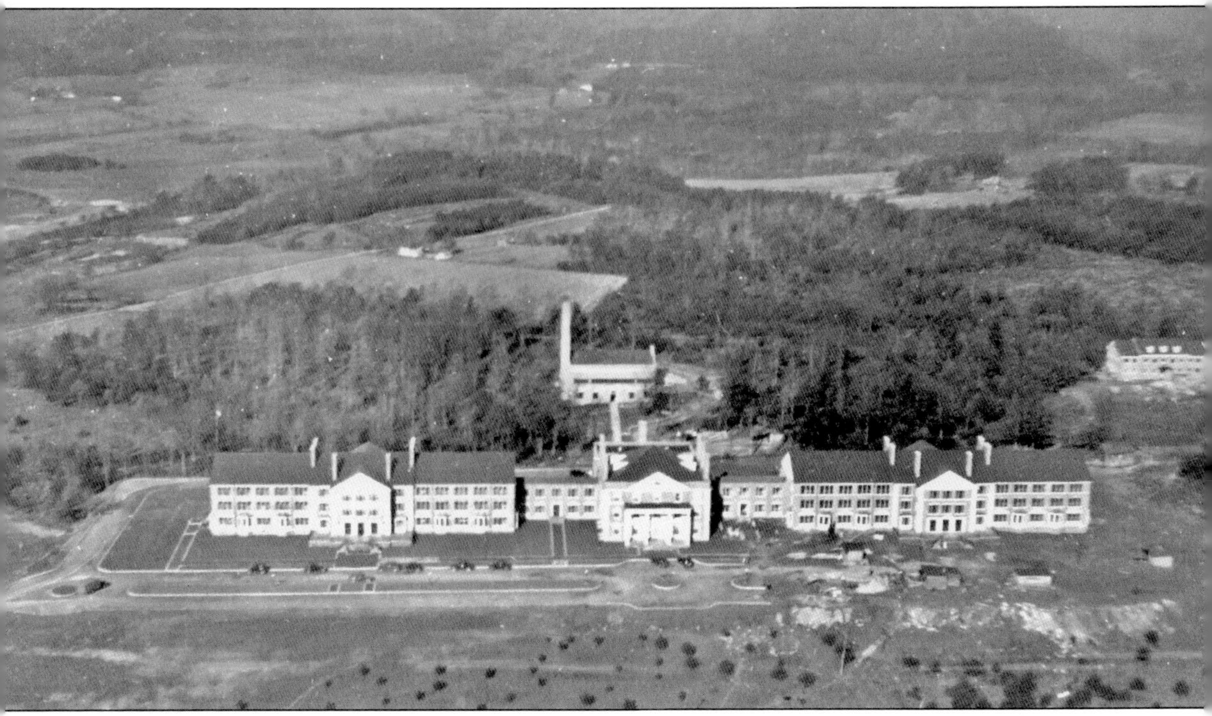

WNC SANATORIUM. In the first three decades of the 20th century, many people came to the Swannanoa Valley for their health. At first, small sanatoriums cared for those stricken with tuberculosis, but as the area's reputation for clean air and restorative health care became wider known, the state built a large sanatorium that provided a higher quality of care to patients. The WNC Sanatorium, as shown in this aerial view, was completed in 1937. (Swannanoa Valley Museum.)

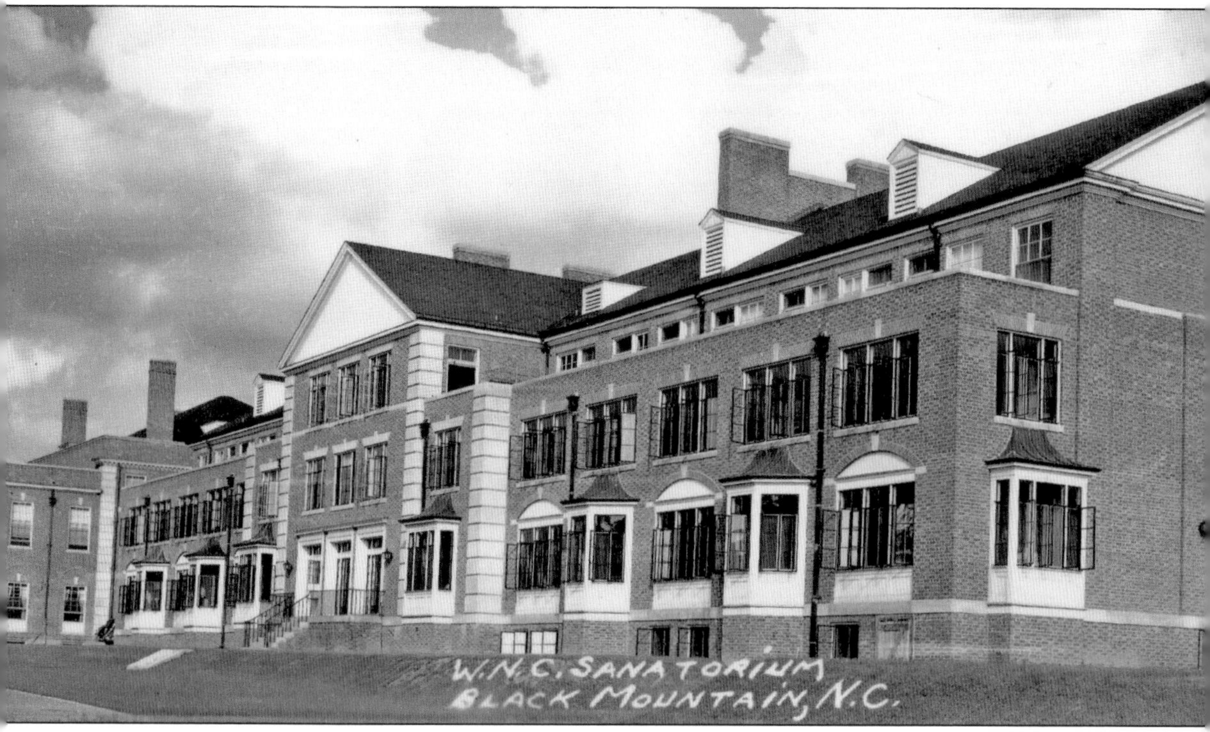

MODERN HEALTH CARE. The handsome facade of the WNC Sanatorium gave hope to hundreds of tuberculosis patients beginning in 1937 until the advent of penicillin brought a cure for that disease. In 1977, the sanatorium became Black Mountain Center but continued to provides health care for valley residents, serving victims of Alzheimer's Disease and people needing drug and alcohol treatment. (Swannanoa Valley Museum.)

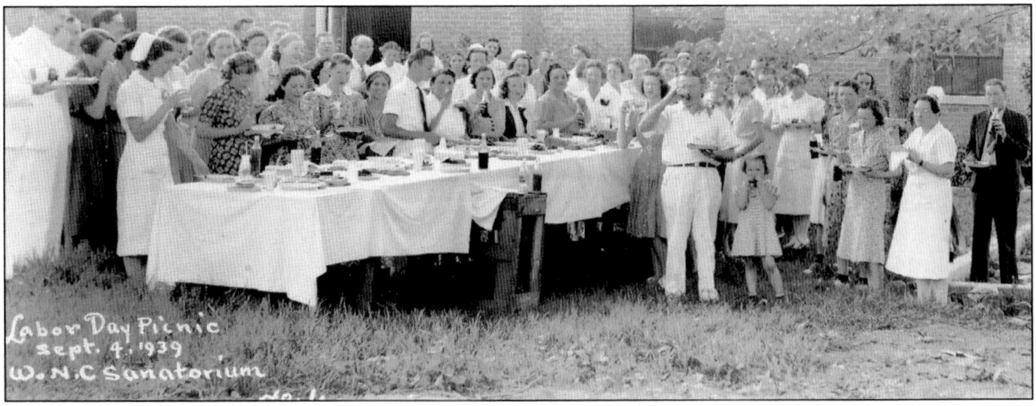

A FAMILY OF HEALERS. Health care workers and staff enjoy leisure time together at a picnic on the grounds of the WNC Sanatorium held on Labor Day in 1939. (Gragg photo, courtesy Mary McMurray.)

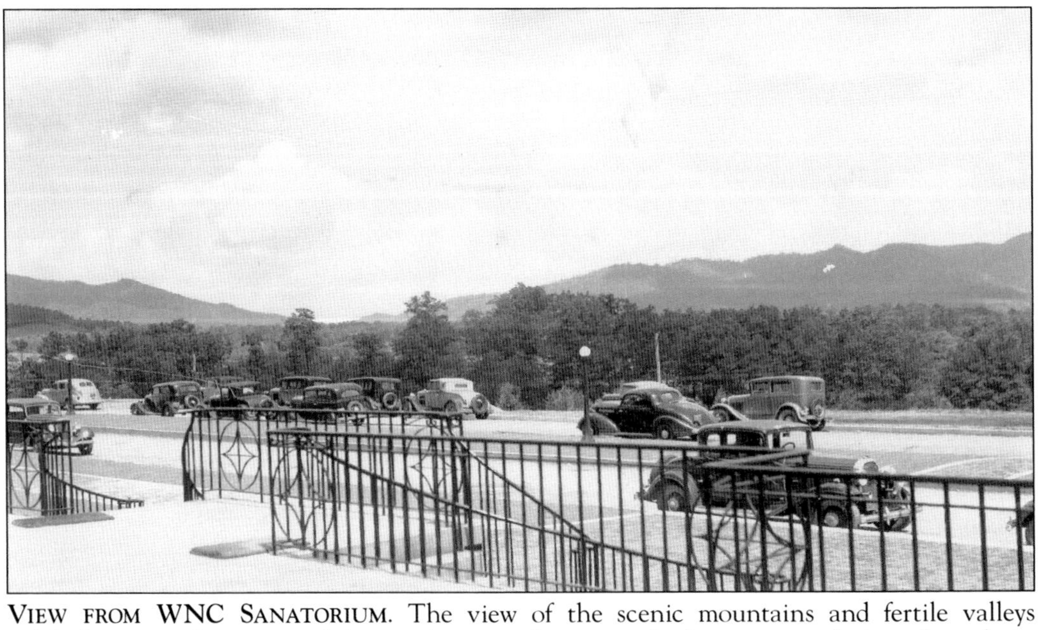

VIEW FROM WNC SANATORIUM. The view of the scenic mountains and fertile valleys uplifted patients' spirits while modern medicine worked to cure their tuberculosis. (Swannanoa Valley Museum.)

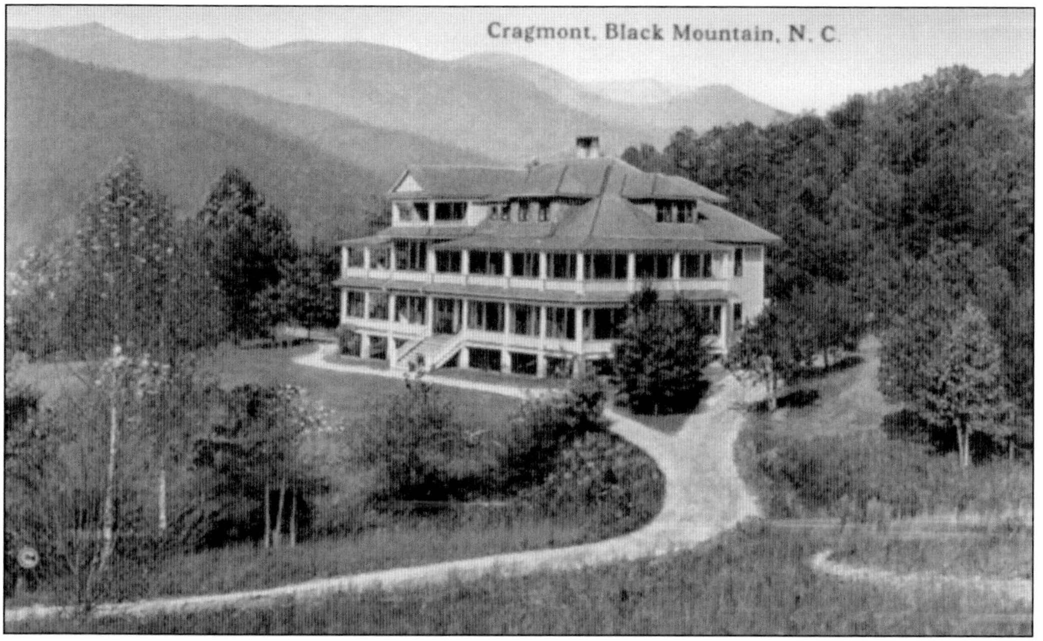

CRAGMONT SANATORIUM, C. 1911. One of several smaller sanatoriums in the Swannanoa Valley, the Cragmont Sanatorium was established by Dr. I.J. Archer and was first known as Harrison Mountain Air Sanatorium Company. (Swannanoa Valley Museum.)

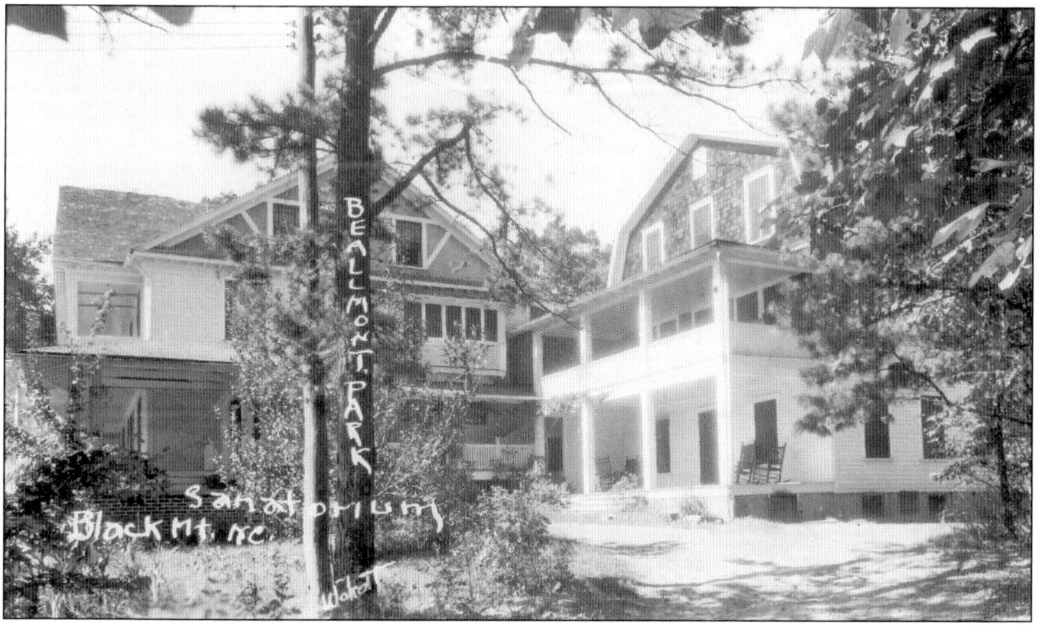

BEALLMONT PARK SANATORIUM. Located in Black Mountain, this small sanatorium treated tuberculosis, alcoholism, and mental conditions.

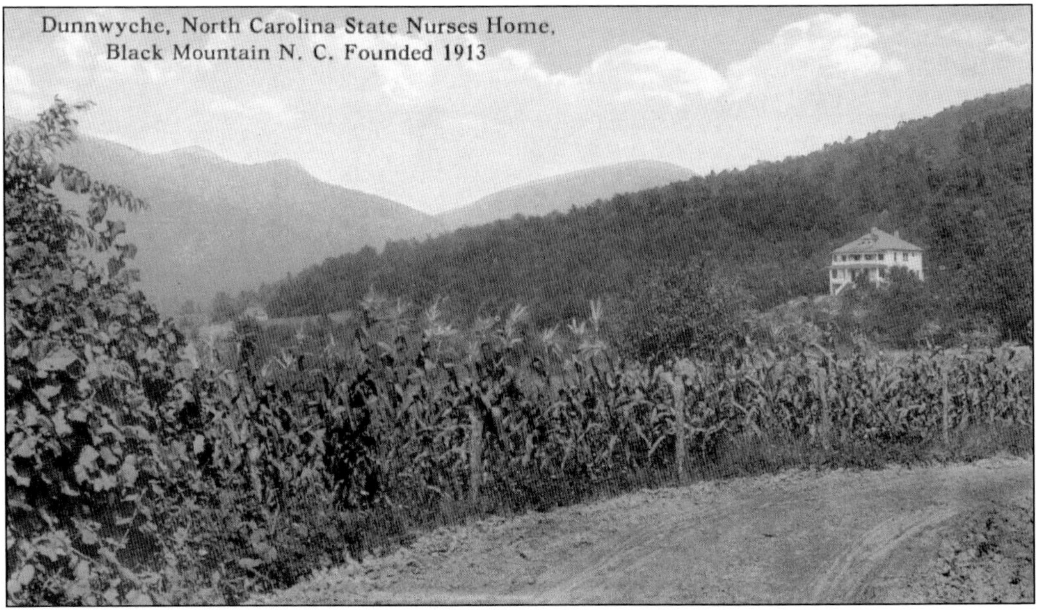

WHO HEALS THE HEALERS? This postcard depicts the North Carolina State Nurses Home, founded in 1913 to treat nurses who became ill during their service to others. (Swannanoa Valley Museum.)

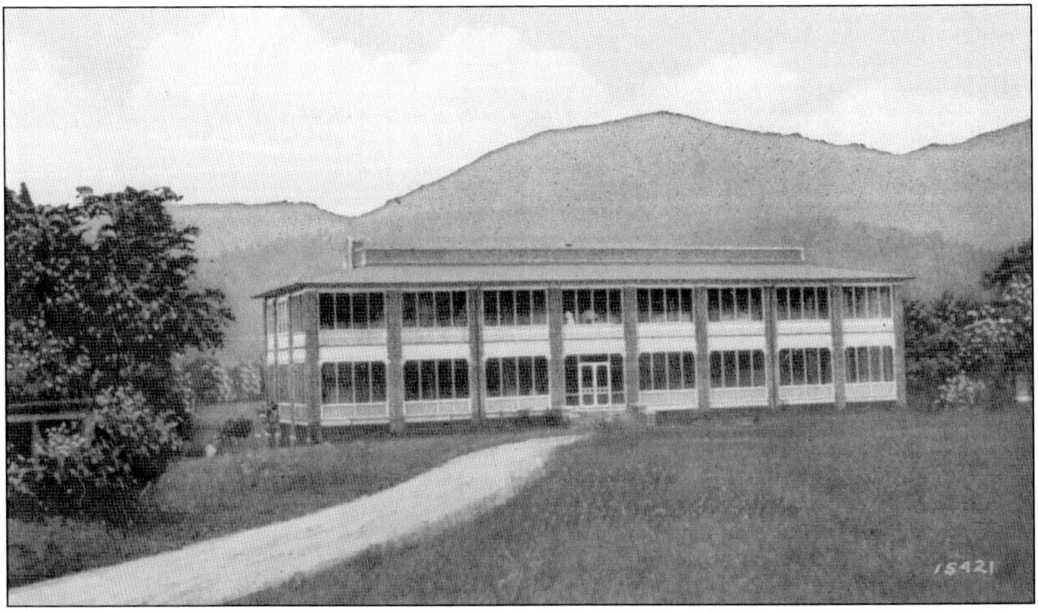

ROYAL LEAGUE SANATORIUM. Now the campus of Camp Dorothy Walls, this sanatorium was established by the Fellowship of the Royal League, a fraternal insurance society in Chicago, Illinois, *c.* 1904. (Swannanoa Valley Museum.)

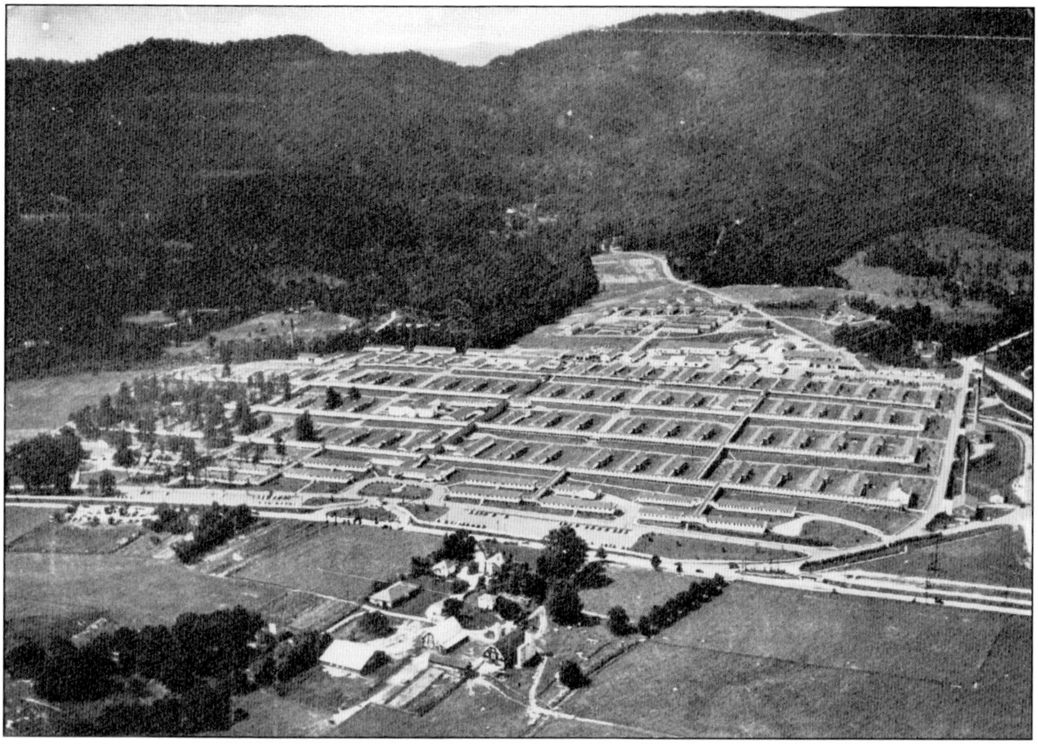

MOORE GENERAL HOSPITAL. Built by the Army Corps of Engineers in only four months in 1942 in Swannanoa, this 1,520-bed hospital operated during World War II. It was named in honor of Dr. Samuel P. Moore, Surgeon General of the Confederacy. After the war, the grounds were used as part of the North Carolina Prison System. (Swannanoa Valley Museum.)

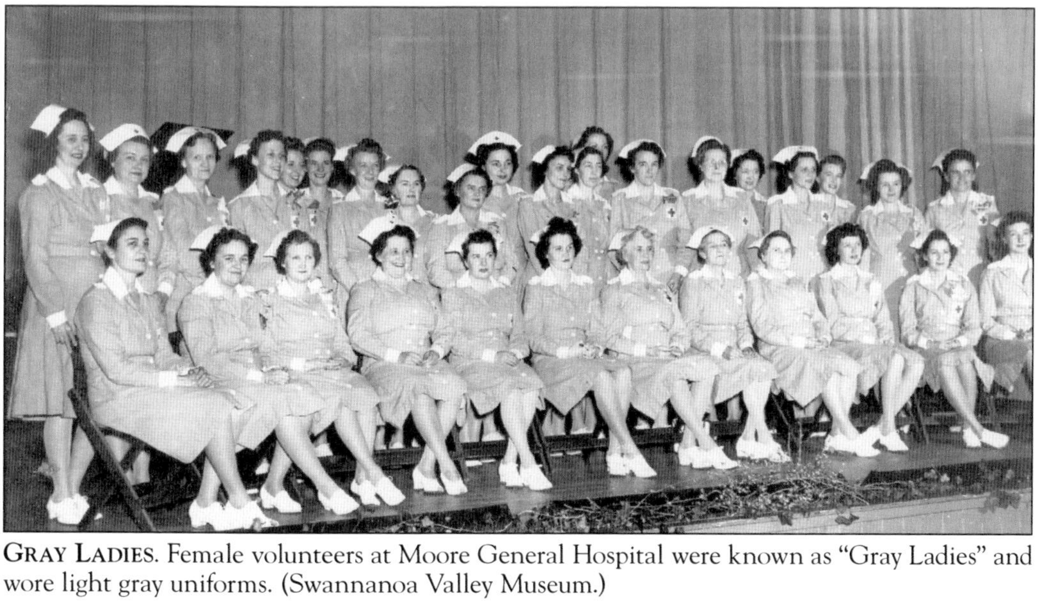

GRAY LADIES. Female volunteers at Moore General Hospital were known as "Gray Ladies" and wore light gray uniforms. (Swannanoa Valley Museum.)

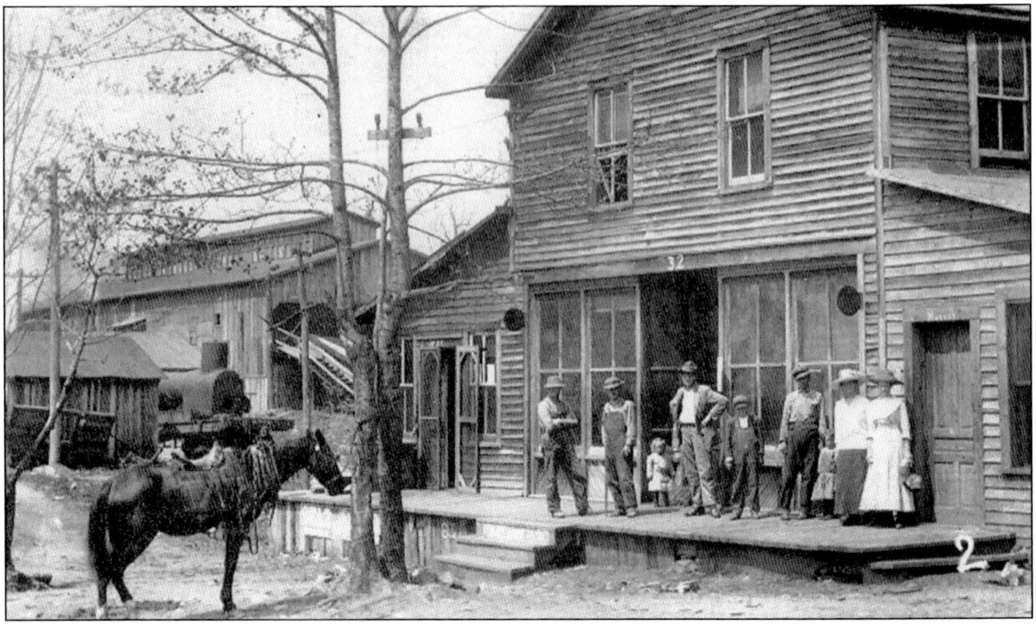

BEE TREE COMMISSARY. During the first two decades of the 20th century, when logging was a major industry in the Bee Tree area, this commissary sold food and other goods needed by the loggers and their families. (Swannanoa Valley Museum.)

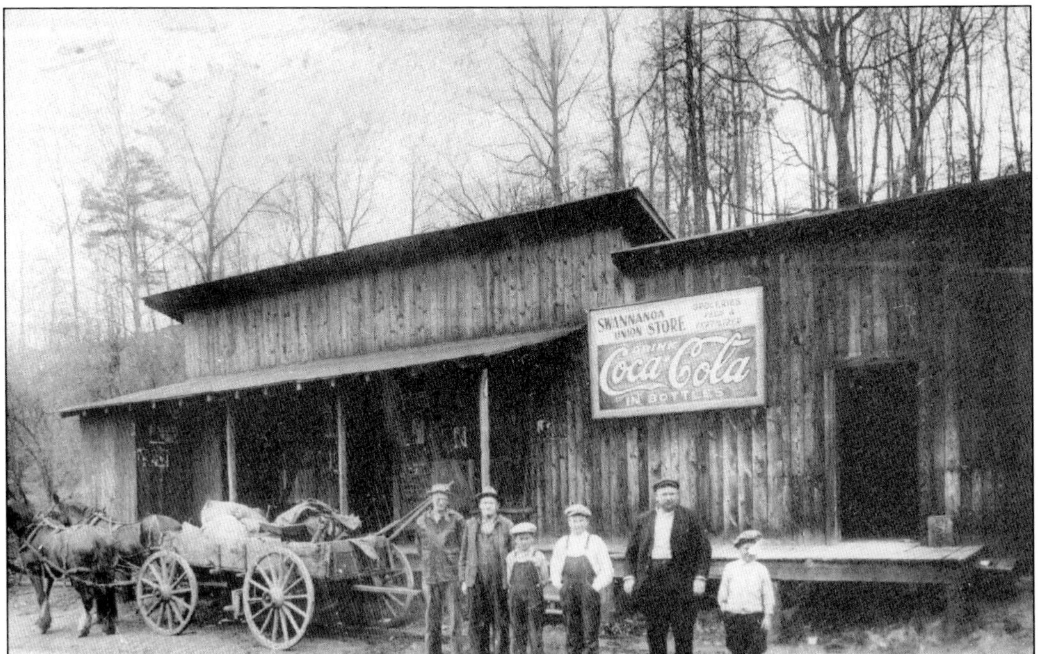

SWANNANOA UNION STORE. Coca-Cola's earliest outdoor advertising was provided to country stores such as the Union Store in Swannanoa. (Swannanoa Valley Museum.)

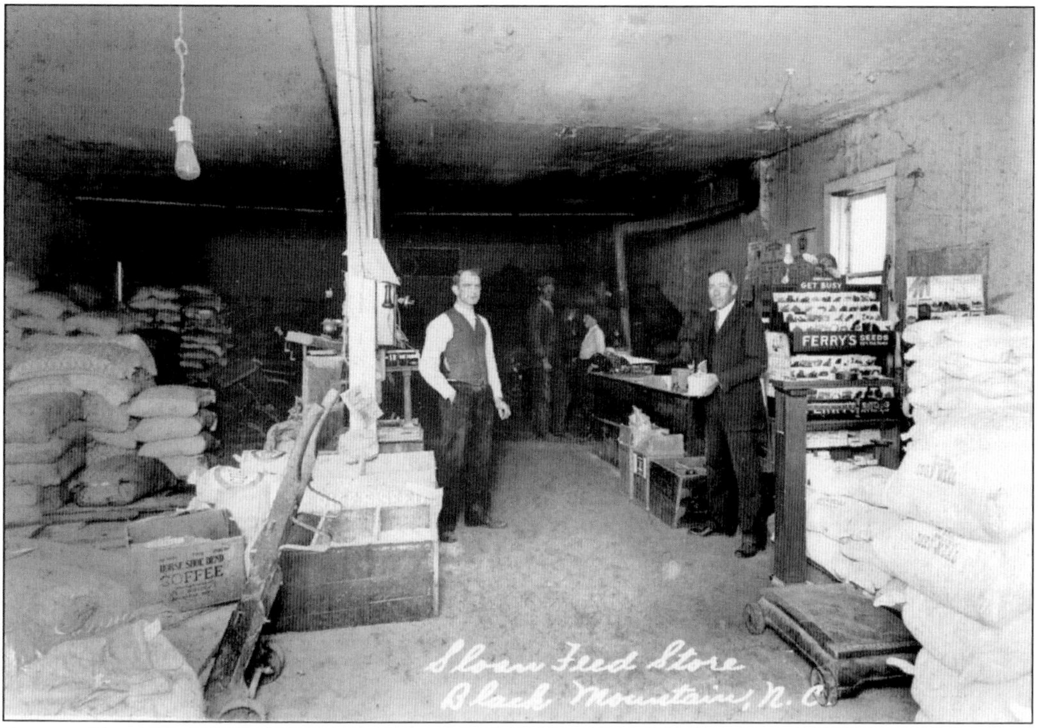

SLOAN FEED STORE. This is an interior view of one of Black Mountain's early feed stores. (Swannanoa Valley Museum.)

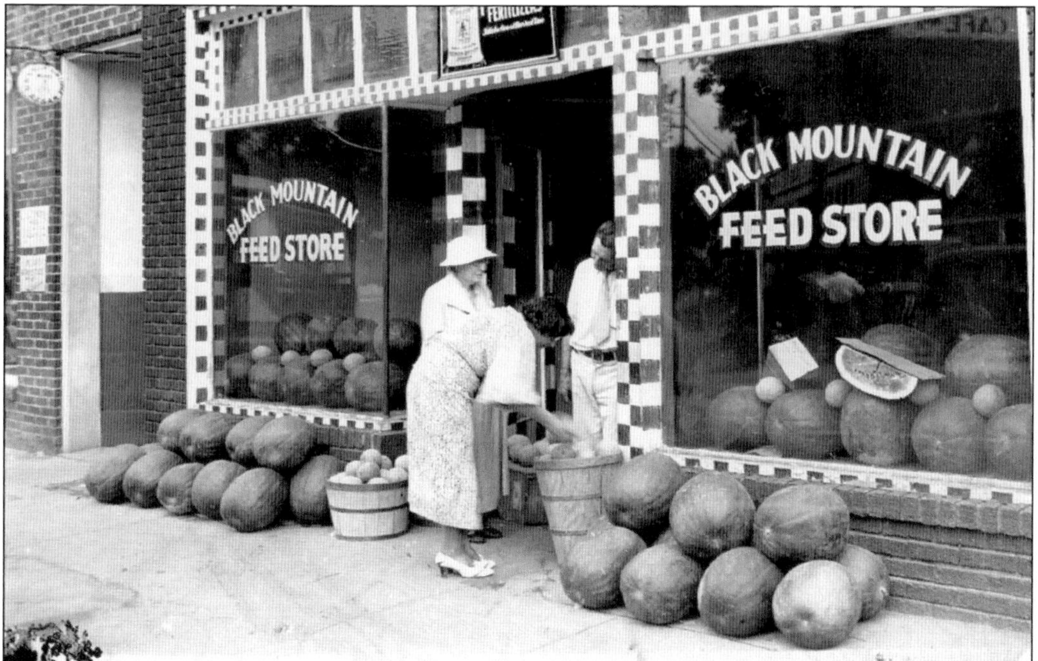

BLACK MOUNTAIN FEED STORE. A late summer harvest of huge watermelons are for sale at another Black Mountain retail store. (Swannanoa Valley Museum.)

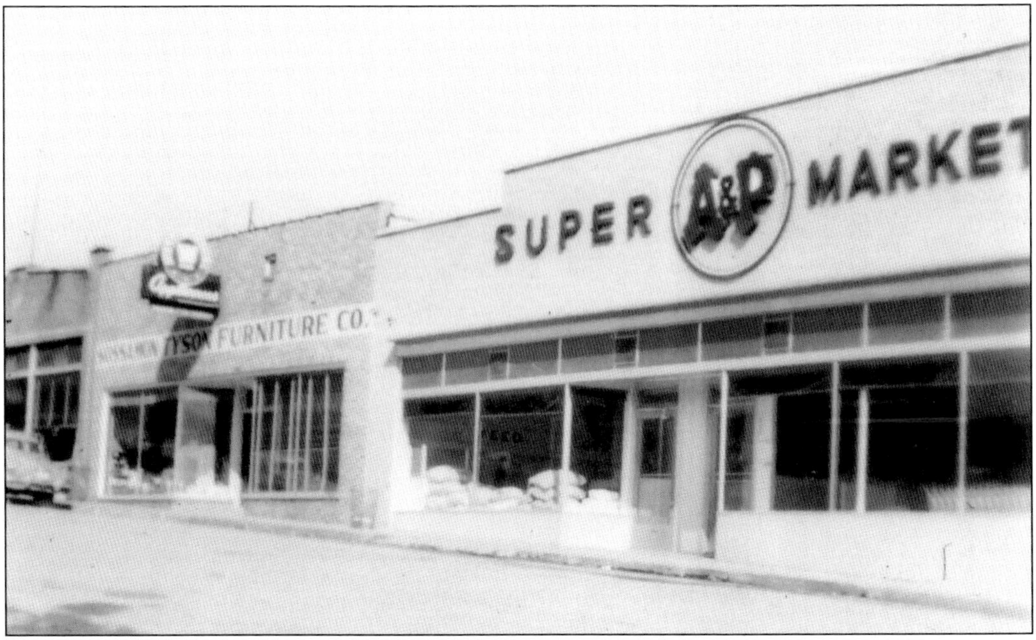

STORES ON BROADWAY. By the mid-1950s, retail shopping was available at the A&P and Tyson's Furniture stores on Broadway. Tyson's remains in this location, having absorbed the grocery store's space. (Courtesy Mary Elizabeth Tyson.)

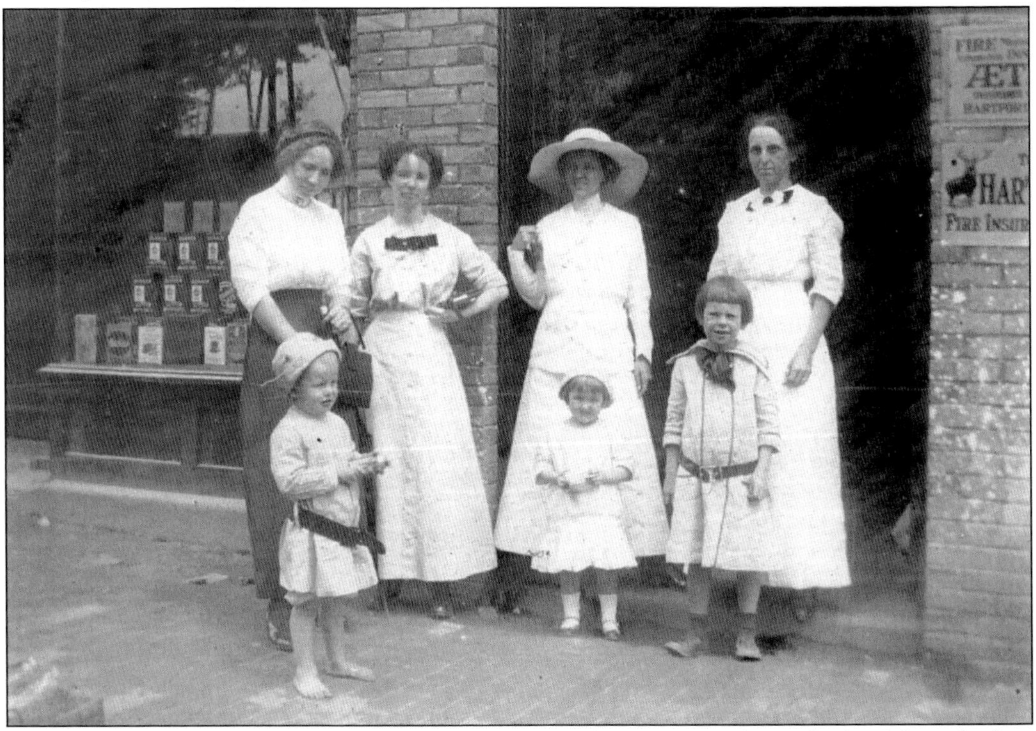

EARLY SHOPPERS. Women and children on a summer shopping trip (note the boy's bare feet) in Black Mountain c. 1910. After most of the town's commercial district burned in 1912, new stores were built on Cherry and State Streets. (Swannanoa Valley Museum.)

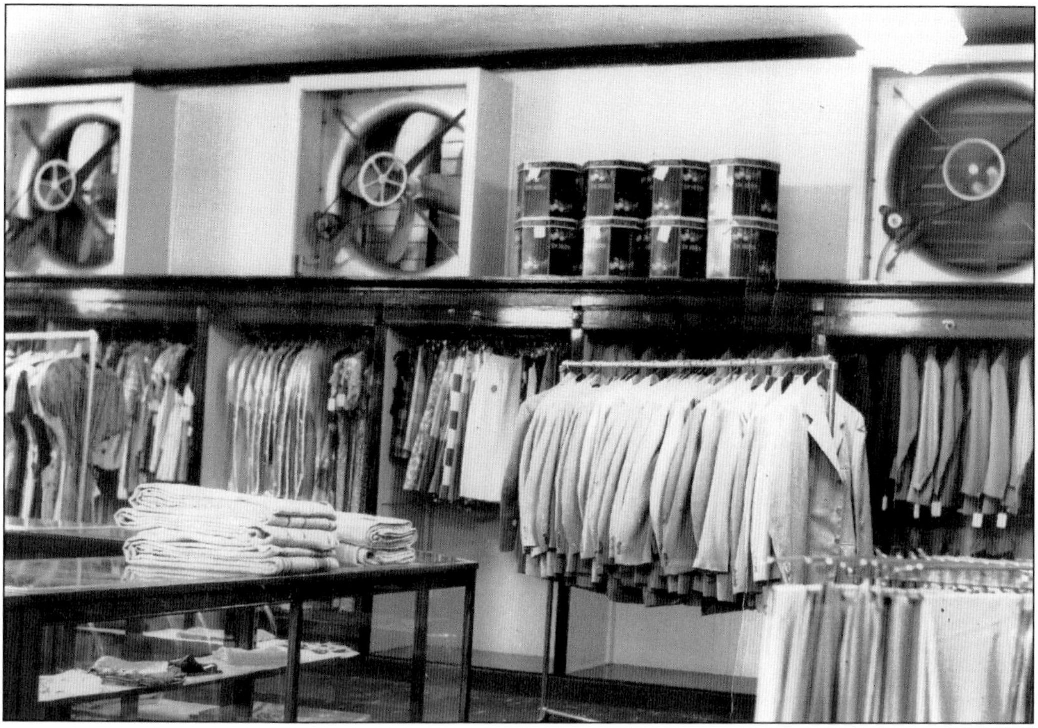

HARRISON'S STORE. This well-stocked Swannanoa clothing store was cooled by large exhaust fans. (Noah Collection, courtesy David Rozzell.)

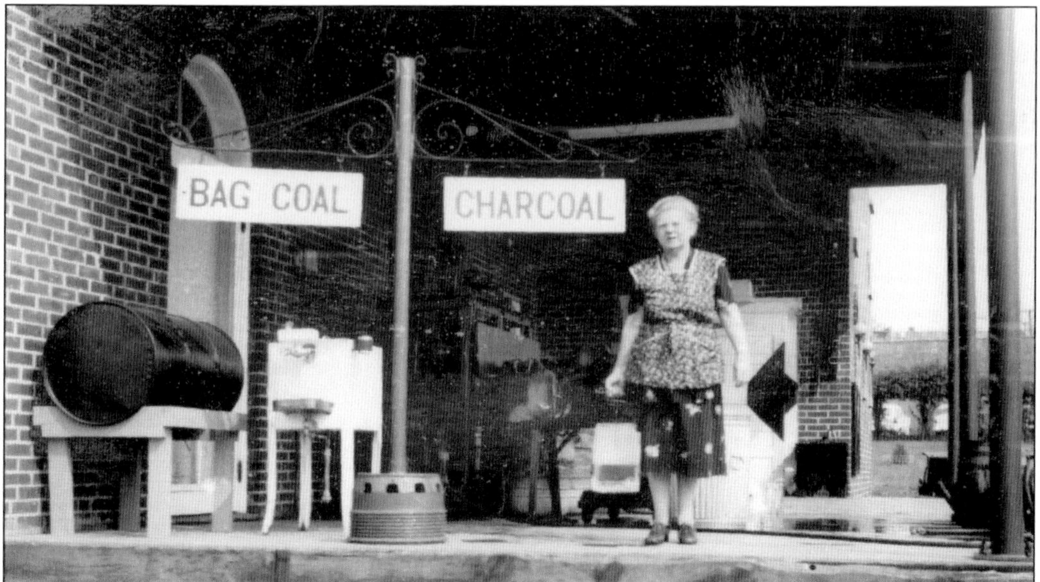

ICE & COAL COMPANY. Mr. and Mrs. Cyril Huffman owned the Black Mountain Ice Company in the 1930s. After the death of her husband, Mrs. Huffman remarried but continued to run the company and added another needed commodity, coal, to her inventory. Shown in this photo is Jennie Huffman Seagle on the front porch of the Ice & Coal Company on Broadway in 1955. The business closed in 1959. (Swannanoa Valley Museum.)

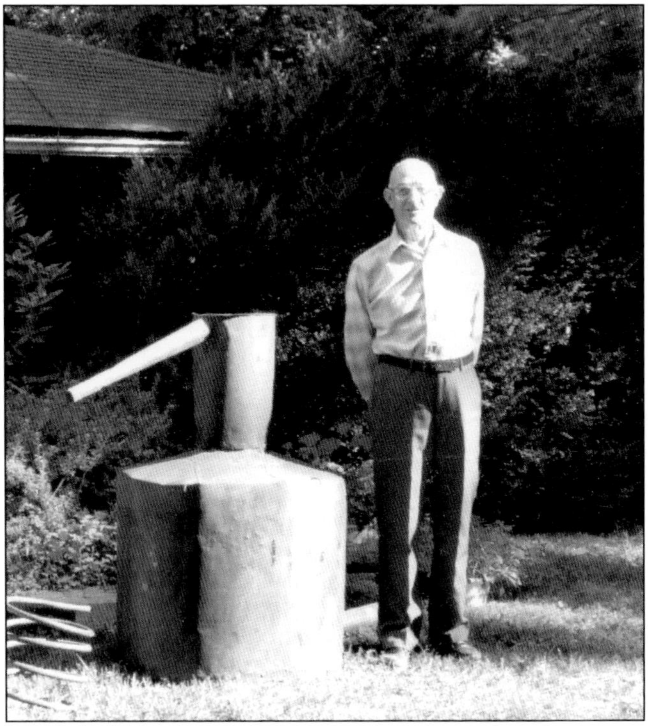

INDIVIDUAL ENTERPRISE. Judge William Styles stands beside a moonshine still given to his father, an Asheville attorney, in payment for having represented two moonshiners in the 1930s. During prohibition and into the present, the making of moonshine whiskey has provided enterprising if illegal entrepreneurs with needed cash. (Courtesy Harriet Styles.)

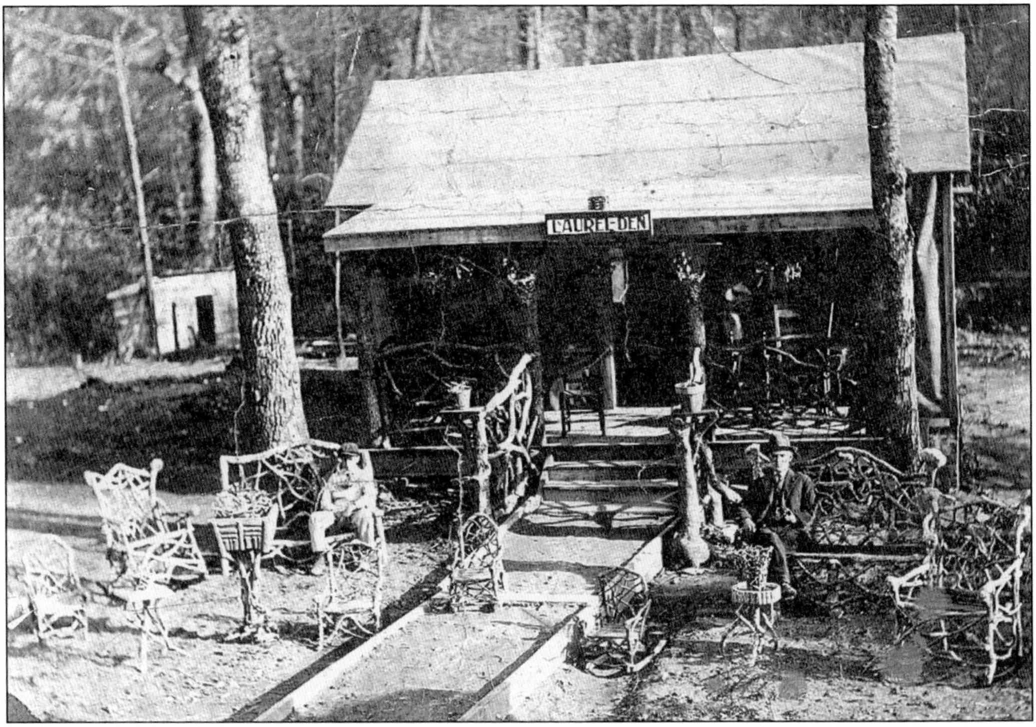

TWIG FURNITURE. In a less risky but still lucrative individually-owned manufacturing business, John Hentschel made and sold furniture he fashioned from native laurel and rhododendron plants. (Swannanoa Valley Museum.)

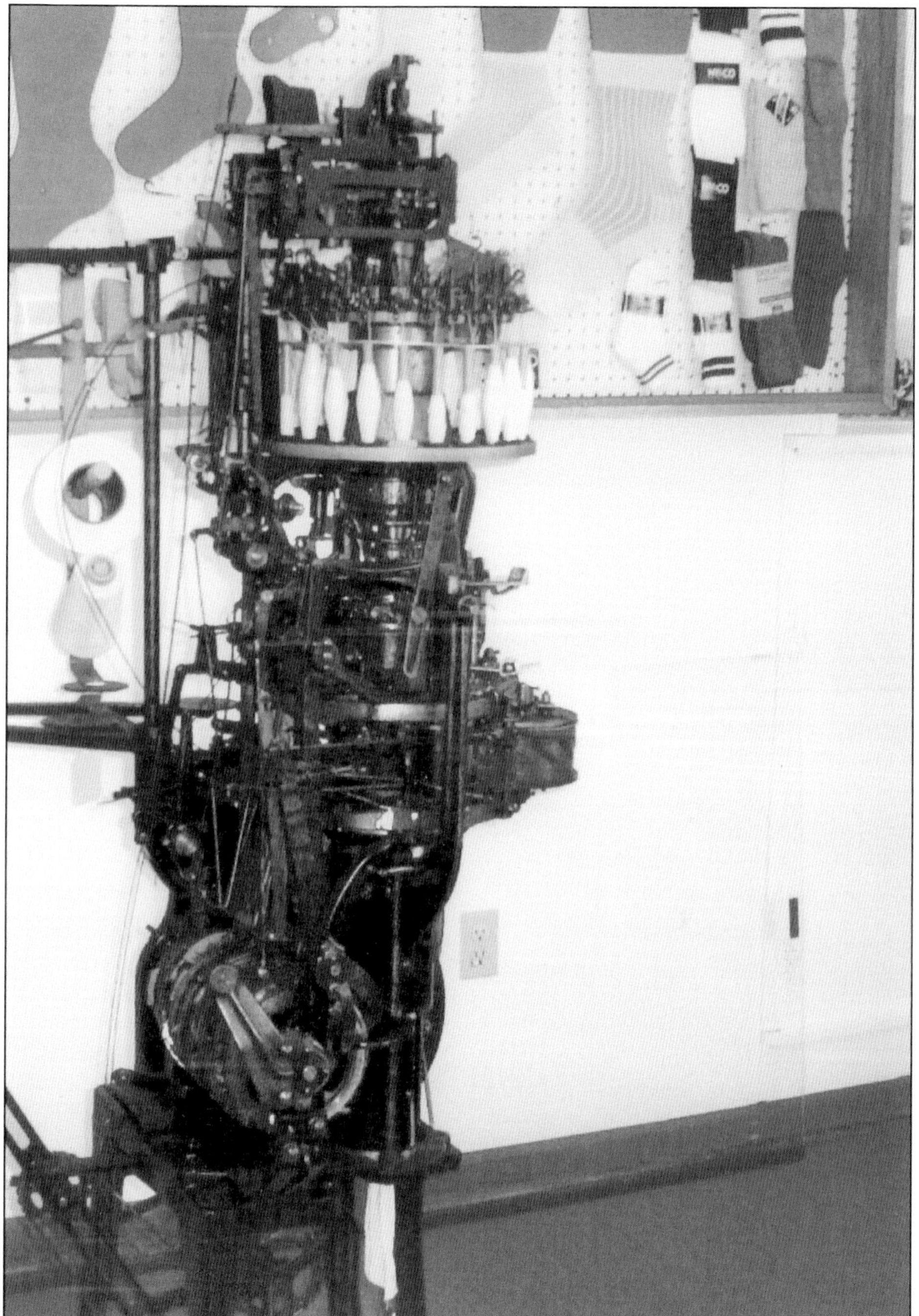

SOCK MACHINE. Among the many textile products manufactured in the Swannanoa Valley in the 20th century were socks. This intricate machine belonged to the Clevenger Sox Company and was donated to the Swannanoa Valley Museum after the company closed. The machine was threaded at the top with various yarns that wound their way through a maze of stitchers and emerged at the bottom as a tube. Stitched across one end, the tube became a sock. (Swannanoa Valley Museum.)

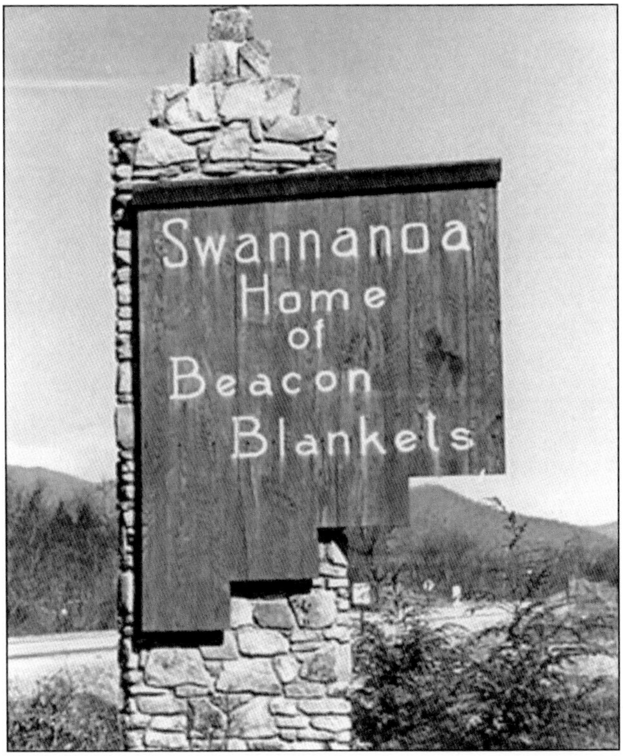

BEACON MANUFACTURING. In 1923, Charles D. Owen passed through the Swannanoa Valley and fell under its charm. He returned to his home in New Bedford, Massachusetts, and decided to move his blanket manufacturing company to Swannanoa. The North Carolina plant opened in 1925, bringing new jobs and prosperity to the valley. (Swannanoa Valley Museum.)

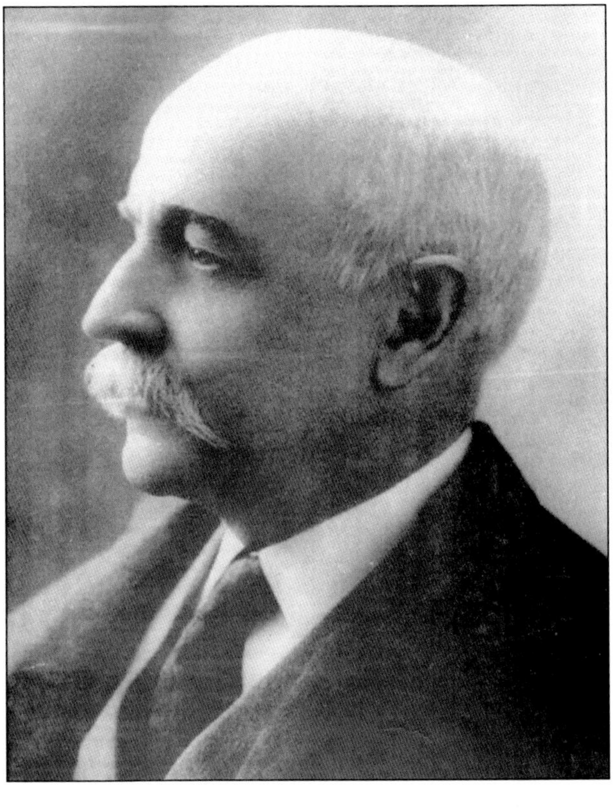

CHARLES D. OWEN. Owen was the founder of Beacon Manufacturing Company in Swannanoa. (Swannanoa Valley Museum.)

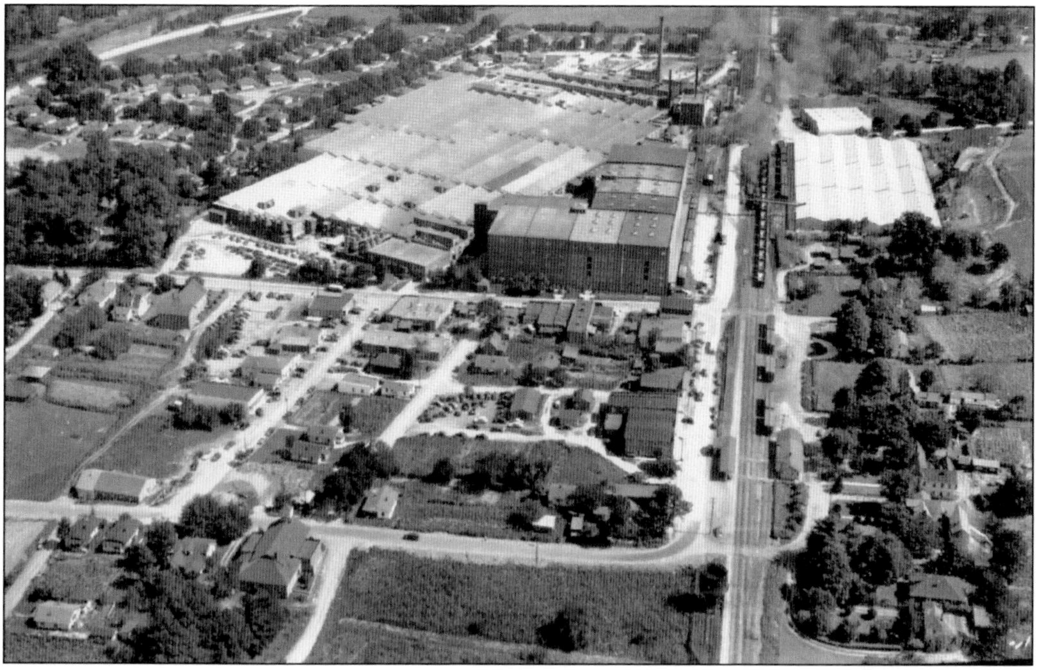

AERIAL VIEW OF BEACON. In this photo, the extent of the Beacon plant can be seen, as can the houses in adjacent Beacon Village (upper left and at far right). Swannanoa was clearly a thriving community at this time. The Beacon plant evolved over the years, changing ownership several times before finally going out of business in 2000. The plant was destroyed by fire in September 2003. (Swannanoa Valley Museum.)

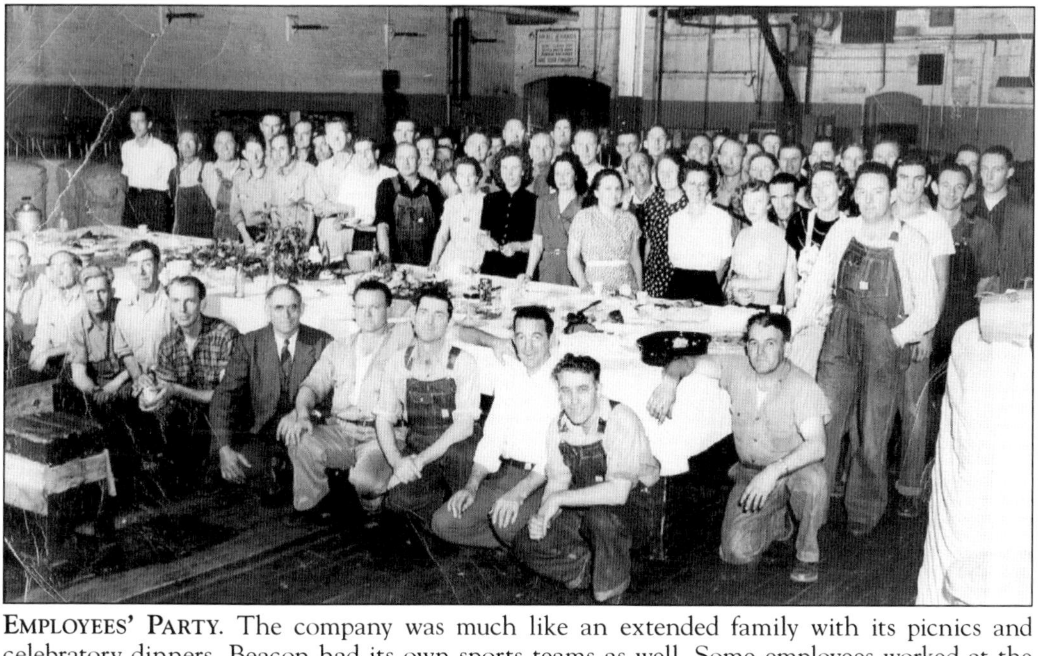

EMPLOYEES' PARTY. The company was much like an extended family with its picnics and celebratory dinners. Beacon had its own sports teams as well. Some employees worked at the plant their entire wage-earning lives, and it was not unusual to find several generations of a valley family employed there at the same time. An annual picnic still reunites the workers.

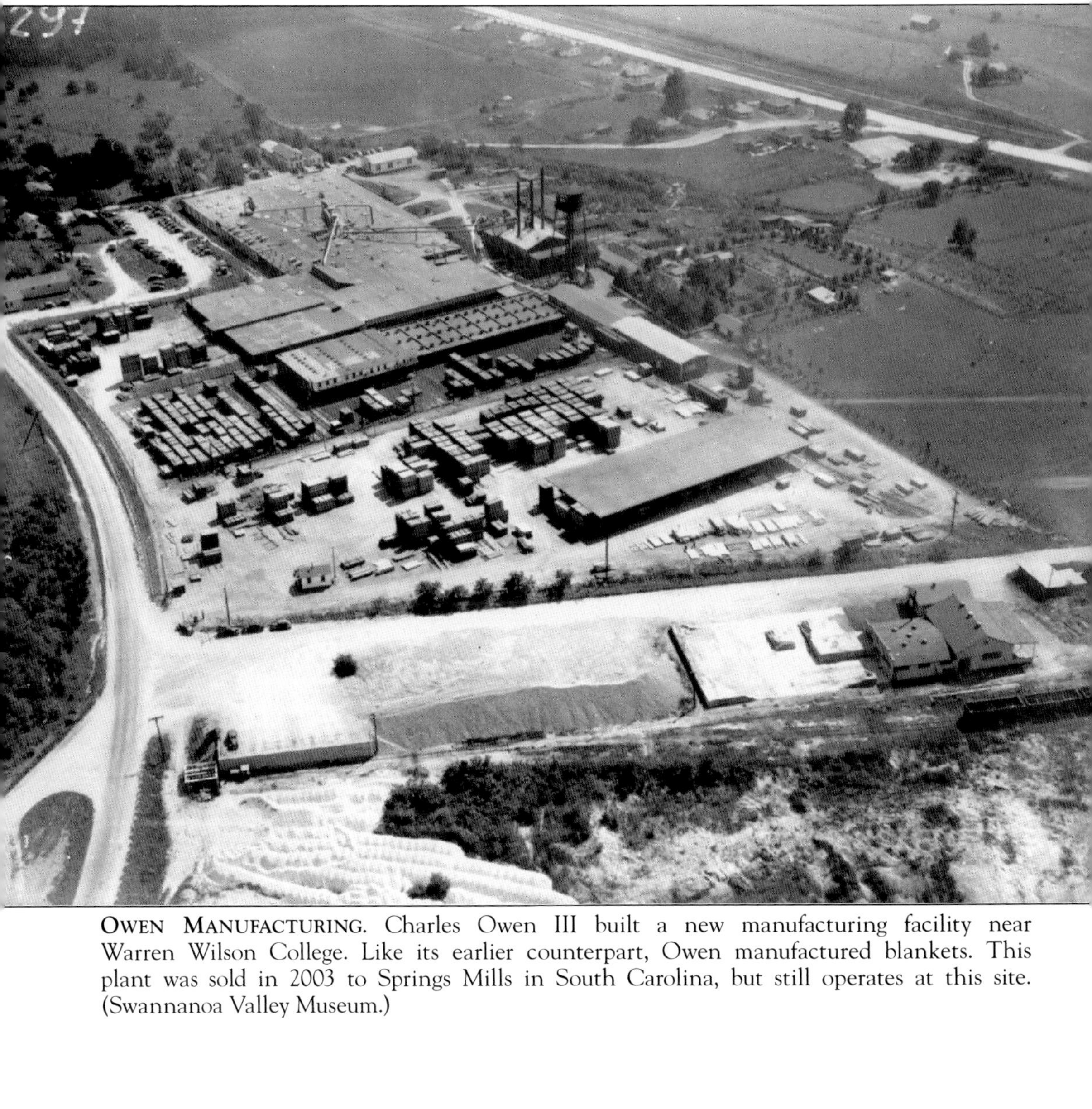

Owen Manufacturing. Charles Owen III built a new manufacturing facility near Warren Wilson College. Like its earlier counterpart, Owen manufactured blankets. This plant was sold in 2003 to Springs Mills in South Carolina, but still operates at this site. (Swannanoa Valley Museum.)

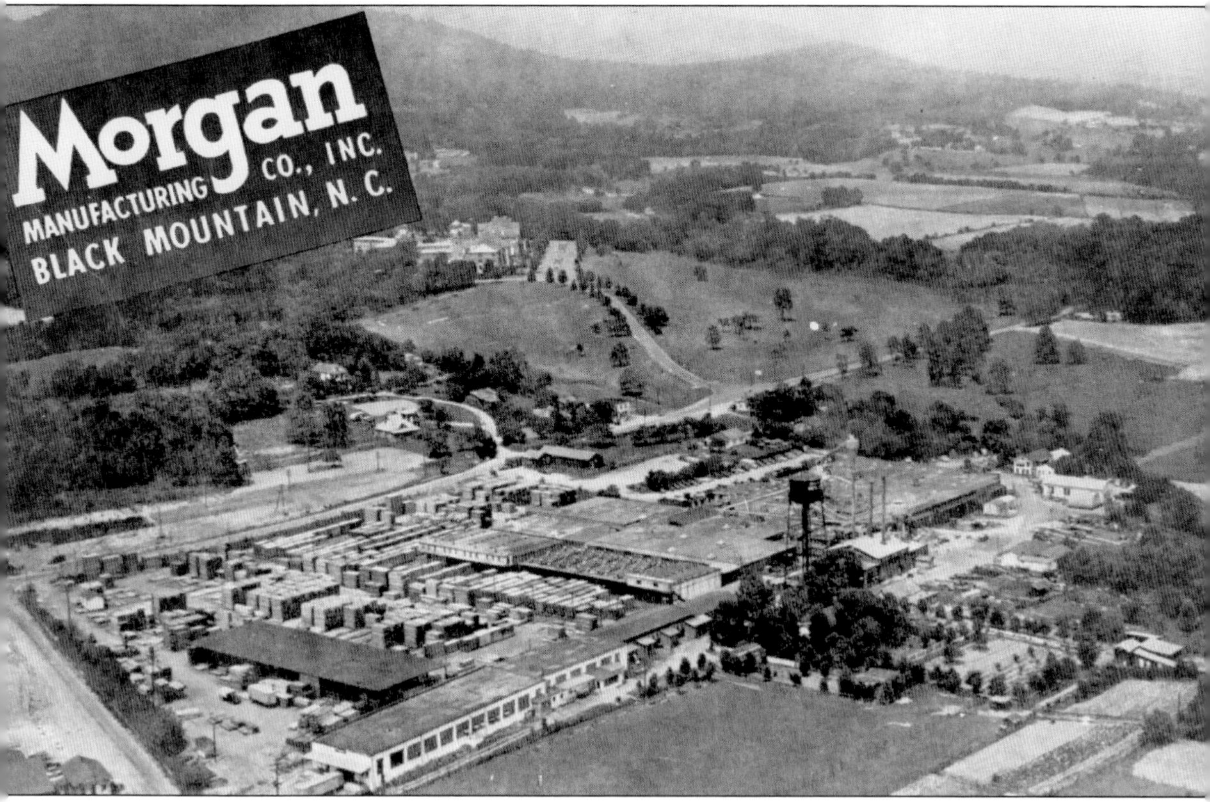

MORGAN MANUFACTURING. A Dimension plant that manufactured wooden furniture parts, Morgan later became part of Drexel Furniture Corporation. (Swannanoa Valley Museum.)

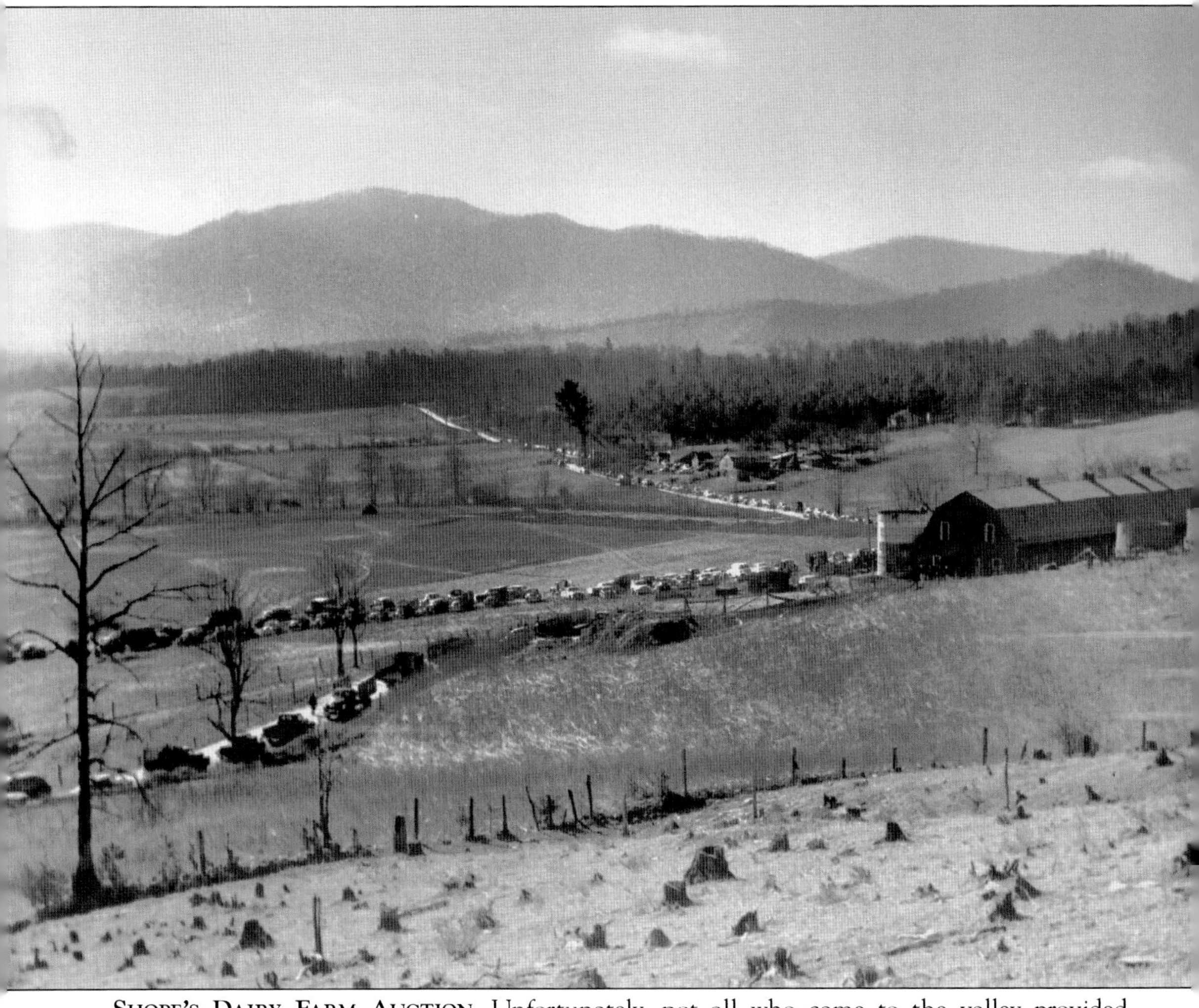

SHOPE'S DAIRY FARM AUCTION. Unfortunately, not all who came to the valley provided stewardship of the land. In 1951, W.C. Shope auctioned his dairy and farm equipment after the Oerlikon Tool and Arms Corp., a Swiss firm, purchased all of the land on Greggs Branch in the Bee Tree community. The facility changed hands several times before Chemtronics purchased it in 1978 and began the production of hallucinogenic chemical warfare agents and tear gas. The site of Shope's dairy and its surrounding land is now a Superfund site containing organic compounds, heavy metals, and dissolved solids. (Noah Collection, courtesy David Rozzell.)

Six

Recreation and Arts and Crafts

For years, people have come to the Swannanoa Valley for rest, relaxation, and recreation. Many of those who are drawn to the valley are artists, writers, poets and musicians. The result has been the development of an area rich in art, culture, and natural recreational opportunities.

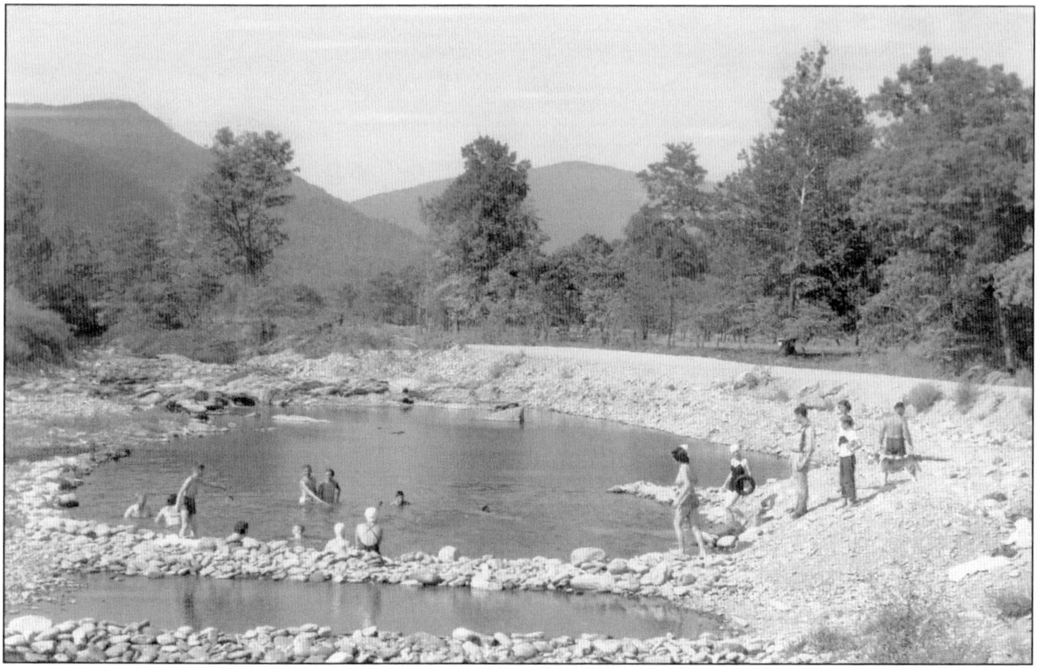

Ole Swimmin' Hole. Many young valley residents learned to swim in this Bee Tree swimming hole. The popular gathering place on hot summer days disappeared with development of an Asheville reservoir. (Noah Collection, courtesy David Rozzell.)

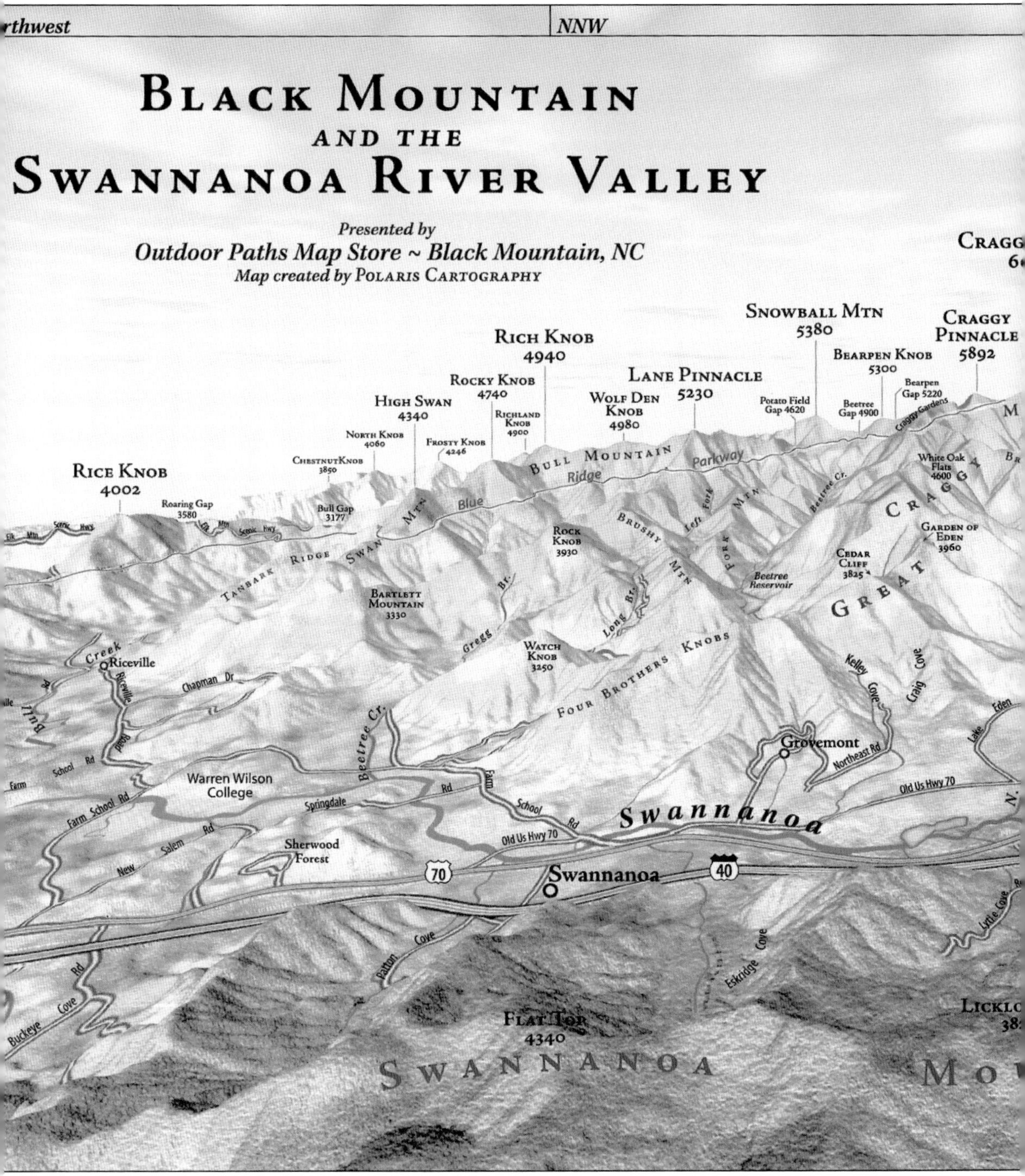

THREE-DIMENSIONAL MAP OF THE SWANNANOA VALLEY. (Copyright 2003, Outdoor Paths

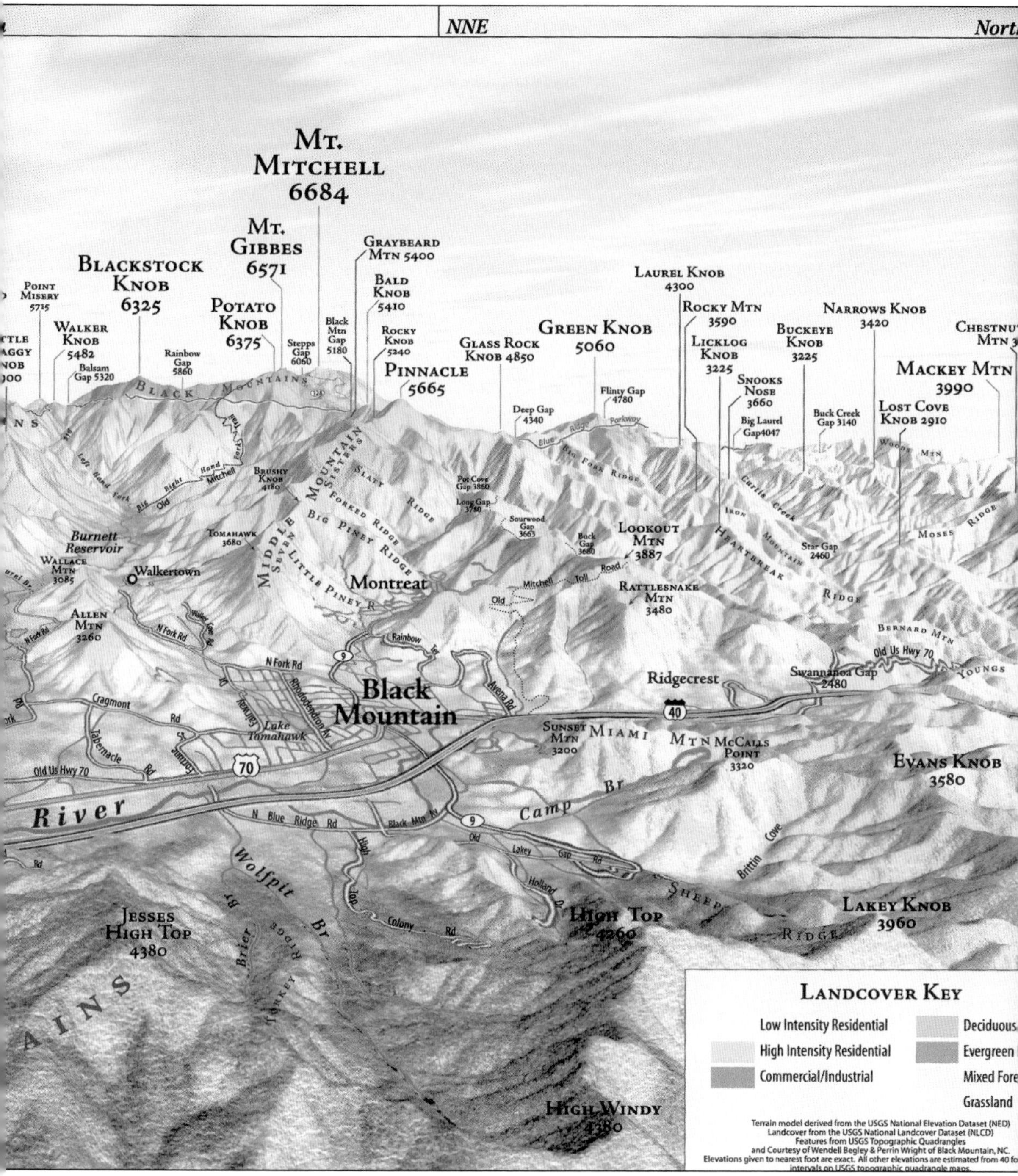

Map Store, Black Mountain. Map by Eric Ringler, Polaris Maps. Visit www.outdoorpaths.com.)

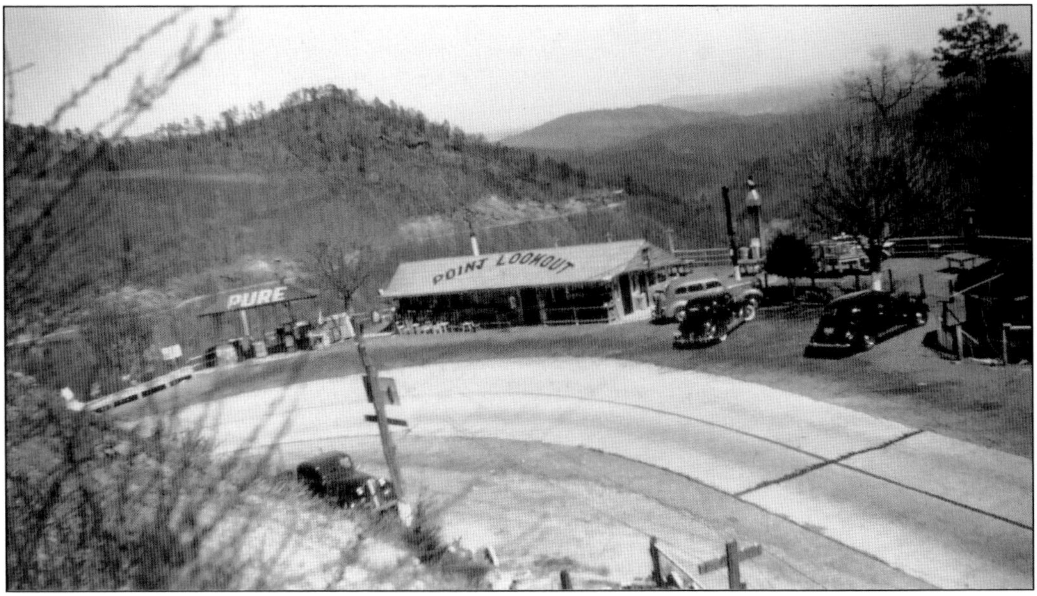

Point Lookout. Although not technically in the Swannanoa Valley, Point Lookout was a favorite destination for visitors and residents alike in the 1930s. Located on old U.S. 70, east of Ridgecrest, Point Lookout offered 5¢ hot dogs, 10¢ sodas, Sally, the cola-drinking bear, and some of the best views of the mountains overlooking the "Royal Gorge." (Swannanoa Valley Museum.)

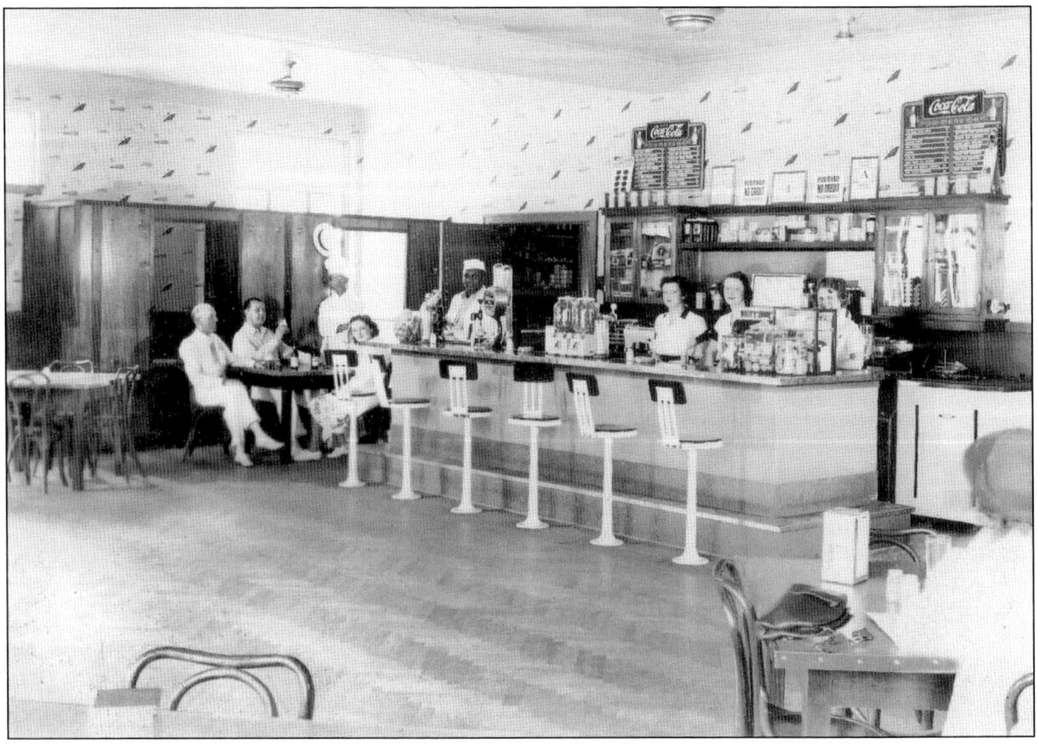

Soda Fountain. In the 1950s, "Roy's Inn," on old U.S. 70, one mile west of Black Mountain, appears to be the perfect place for a cola and a sock-hop. (Courtesy Joe Lance.)

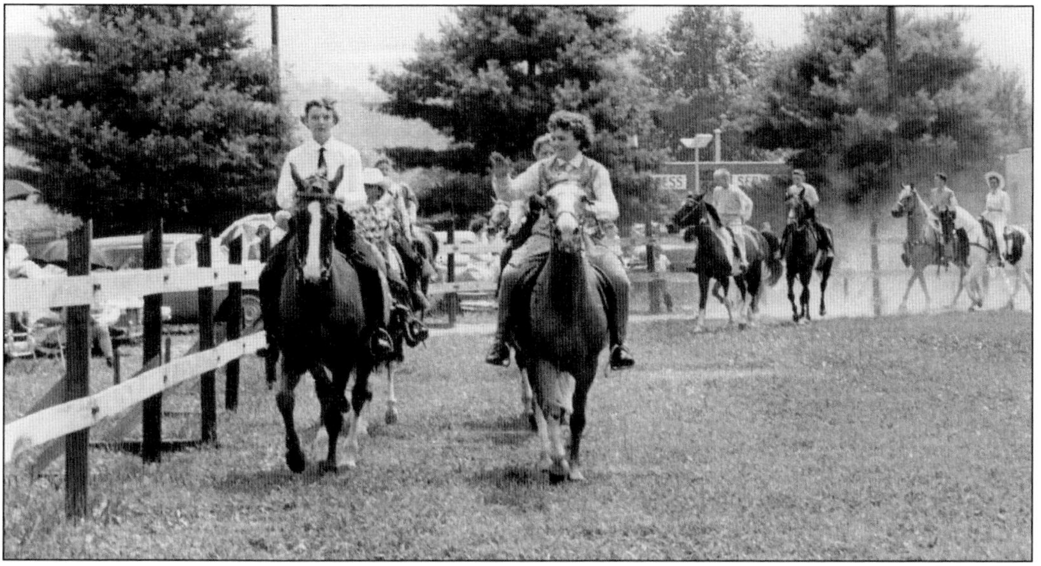

Horse Show. Not all recreation is in the wilds of the Swannanoa Valley. Shown here is a horse show presented by the Black Mountain PTA in 1959. Initiated by the Young Women's Equestrian Club and at first sponsored by the PTA, a later committee was formed to hold more professional shows at the Monte Vista Farms. (Dupuy photo, courtesy Harriet Styles.)

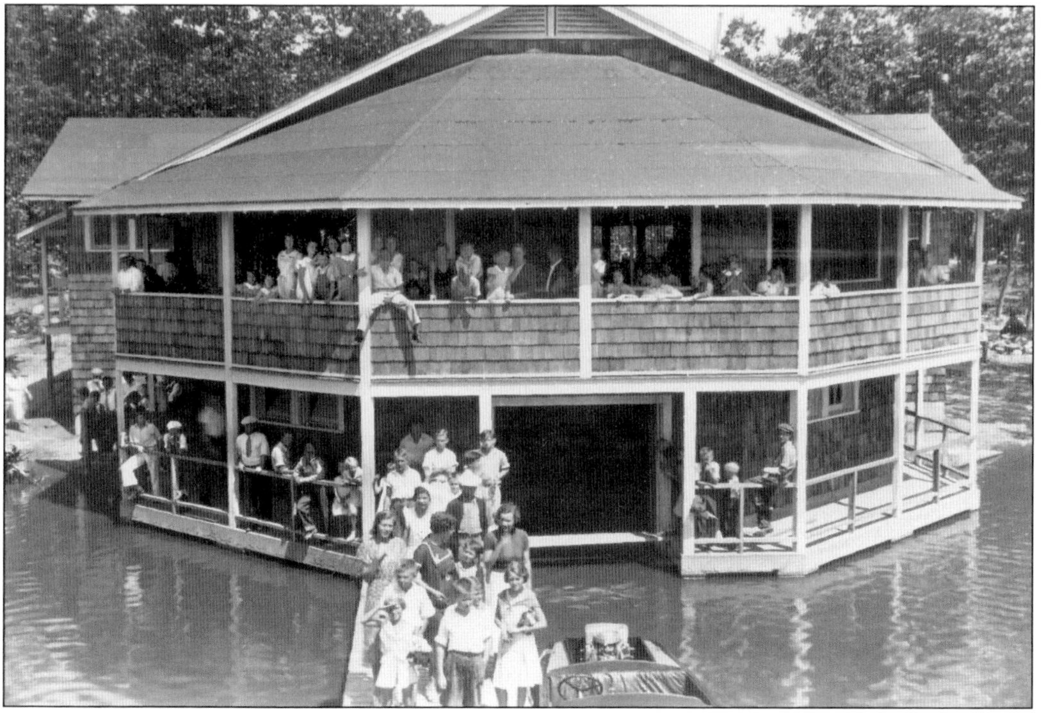

The "Jewel of Black Mountain." Lake Tomahawk, in the center of the Town of Black Mountain, is a man-made lake, a WPA project of the 1930s. After the lake was constructed the town added another gem, a multi-use facility, the Recreation Center shown here. Today, the area includes a public swimming pool, walking path, covered pavilion, and a whole lot of ducks. (Swannanoa Valley Museum.)

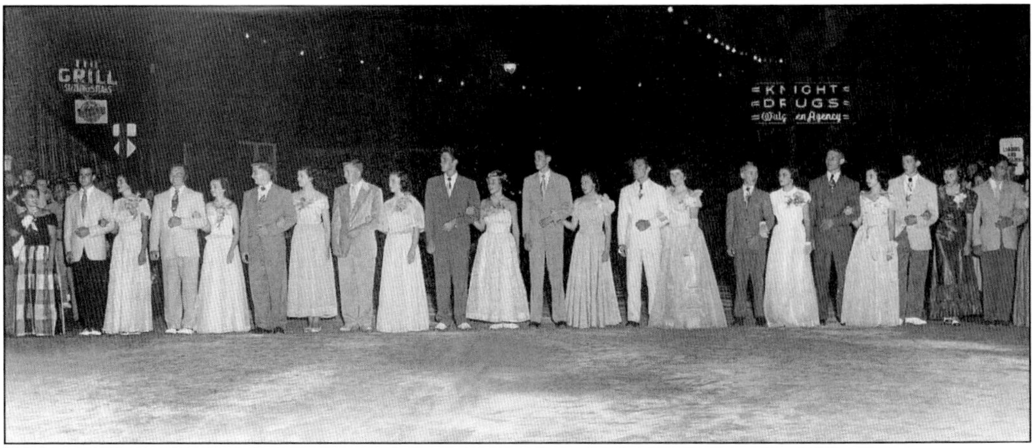

STREET DANCE. Decked out in formal attire, these 1950s party goers stopped traffic on State Highway 70 for a night. (Swannanoa Valley Museum.)

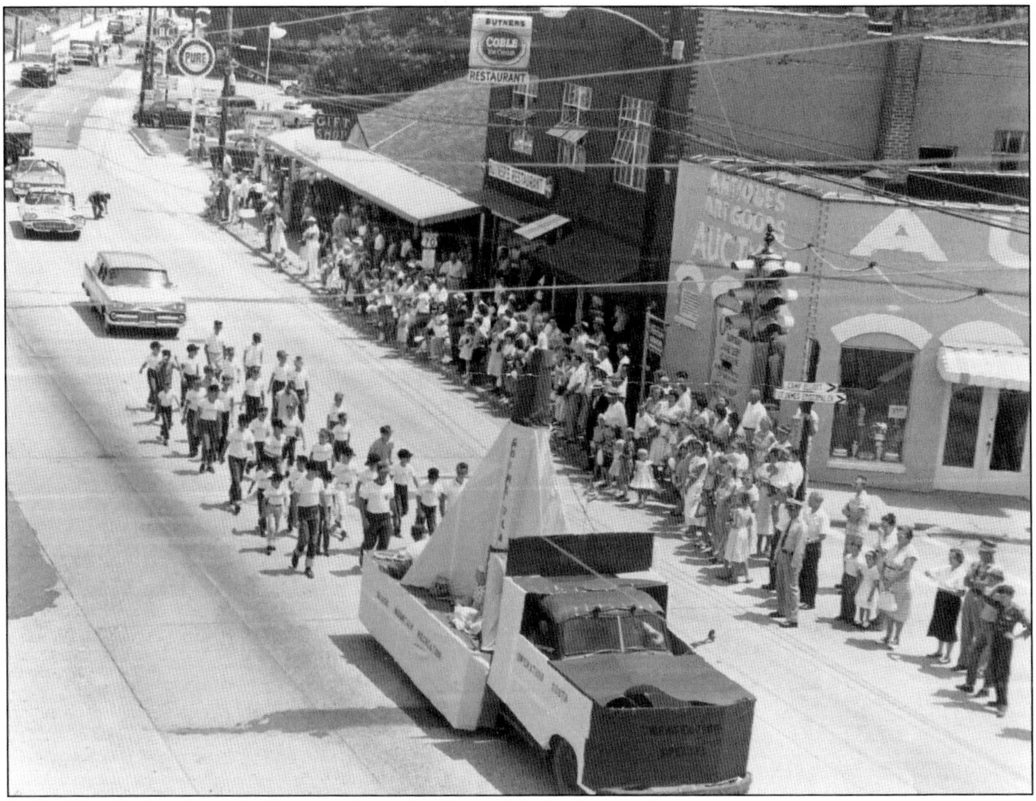

BLACK MOUNTAIN PARADE. The parade was held in celebration of the local fair, c. 1950s. (Courtesy Mary Elizabeth Tyson.)

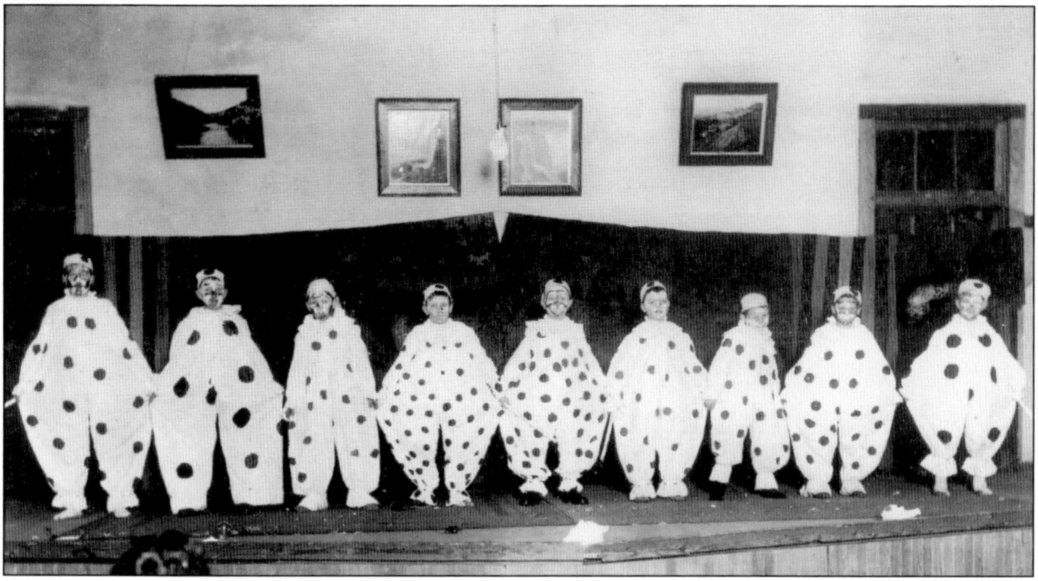

KID CLOWNS. Theater and the performing arts have long had a place in early education in the Swannanoa Valley. These young performers at Black Mountain School show off in their clown suits in the 1950s. (Swannanoa Valley Museum.)

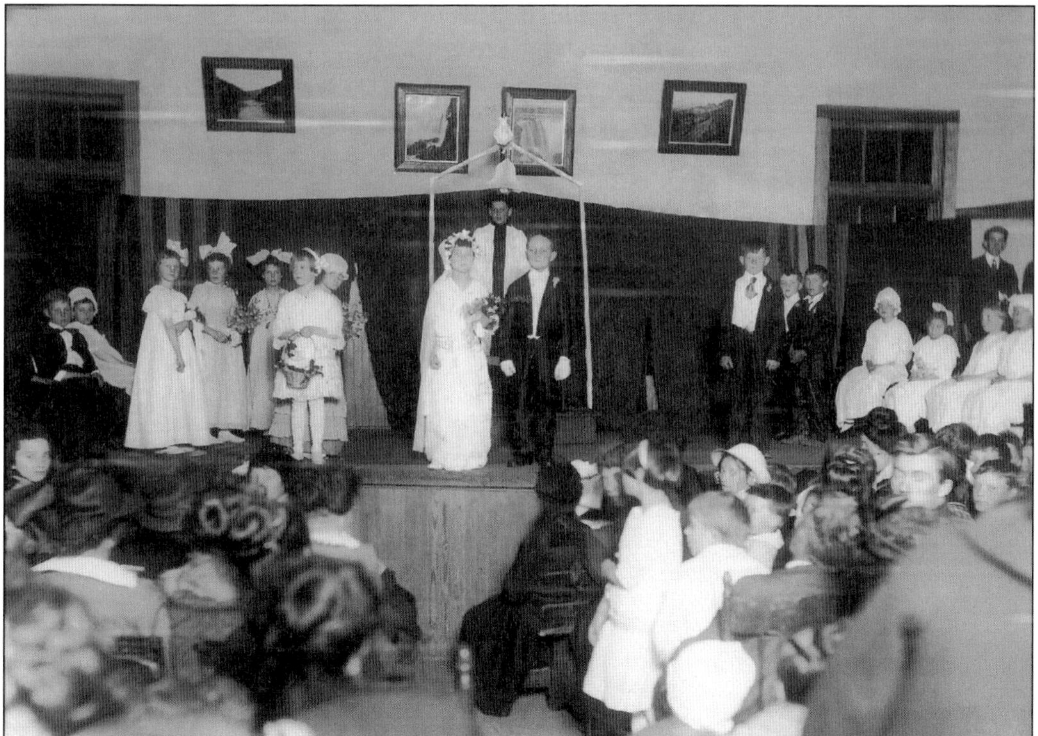

TOM THUMB WEDDING. Before television brought automatic entertainment to the valley, residents created their own. Despite the pained looks on several participants' faces in this photo, the theatrical event was the pride of many parents in the audience, *c.* 1950s. (Swannanoa Valley Museum.)

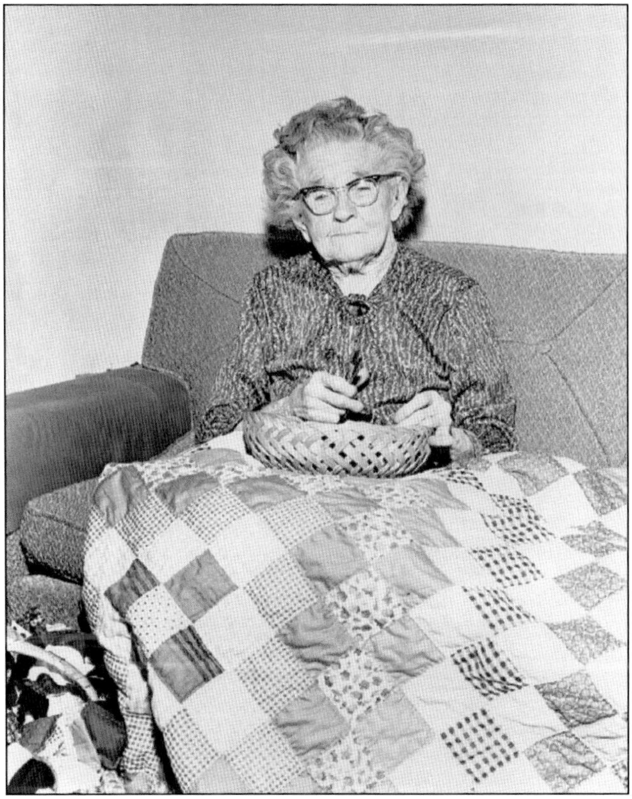

QUILTER AT WORK. Among the many arts and crafts to be found in the Swannanoa Valley, quilting is one of the most popular. Here, 100-year-old Ella Kerlee stitches away. (Swannanoa Valley Museum.)

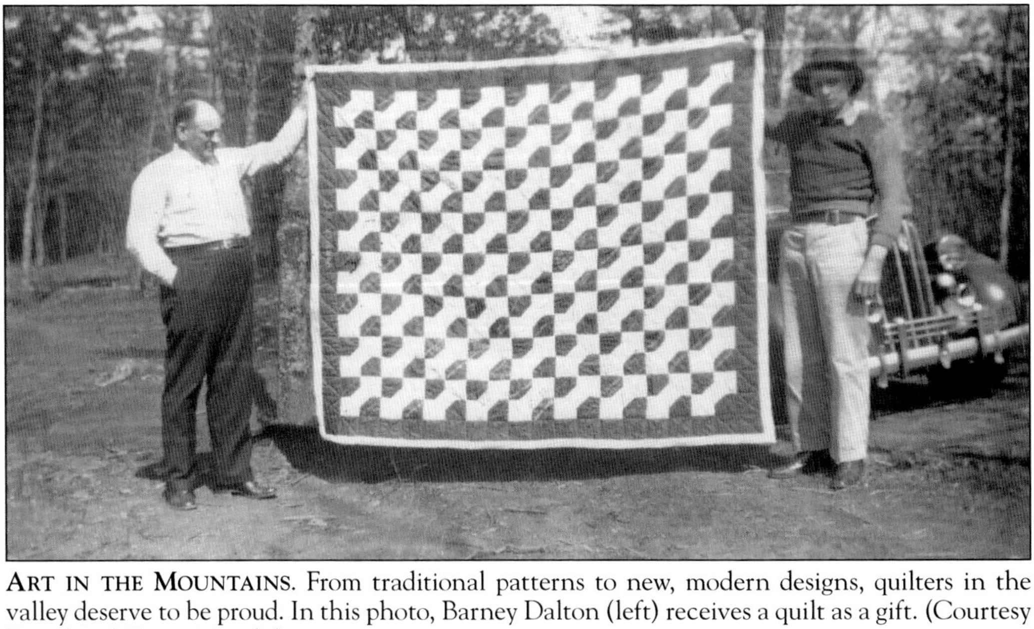

ART IN THE MOUNTAINS. From traditional patterns to new, modern designs, quilters in the valley deserve to be proud. In this photo, Barney Dalton (left) receives a quilt as a gift. (Courtesy David and Tressy Mundy.)

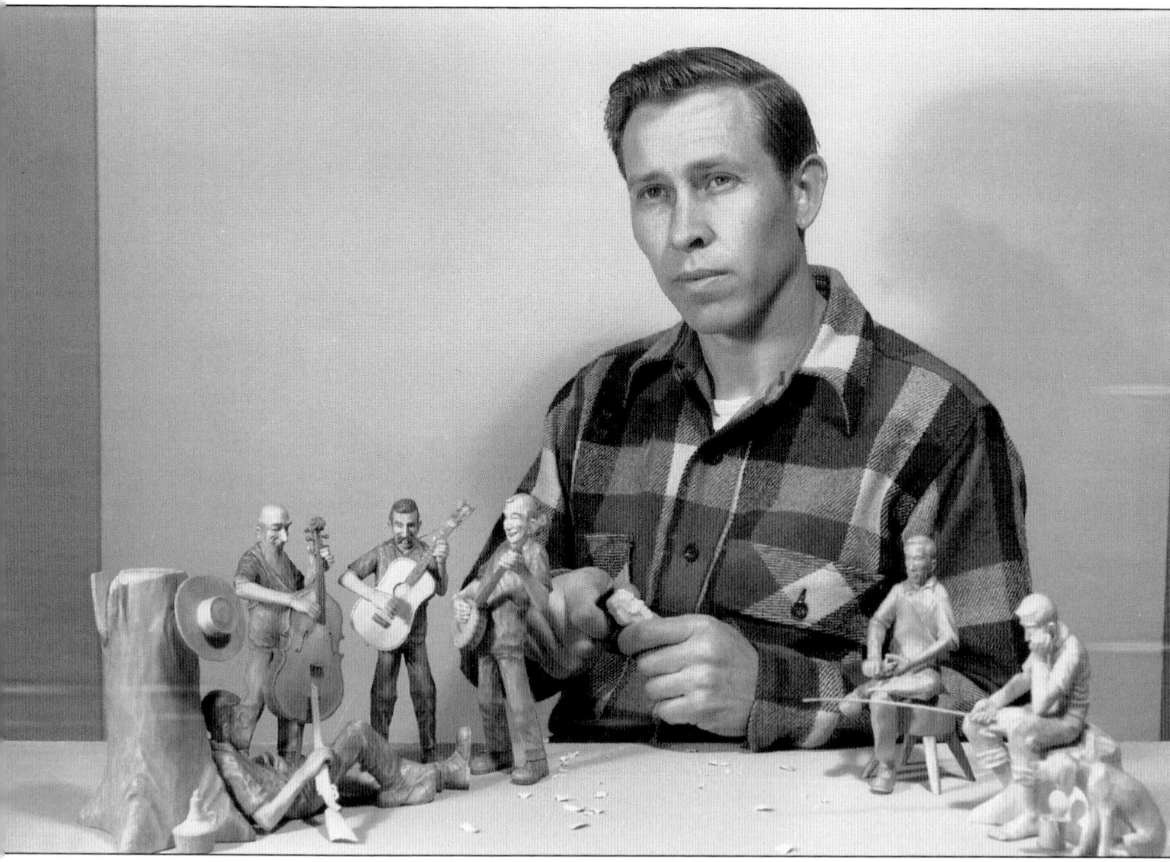

WADE MARTIN. Among the Swannanoa Valley's most revered artists is Wade Martin, carver of intricate figures that represent the people of the valley. (Wade Martin Collection, Swannanoa Valley Museum.)

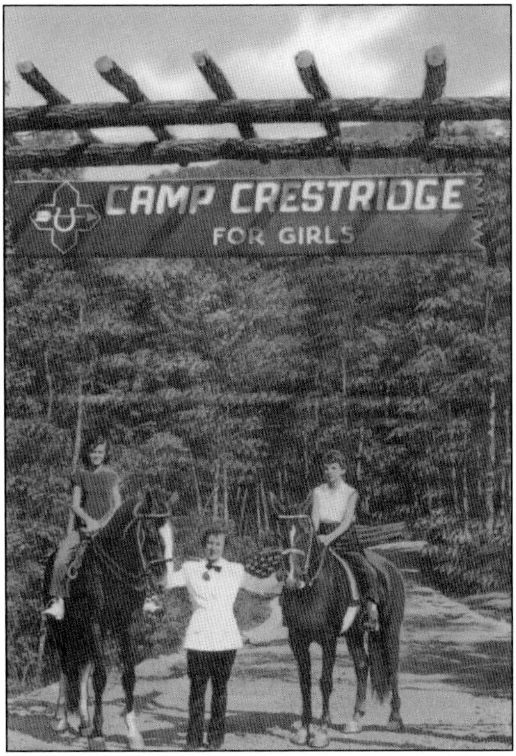

CAMP CRESTRIDGE. Private summer camps have long drawn people to the Swannanoa Valley. In addition to Camp Crestridge, campers attend Camp Merrimac for Girls, Camp Timberlake for Boys (both located near Montreat), Camp Rockmont for Boys on Lake Eden, Camp Ridgecrest for Boys, and Camp Awaniko, the 4-H camp in Swannanoa. (Swannanoa Valley Museum.)

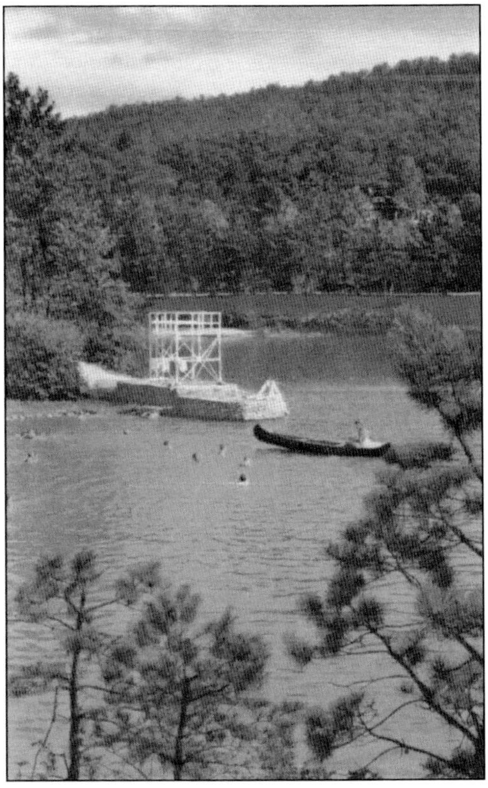

CAMP RIDGECREST. Many of the area assemblies and conference centers offer youth camps every summer. Shown in this historic postcard is Camp Ridgecrest for Boys, with a private lake perfect for swimming and canoeing. (Swannanoa Valley Museum.)

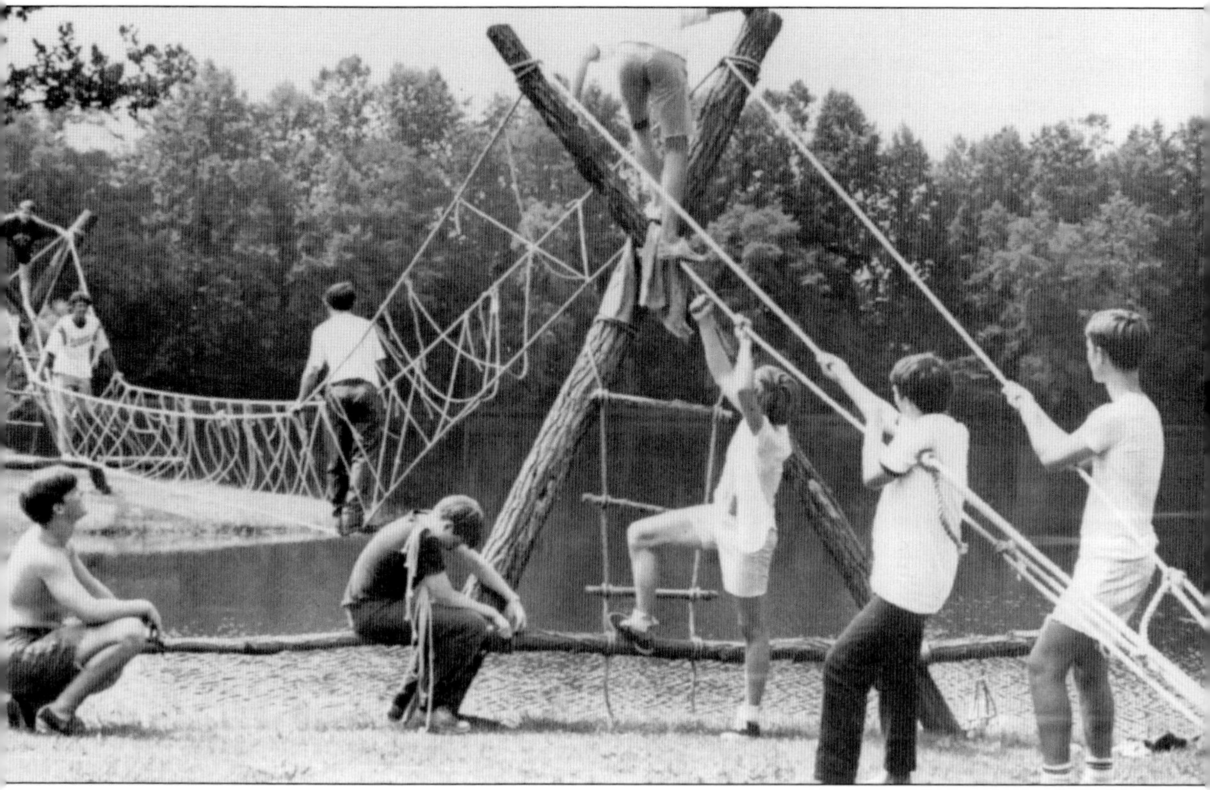

Bridge Building. Before the popular "Outward Bound" type of trust and confidence building programs, Swannanoa Valley conference centers were engaged in helping young people gain these skills by literally building bridges together. (Courtesy YMCA Blue Ridge Assembly.)

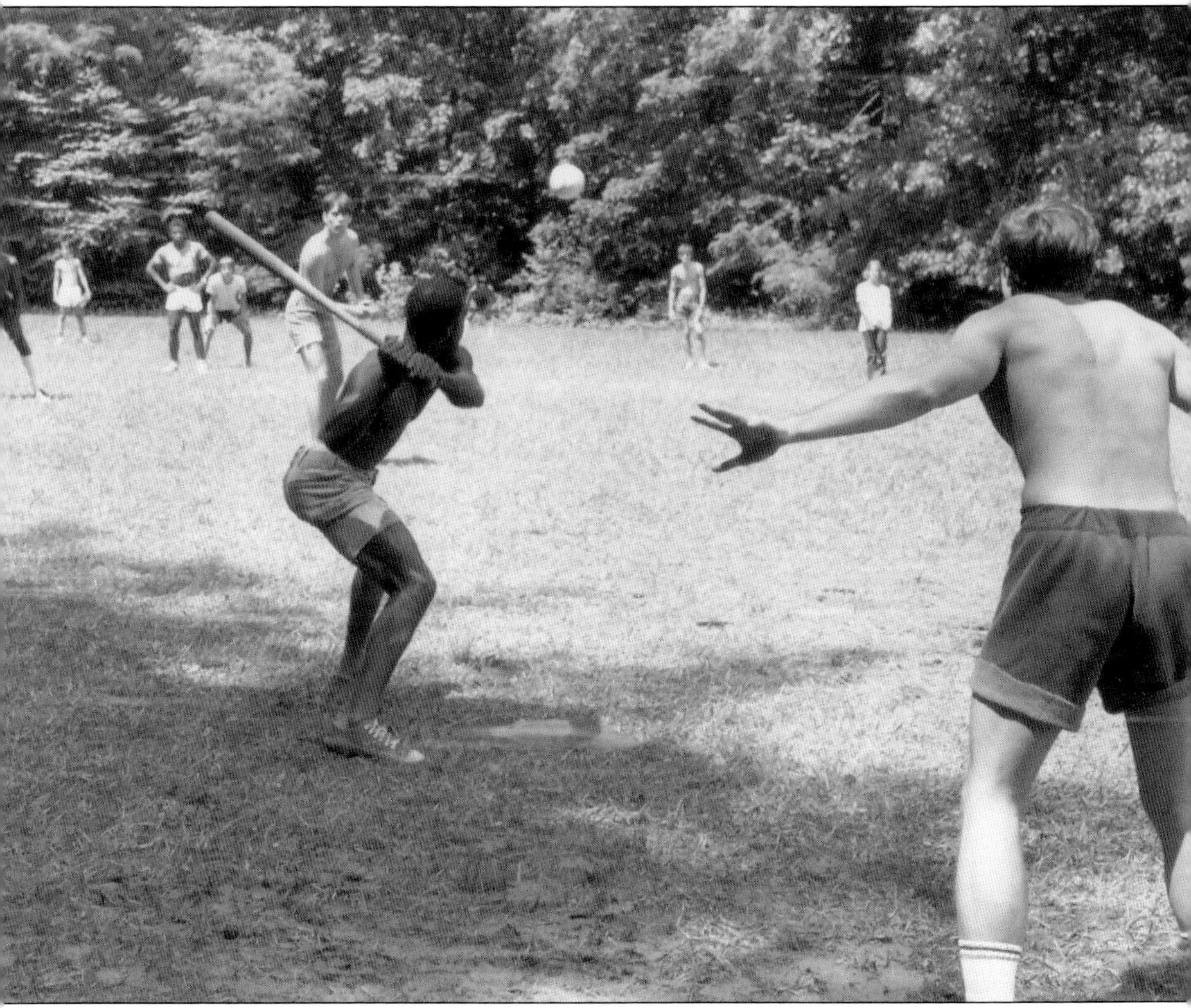

STRIKE! A softball game at YMCA Blue Ridge Assembly is typical of the many sports opportunities offered by Swannanoa Valley camps and conference centers. (Dupuy photo, courtesy YMCA Blue Ridge Assembly.)

PRETEND INDIANS. Part of the magic of summer camps for kids is stepping back in time and trying to understand what life was like in the valley for other people. Here, young campers adorn themselves with face paint and costumes and learn about native cultures. (Swannanoa Valley Museum.)

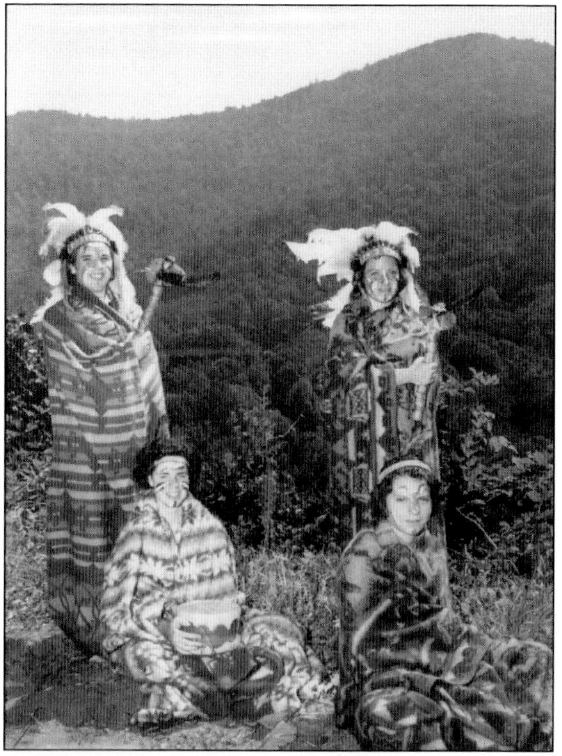

BULLSEYE! Archery is another sport offered by area camps and recreational facilities. (From camp brochure.)

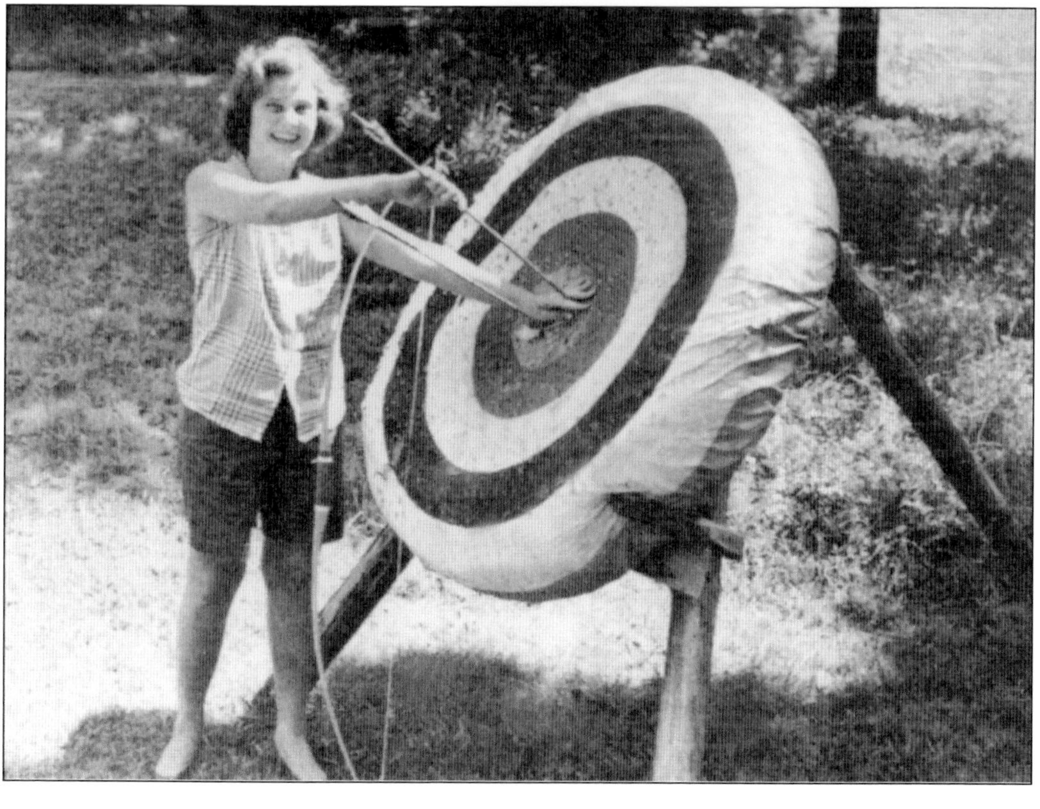

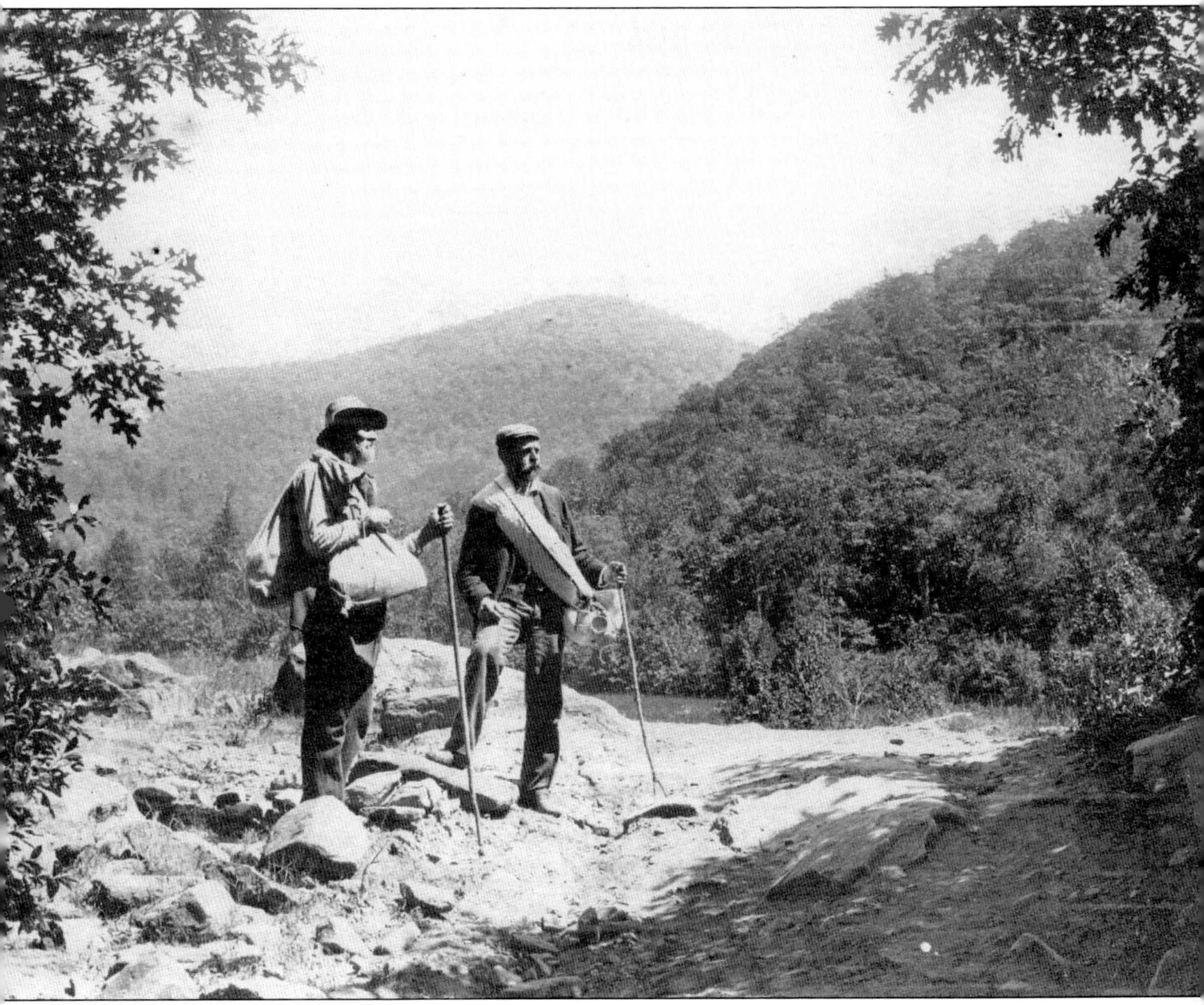

Early Hikers. Once again, the cyanotype images of Gertrude Sprague take us back in time and show that hikers have loved this valley for decades. These unidentified hikers pause to peruse the natural wonders that surround them on every side c. 1900. (Swannanoa Valley Museum.)

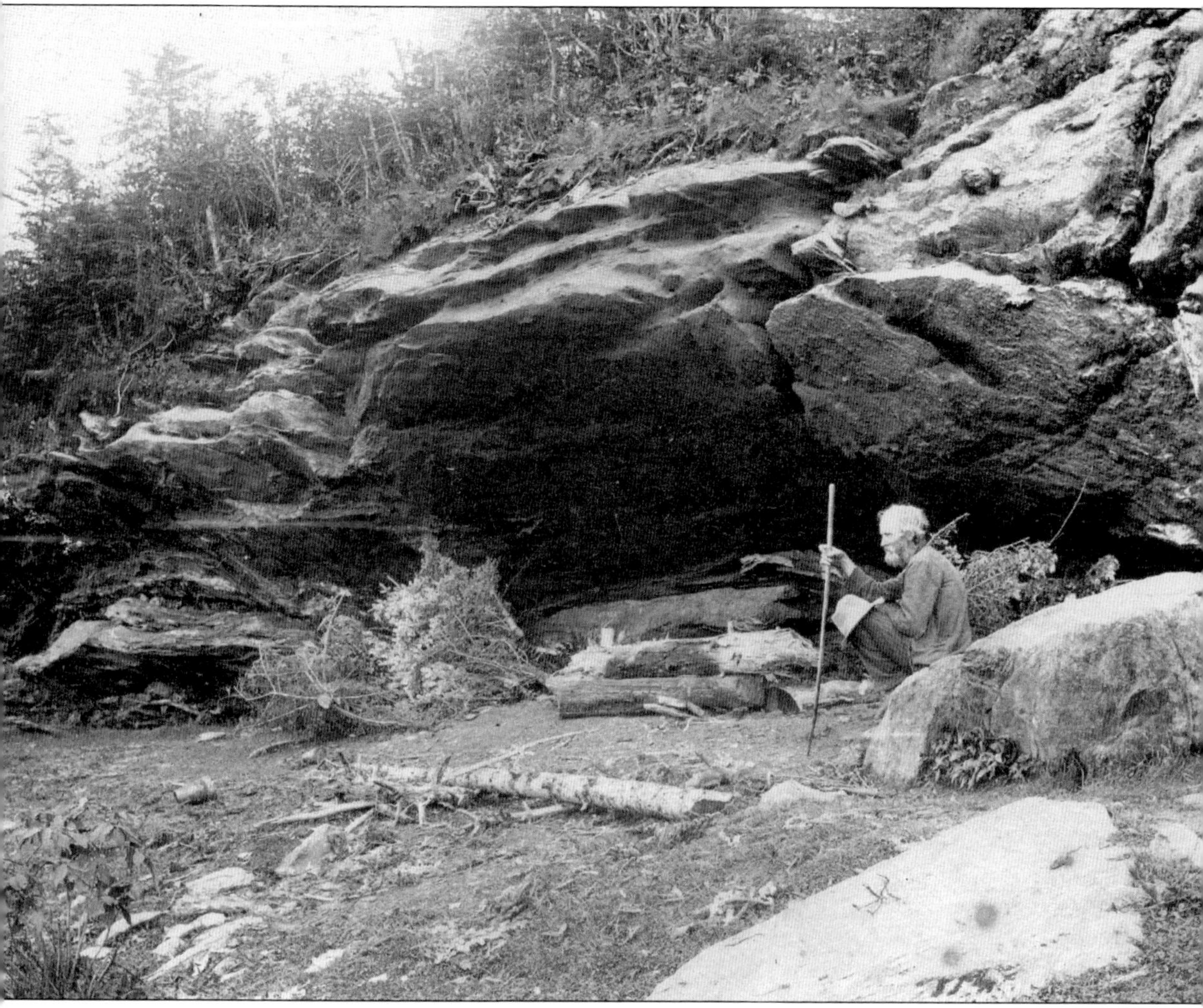

CAMP ROCK. Another Sprague image shows a hiker/camper resting beneath a famous landmark on Craggy Pinnacle, *c.* 1900. (Swannanoa Valley Museum.)

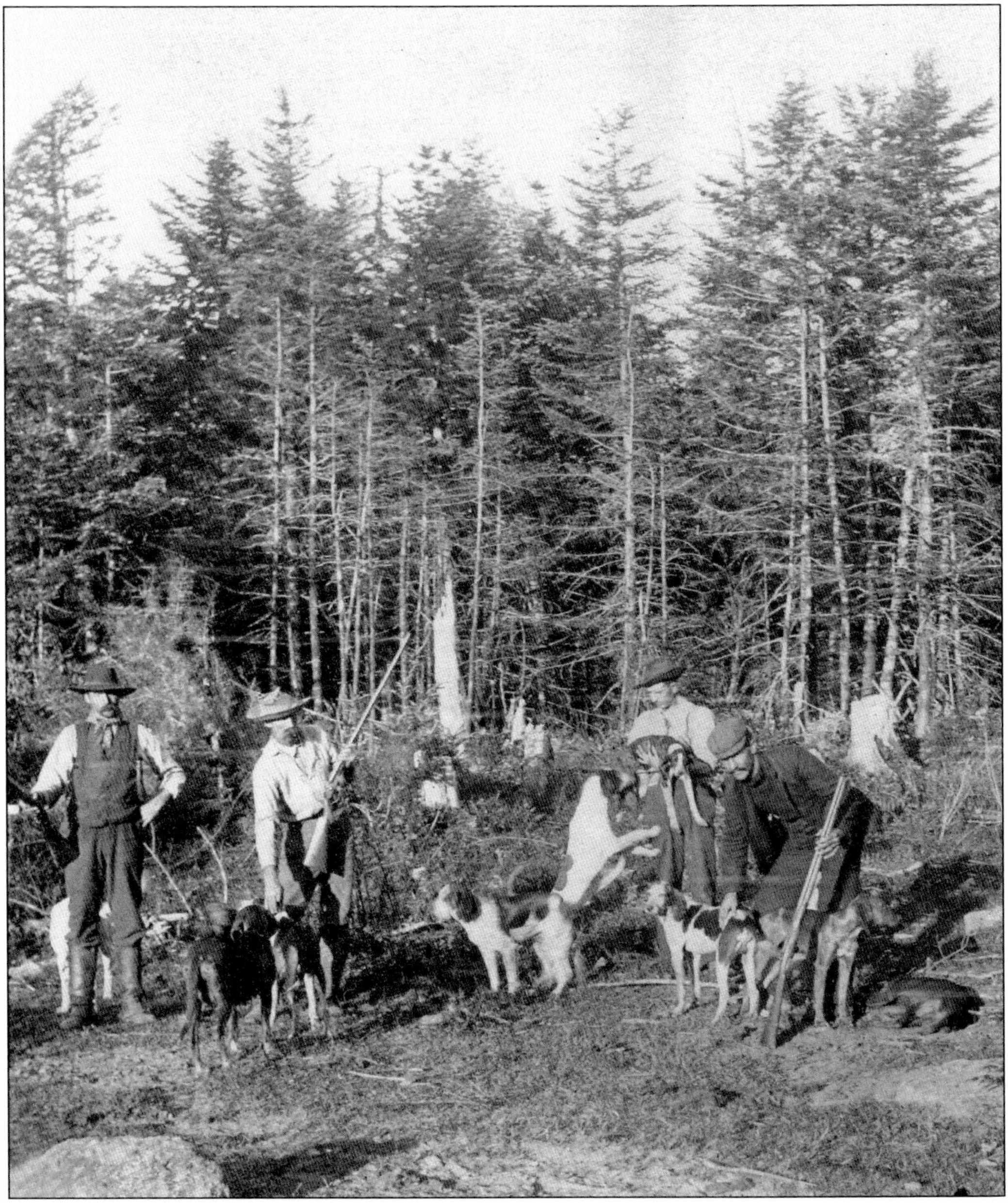

LOOKING FOR BEAR. Hunters and their dogs prepare for a big bear hunt in the high mountains, seen in another Cyanotype by Gertrude Sprague, *c.* 1900. (Swannanoa Valley Museum.)

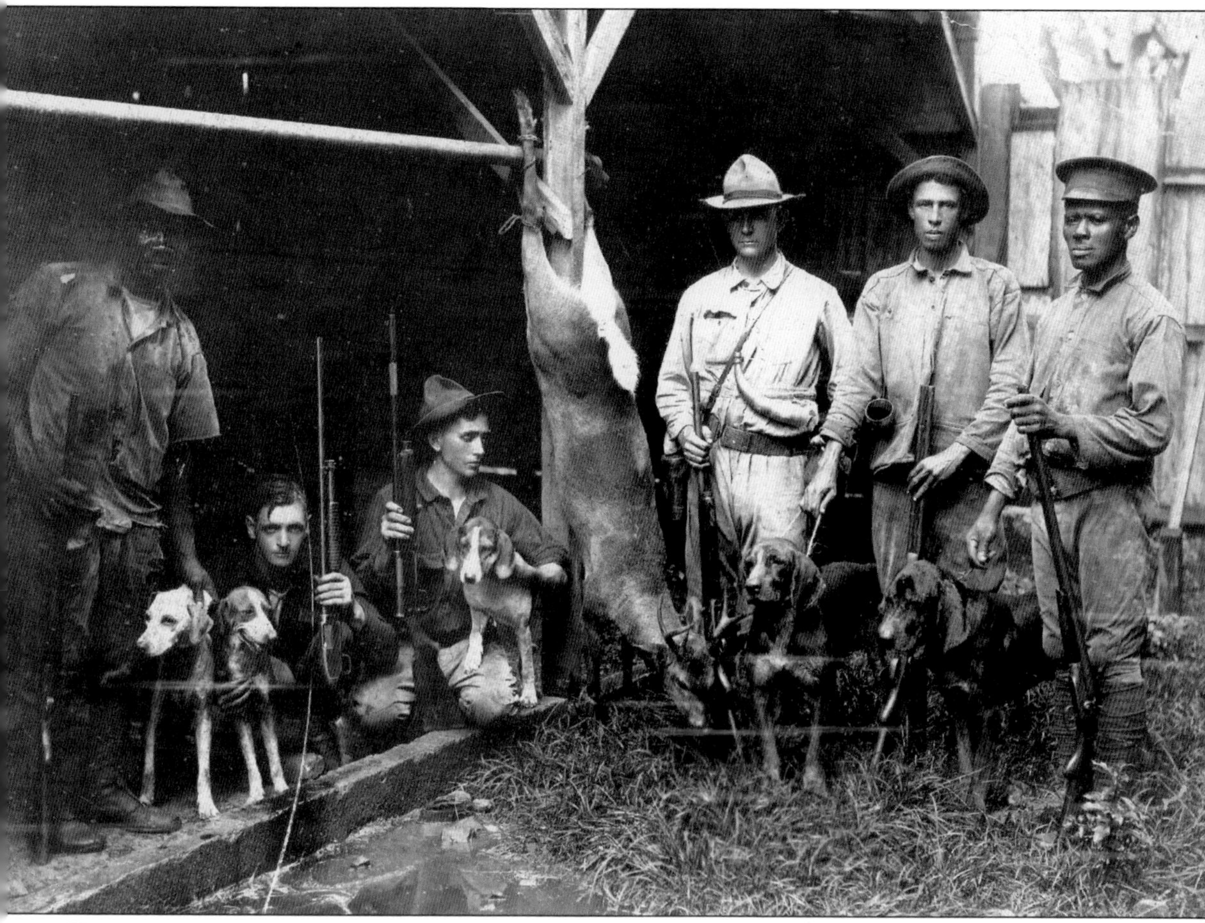

The Lure of the Hunt. Some things never change, and in the Swannanoa Valley, the lure of the hunt has tempted residents from the early native peoples to today's sportsmen. In this early 20th-century photo, hunters and their dogs pose with their trophy deer. (Courtesy Willie Kerlee Headley.)

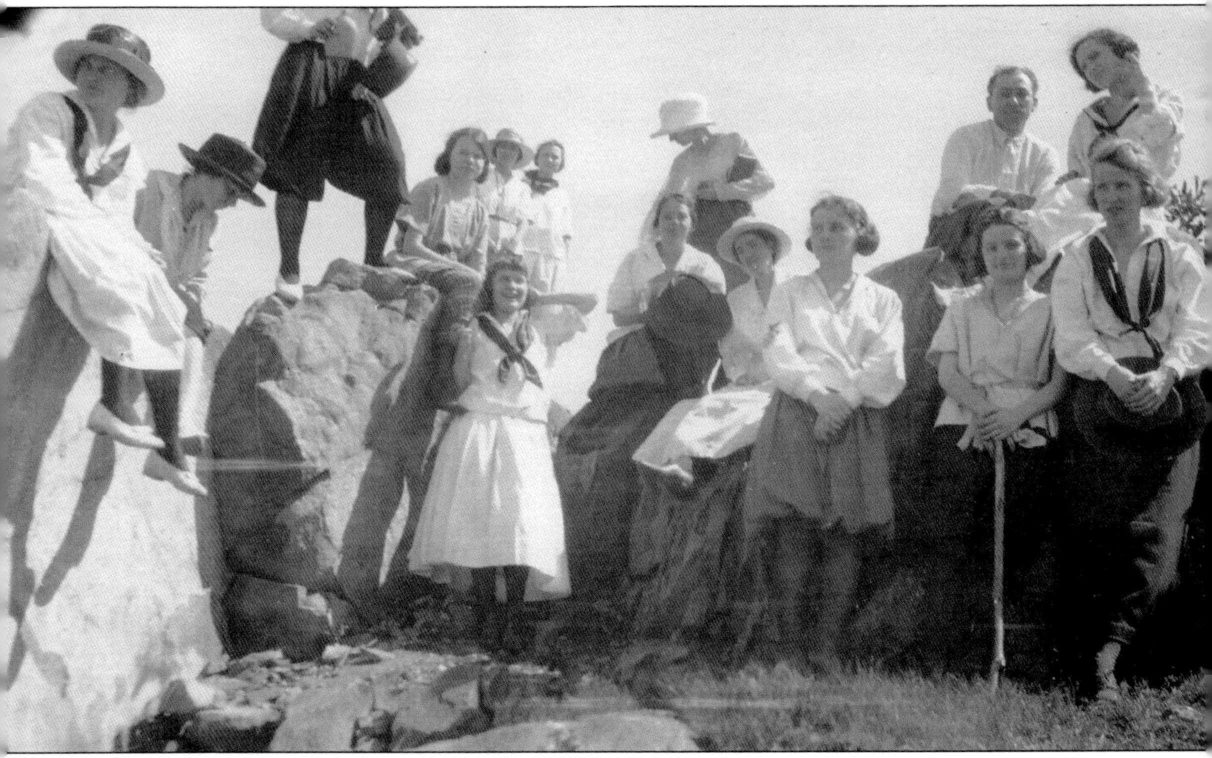

WOMEN HIKERS. Summer students from Asheville Normal School, wearing middie blouses and bloomers, have reached a resting spot on their hike to Graybeard. (Courtesy Harriet Styles.)

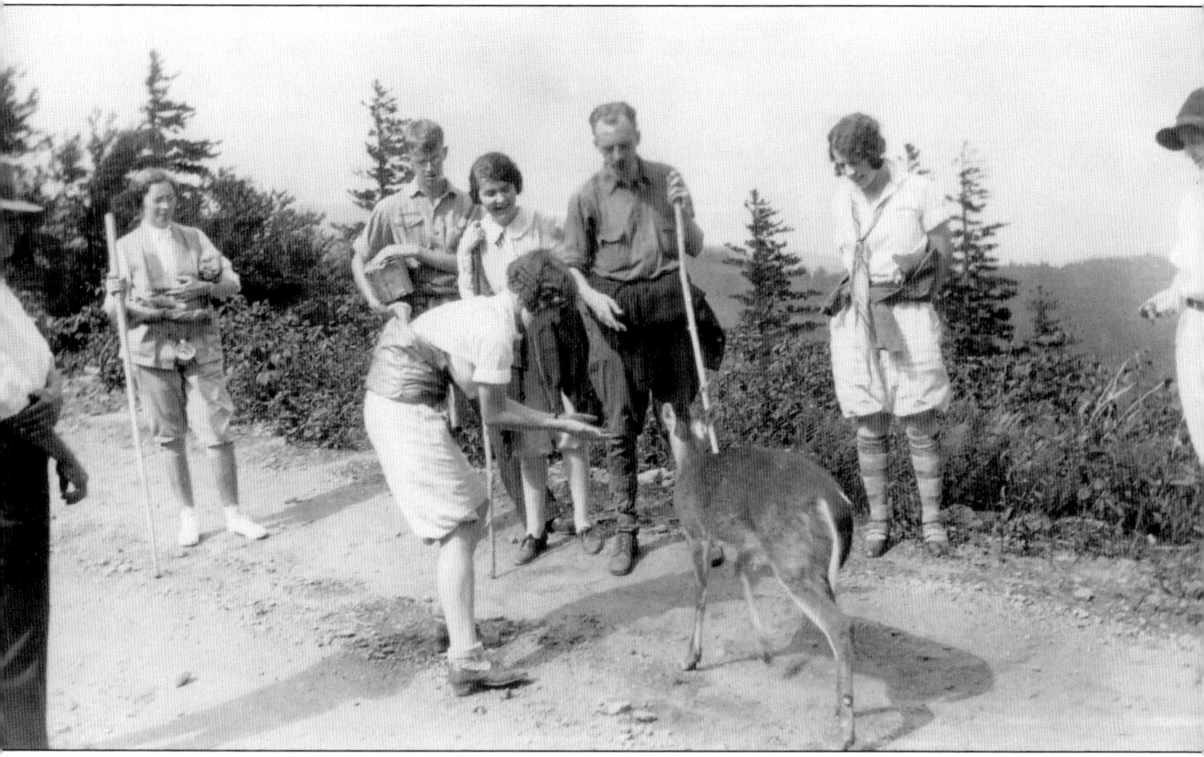

HIKERS MEET NATIVE. It's a conference between species on a high country trail when hikers meet up with a deer. The challenge is for each to go its own way, maintaining respect for the wildness of habitat. Not feeding the deer and other wildlife frees them from becoming dependent upon humans for their subsistence. (Courtesy Harriet Styles.)

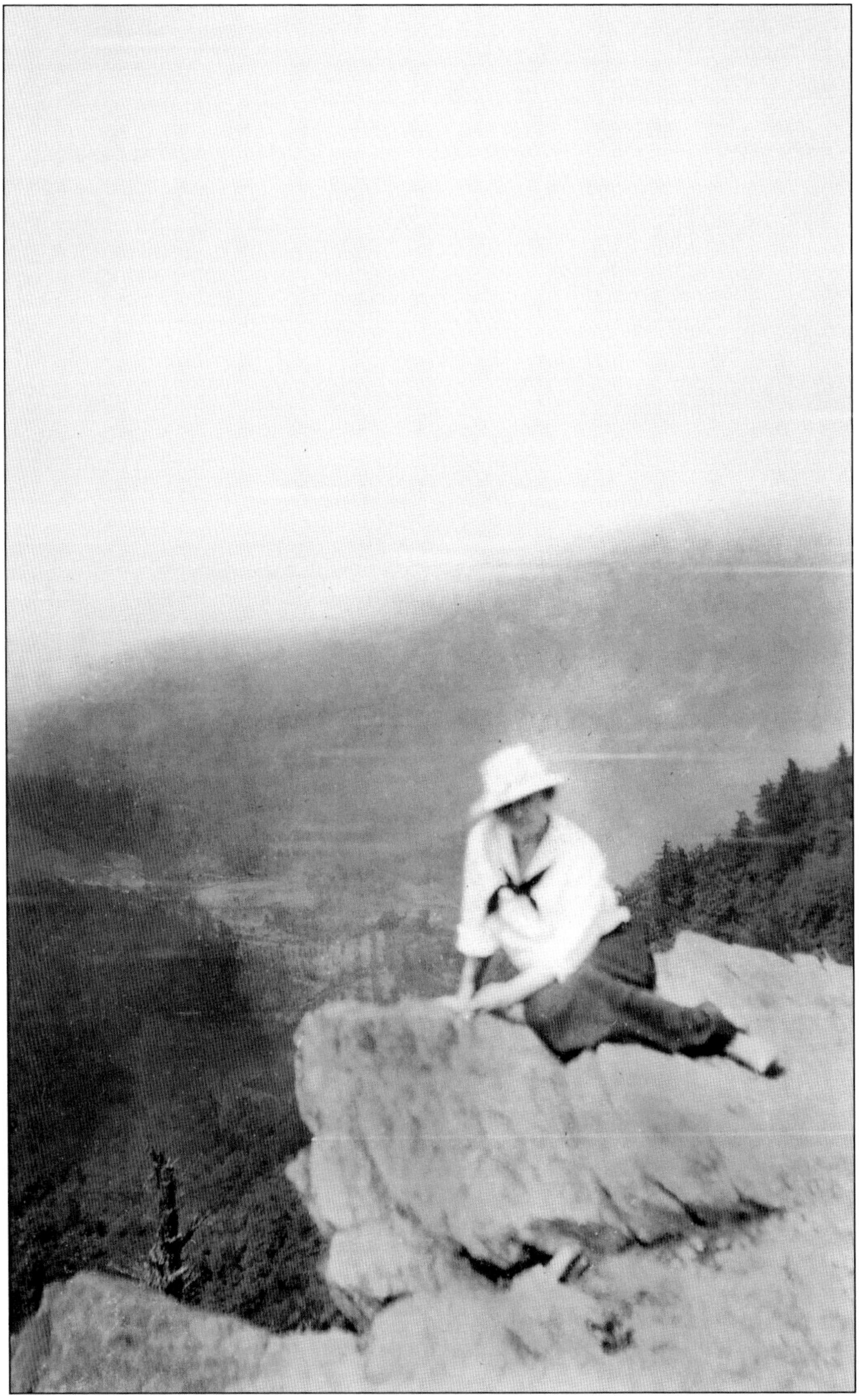

THE LONG VIEW. From her peaceful repose high on the cedar cliffs above Blue Ridge Assembly, Mabel Allen appears to be reflecting on the beauty of the mountains and the valley below, which continues to bring people to Black Mountain and the Swannanoa Valley. (Courtesy Harriet Styles.)